Critical Perspectives on Canadian Theatre in English

General Editor Ric Knowles

2005

volume one	***Aboriginal Drama and Theatre***, ed. Rob Appleford 0-88754-792-3
volume two	***African-Canadian Theatre***, ed. Maureen Moynagh 0-88754-794-X
volume three	***Judith Thompson***, ed. Ric Knowles 0-88754-796-6

2006

volume four	***Feminist Theatre and Performance***, ed. Susan Bennett 0-88754-798-2
volume five	***George F. Walker***, ed. Harry Lane 0-88754-800-8
volume six	***Theatre in British Columbia***, ed. Ginny Ratsoy 0-88754-802-4

2007

volume seven	***Queer Theatre***, ed. Rosalind Kerr 0-88754-804-0
volume eight	***Environmental and Site Specific Theatre***, ed. Andrew Houston 0-88754-806-7
volume nine	***Space and the Geographies of Theatre***, ed. Michael McKinnie 0-88754-808-3

416-703-0013 • orders@playwrightscanada.com • www.playwrightscanada.com

Feminist Theatre and Performance

Critical Perspectives on Canadian Theatre in English

volume four

Feminist Theatre and Performance

Edited by Susan Bennett

Playwrights Canada Press

Toronto • Canada

Playwrights Canada Press
215 Spadina Avenue, Suite 230, Toronto, Ontario CANADA M5T 2C7
416-703-0013 fax 416-408-3402
orders@playwrightscanada.com • www.playwrightscanada.com

Financial support provided by the taxpayers of Canada and Ontario through the Canada Council for the Arts and the Department of Canadian Heritage through the Book Publishing Industry Development Programme, and the Ontario Arts Council.

Cover image: Jin-me Yoon, between departure and arrival, 1996/1997. Partial installation view, Art Gallery of Ontario. Video projection, video montage on monitor, photographic mylar scroll, clocks with 3-D lettering, audio. Dimensions variable. Courtesy of the artist and Catriona Jeffries Gallery, Vancouver.
Production Editor/Cover Design: JLArt

Library and Archives Canada Cataloguing in Publication

Feminist theatre and performance / edited by Susan Bennett.

(Critical perspectives on Canadian theatre in English ; v. 4)
Includes bibliographical references.
ISBN 0-88754-798-2

1. Feminist theater--Canada--History. 2. Canadian drama (English)--Women authors--History and criticism. 3. Canadian drama (English)--20th century--History and criticism. I. Bennett, Susan, 1955- II. Series. Critical perspectives on Canadian theatre in English.

PN2304.2.F44 2006 792.082'0971 C2006-902360-3

First edition: May 2006
Printed and bound by Hignell Printing at Winnipeg, Canada.

Table of Contents

General Editor's Preface

Critical Perspectives on Canadian Theatre in English sets out to make the best critical and scholarly work in the field readily available to teachers, students, and scholars of Canadian drama and theatre. In volumes organized by playwright, region, genre, theme, and cultural community, the series publishes the work of scholars and critics who have, since the so-called renaissance of Canadian theatre in the late 1960s and early 1970s, traced the coming-into-prominence of a vibrant theatrical community in English Canada.

Each volume in the series is edited and introduced by an expert in the field who has selected a representative sampling of the most important critical work on her or his subject since circa 1970, ordered chronologically according to the original dates of publication. Where appropriate, the volume editors have also commissioned new essays on their subjects. Each volume also provides a list of suggested further readings, and an introduction by the volume's editor.

It is my hope that this series, working together with complementary anthologies of plays published by Playwrights Canada Press, Talonbooks, and other Canadian drama publishers, will facilitate the teaching of Canadian drama and theatre in schools, colleges, and universities across the country for years to come. It is for this reason that the titles so far selected for the series—*Aboriginal Drama and Theatre, African-Canadian Theatre, Judith Thompson, Feminist Theatre and Performance, George F. Walker, Theatre in British Columbia, Queer Theatre, Environmental and Site Specific Theatre*, and *Space and the Geographies of Theatre*—are designed to work as companion volumes to a range of Canadian drama anthologies recently published or forthcoming from the country's major drama publishers that complement them: *Staging Coyote's Dream: An Anthology of First Nations Drama in English* (Playwrights Canada, 2003); the two volumes of *Testifyin': Contemporary African Canadian Drama* (Playwrights Canada, 2000, 2003); *Judith Thompson: Late 20th Century Plays* (Playwrights Canada, 2002); the various collections of plays by George F. Walker published by Talonbooks; *Playing the Pacific Province: An Anthology of British Columbia Plays, 1967-2000* (Playwrights Canada, 2001), and other projected volumes. I hope that with the combined availability of these anthologies and the volumes in this series, courses on a variety of aspects of Canadian drama and theatre will flourish in schools and universities within Canada and beyond its borders, and scholars new to the field will find accessible and comprehensive introductions to some of the field's most provocative and intriguing figures and issues.

Finally, the titles selected for *Critical Perspectives on Canadian Theatre in English* are designed to carve out both familiar and new areas of work. It is my intention that the series at once recognize the important critical heritage of scholarly work in the field and attempt to fill in its most significant gaps by highlighting important work from and about marginalized communities, work that has too often been neglected in courses on and criticism of Canadian drama and theatre. In its nationalist phase in the late 1960s and 70s, English-Canadian theatre criticism tended to neglect work by women, by First Nations peoples and people of colour, by Gay, Lesbian, Bi- or Transsexual artists, and by those working in politically, geographically, or aesthetically alternative spaces. While respecting, honouring, and representing important landmarks in Canadian postcolonial theatrical nationalism, *Critical Perspectives on Canadian Theatre in English* also sets out to serve as a corrective to its historical exclusions.

Ric Knowles

Acknowledgements

I was an undergraduate student in England when I saw the Women's Theatre Group perform on campus and in many ways everything I believe about the importance and impact of feminist theatre began that evening. And, since that time and especially in the last twenty years or so that I've lived in Canada, I've had an extraordinary opportunity to engage with feminist theatre and performance. Putting together this volume has been a reminder of how much I've learned and what fun it's been along the way. Practitioners and critics alike, feminists in Canada have created a passionate, engaged, vital, and provocative community in which it is a privilege to participate. An especial debt goes to the Women's Caucus of the Association for Canadian Theatre Research that has, over the years, made a place for the conversations that insist on feminist perspectives and to the women of the late-lamented Maenad Theatre who made great work happen.

My thanks go to Playwrights Canada Press for supporting this series of volumes, to the general editor Ric Knowles for giving me this opportunity, and to Jean-Sébastien Windle who has been a research assistant par excellence.

"Messages in the Wilderness" by Cindy Cowan was first published in *Canadian Theatre Review* 43 (1985): 100-10; "Fear of Feminism" by Kate Lushington was first published in *Canadian Theatre Review* 43 (1985): 5-11; "The Body as Spectacle: Women's Theatre in Quebec" by Jane Moss was first published in *Women & Performance: A Journal of Feminist Theory* 3.1 (1986): 5-16; "The Company of Sirens: Popular Feminist Theatre in Canada by Kym Bird was first published in *Canadian Theatre Review* 59 (1989): 35-37; "Getting the Message: The NAAGs of Halifax" by Donna E. Smyth was first published in *Canadian Theatre Review* 59 (1989): 29-34; "Women's Circle, Women's Theatre" by Wendy Philpott was first published in *Canadian Theatre Review* 69 (1991): 5-14; "Playing Solitaire: Spectatorship and Representation in Canadian Women's Monodrama" by Patricia Badir was first published in *Theatre Research in Canada* 13 (1992): 120-33; "Naming Names: Black Women Playwrights in Canada" by Djanet Sears was first published in *Women on the Canadian Stage: The Legacy of Hrotsvit*. Ed. Rita Much. Blizzard Publishing, 1992: 92-103; "Critical Revisions: Ann-Marie MacDonald's *Goodnight Desdemona (Good Morning Juliet)*" by Ann Wilson was first published in *Women on the Canadian Stage: The Legacy of Hrotsvit*. Ed. Rita Much. Blizzard Publishing, 1992: 1-12; "Making It Happen: A Commercial Model for Self-Production" by Shawna Dempsey and Lorri Millan was first published in *Canadian Theatre Review* 82 (1995): 23-25; "Diversity and Voice: A Celebration of Canadian Women Writing for Performance" by Susan

Bennett was first published in *On-Stage and Off-Stage: English Canadian Drama in Discourse.* Ed. Albert-Reiner Glaap with Rolf Althof. St. John's: Breakwater, 1996: 60-75; "A Clash of Symbols: When I Put on What I Want to Put on" by Louise H. Forsyth was first published in *Canadian Theatre Review* 92 (1997): 27-33; "Collective Creation and the Changing Mandate of Nightwood Theatre" by Shelley Scott was first published in *Theatre Research in Canada* 18 (1997): 191-207; "A Feminist Absurd: Margaret Hollingsworth's *The House That Jack Built*" by Celeste Derksen was first published in *Modern Drama* 45 (2002): 209-30; "Still 'Activist' after All These Years? Reflections on Feminism and Activist Theatre, Then and Now" by Cynthia Grant was first published in *Canadian Theatre Review* 117 (2004): 4-6; and "Still Acting Out After 25 Years" by Jennifer O'Connor was first published in *Herizons* (Fall 2004): 9. All are reprinted here by permission.

Introduction

by Susan Bennett

> I am hearing from feminists in theatre across the country and I am taking heart. True, these women are largely disenfranchised from the established theatre, but not, we hope, permanently. (Rina Fraticelli 18)

Critical perspectives on theatre practices have changed and diversified in the last 30 years of the twentieth century, due in no small part to the contributions of feminist criticism and theory. New attention to the representation of women on stage as well as, more broadly, women working in the theatre radically shifted not only the terms of analysis, but also the range and variety of theatrical work given scholarly consideration. Not surprisingly, an important emphasis of feminist critical work has been feminist theatre and performance practice. This volume collects some of the essays published over this period and so seeks to contribute to a history of feminist theatre in Canada.

It is significant, then, to note that elsewhere in the English-speaking world, there have already been book-length studies of this topic: Charlotte Canning's *Feminist Theaters in the USA* (first published in 1995), Lizbeth Goodman's *Contemporary Feminist Theatres: To Each Her Own* (1993), and Peta Tait's *Converging Realities: Feminism in Australian Theatre* (1994) the best known. And, given these three books all appeared more than a decade ago, a similar book chronicling feminist theatre and performance across Canada and Québec is surely long overdue. This is not that book but it is, nonetheless, evidence of a strong tradition of critical interest and the essays here show the diversity of perspective, geography, and performance method that falls under the rubric of "feminist theatre in Canada."

Of course, the mere mention of that rubric still prompts the question "what is feminist theatre in Canada?" As Canning writes in her study of feminist theatres in the USA, "I became more and more disenchanted with the project of struggling toward a definition, however provisional, as ultimately artificial, exclusionary, and discriminatory" (29). Instead, in a recognition that categorization is, by definition, limiting, Canning proposes a narrative that "identifies practices, relationships, and methods that characterize the process of doing feminist theatre" (29). In short, then, feminist theatre is a lot of different things—creators, communities, practitioners, audiences, styles, practices, critics. The essays in this volume follow the same principle as Canning's narrative and I hope that collectively they demonstrate at least as much about process as they do about product. In any event, it is impossible, in a single book, to do justice either to the range of feminist work in Canadian theatre or the breadth of scholarship this work has provoked. Instead this is best seen as a sampler of critical engagements with that very "process of doing feminist theatre."

Still, however, histories of women's contributions to theatre for any nation and in any historical period remain scant, and it is certainly true that the three books cited above have, despite the authors' intentions, come to stand for those histories in the countries they address as if they were the last—or, at least, the only necessary—word on their subject. Tait suggests her book "cannot encompass all those pioneering women who work in theatre, successfully breaking down barriers to women's inclusion in non-traditional fields such as directing, designing, writing and technical areas. Nor does it set out to document all the areas of theatre work in which feminists have made significant contribution in recent years" (22). Yet it is without question that we owe these authors a considerable debt for entering at least some of their countries' feminist theatres into significant and accessible historical record, for providing what Canning hopes is "a possible collective memory" (7). It is worrying, then, that no book-length record—even a partial one—exists for this theatre work in Canada, even if we can surely celebrate how much strong critical writing has appeared in print and that cumulatively this work has sketched in some of the achievements, challenges, and contributions of feminists working in theatres and other traditional and non-traditional performance spaces across Canada. I have chosen essays to represent a number of key critical approaches and in the context of other volumes in this series that will address work by lesbians and women of colour—many of whom are explicitly feminist and all of whom address many of the same issues that emerge in the essays here.

It is also relevant to observe, more generally, that while most "comprehensive" theatre histories now include reference to feminist theatre, this has not meant any widespread revision to account more inclusively for women's contributions to the theatre. Indeed, women's work often tends to be ghettoized in a single chapter devoted to this period-inscribed phenomenon of feminist theatre (predominantly 1970s and 1980s), something that seems to assure the continued absence of women elsewhere. This is, among other things, confirmation that not much—or at least not enough—has changed since Rina Fraticelli noted, in 1983, "[t]he exclusion of women's contribution from the cultural bank negates and undermines the version of reality which is actually lived by the women who comprise the vast majority of Canadian theatre audiences" (10).

Canada had its first feminist theatre companies in Winnipeg's Nellie McClung Theatre (1968) and Toronto's Redlight Theatre (1974). At the same time, in Québec, the Théâtre Expérimental des Femmes was an important model both within and outside that province—an inspiration for women working in theatre elsewhere in Canada and also across the world. Redlight, for example, created a new work to perform at Théâtre Expérimental des Femmes's 1982 festival of ten-minute plays. But it was Fraticelli's 1982 report *The Status of Women in Canadian Theatre*, commissioned by the federal government, that might be best described as a lightning rod for the growth and development of feminist theatre in this country. A national survey of 1156 productions staged at 104 Canadian theatres between 1978 and 1981, hers was a stark account of the extraordinary under-representation of women in the categories of playwright (10%), director (13%), and artistic director (11%). While Fraticelli's report did not garner the traction in the mainstream that might have been expected, it undoubtedly inspired both women working in the theatre and in the academy. For women working in theatre, the report gave weight and presence to what they already knew—opportunities were few in mainstream Canadian theatre and were often limited by theatre practices that did not fit with social, political, and aesthetic aims women had for their art. Fraticelli's report confirmed a need to create what was apparently unavailable and/or inaccessible in much of Canadian theatre.

Fraticelli's statistical evidence was also a clarion call to theatre scholars in the academy, to begin to address some of the feminist questions her report raised. In his introduction to the landmark volume of *Canadian Theatre Review* addressing "Feminism & Canadian Theatre" (which appeared in Summer 1985), Robert Wallace observed:

> The genesis of this issue was my discovery last year that Rina Fraticelli's invaluable report *The Status of Women in the Canadian Theatre*, which she prepared for the Status of Women Canada in 1982, had never been published. When I proposed to her that *CTR* publish parts of this report, she suggested that, at this late date, it would be more constructive to address the current status of women in Canadian theatre and to explore the ways in which feminism connects with or influences their work. (4)

Two articles from that *CTR* issue appear here. In one, Cindy Cowan looks at the contributions of women to Nova Scotia's theatre, how women there have necessarily had to work within the structures of existing theatres—"Nova Scotia is too sparsely populated and the theatre profession too small for women to avoid working with men" (3)—and she suggests that networking and mutual support are essential if feminist-inspired work is to flourish. Perceptively, Cowan notes that this will require not just concerted networking among women in Nova Scotian theatre, but larger social changes that might encourage the production of more plays by women and more receptive audiences, in the broadest sense, for that work. This reminds us of the importance of local and regional realities to any notion of feminist theatre, as well as the complexity of coalition that this requires. In the other, Kate Lushington explores the knotty question of what exactly a feminist might be and why was everyone so scared of her? Using Fraticelli's statistics as the basis for her own argument, Lushington looks at an anti-intellectualism that she sees as "intrinsic to the Canadian theatre" (16). Moreover, she observes that "[t]he silence which greeted the release of the [Fraticelli] report was (and has remained) deafening" (15). Yet Lushington ends on an optimistic note—one that rightly anticipates the wealth of activity, both creative and critical, that would follow through the 1980s and far beyond. Nonetheless, history has shown us that notwithstanding the quantity and quality of work undertaken by feminist theatres in Canada, the statistical landscape has not much changed since the Fraticelli report and that the opportunities for women in Canadian theatre at the beginning of the twenty-first century are certainly no better than they were when Fraticelli prepared her report. As Jennifer O'Connor's 2004 update on Nightwood Theatre (the final piece in this volume) indicates, a recent poll of twenty-six Canadian theatres produced equally depressing figures: less than 25% of artistic directors were women, 75.8% of plays performed were written by men, and so on (154). This has provoked a new initiative, "Equity in Canadian Theatre" (a coalition of theatre professionals and scholars), to reinvigorate a project Fraticelli initiated now more than twenty years ago.

This volume's next essay is a survey of women's theatre in Québec, written by Jane Moss and first published in 1986. Her essay, "The Body as Spectacle," first appeared in the important periodical *Women & Performance: A Journal of Feminist Theory* published out of the Department of Performance Studies at Tisch School for the Arts, New York University. Moss introduces readers to Québec theatremakers, strongly influenced by French feminist theory, creating "gynocentric plays in which women authors and performers invite women spectators to see themselves mirrored in the spectacle of the female body" (18). This (and Louise Forsyth's "A Clash of Symbols: When I Put on What I Want to Put on," included later in this collection) records the innovative and overtly feminist performances that have characterized Québec women's work. Certainly this has had an important influence on women working in English Canada as well as feminist critical writing (see, in particular, Patricia Badir's essay "Playing Solitaire: Spectatorship and Representation in Canadian Women's Monodrama" which discusses both Anglophone and Francophone work). Also, Moss's essay drew attention, for an international readership, to Québec as a location at the forefront of new performance directions in feminist theatre, with a commonality based on a commitment to feminist theory. It is important here, then, to remember the significance of Marie Savard, Pol Pelletier, Nicole Brossard and other Québec women in the landscape of feminist theatre in Canada. In this regard, it is worth noting that *Jeu*, the leading journal for Québec theatre, published its first special issue on "théâtre-femmes" (a bumper 250 pages) in 1980, a full five years before *Canadian Theatre Review* explored a similar terrain for English Canada. Forsyth's retrospective gives a wonderful sense of just how experimental and challenging was the work by women in Québec in the 1970s and 1980s, tempered by the author's sense that the 1990s have seen a downturn in that success—something that is substantiated by the quotation from Pol Pelletier that ends Forsyth's piece.

If the 1985 "Feminism & Canadian Theatre" special issue of *Canadian Theatre Review* had, for the most part, addressed the opportunities—or lack of them—for women within mainstream theatre, then later work began to look at the more alternative venues feminists had identified and established for performance creation. Kym Bird's article on The Company of Sirens introduced to the *CTR* readership the Toronto-based feminist theatre company that had been in existence since 1985. She describes the Sirens's emphasis on topic-based work (including shows addressing, among other things, sexual harassment, poverty, female work ghettos, and pay equity) and celebrates that the company "manages such important pedagogical work with an ease and lightness of tone" (30). This, as Bird shows, involves a wide variety of dramatic styles and approaches, as well as the active identification of non-traditional audiences. This is feminist theatre outside the theatre—appearing in union halls, schools, women's shelters, and conferences rather than behind the proscenium arch. Donna Smyth's essay on "Getting the Message: The NAAGs of Halifax" looks at street theatre "to raise public consciousness about peace issues from a feminist point of view" (32). Her account looks at the process (Smyth herself was a member of the NAAGs—Never Again Affinity Group) over four years of creating work in opposition to the nuclearism and militarism rampant in the early 1980s, culminating in a street performance to coincide with a meeting of NATO foreign ministers in Halifax. As Smyth points out, their kind of theatre faced particular kinds of challenges in its determination to be on the streets or in the shopping malls—taking it to their audiences—since so-called public space comes with all kinds of restrictions and controls. In short, there was a price to be paid for their feminist activist message. Women have, however, persisted in this kind of street comedy (as Smyth herself notes, the NAAGs resembled the Raging Grannies—an activist performance group that has had troupes in a number of Canadian cities) and this has been one site where feminist performance has, from time to time, flourished.

In "Women's Circle, Women's Theatre," Wendy Philpott describes another process-based feminist theatre, this time in Edmonton, to bring together women in participatory performance "to initiate action for justice" (41). Philpott's essay is based on individual interviews with each member of Catalyst Theatre's Women's Circle Collective—Marilyn McLean, Patricia Darbasie, Patricia Drake, Jane Heather, Jan Selman, Lise-Ann Johnson and Shirley Barrie—a strategy that compels the reader to wrestle with the complexities of process in creating performance work of this kind. In Shawna Dempsey and Lorri Millan's "Making It Happen: A Commercial Model for Self-Production," part of the creative process is thinking about where the work should appear—not in a conventional performance space or part of any theatre season but instead they have "opened for bands in bars, performed in classrooms as part of women's studies programs, or entertained participants of a United Church conference" (81). The commitment by these Winnipeg-based artists to take work to potential audiences is, it seems to me, as much a creative act as devising the performance itself.

These accounts of different strategies of production and reception indicate how local communities and individuals and groups of artists have found ways to create feminist performance in the logic of their own circumstances. Often this is done in relative isolation, a problem compounded by the geography of Canada. It is hard to know the full range of work being done at any one time, now or in the past. I have included in this collection an essay I wrote in 1995 (the opportunity to represent "women" in a volume on contemporary Canadian theatre) where I tried to suggest some of the diversity of theatre by women across the country. My goal was to anchor contemporary work to a tradition of Canadian women's playwriting and to demonstrate a proliferation of newer (alternative) practices that had emerged over recent years—in particular, performance art and collective creation—and the alternative venues in which these practices found their audiences: "In so many communities, inside and outside of Canada's major urban centres, women are claiming their own performance spaces, some of which they name as theatres and some not" (92). I remember well the difficulty in writing that essay, because of the compelling need to name names—to enter women's dramatic writing and performance into the historical record of Canadian theatre. More than ten years ago now, I worried about how much of this work was being lost and the accidental nature of what was being recorded. Feminist theatre scholars have a responsibility to think ahead, to allow for future theatre historians (and future artistic directors) to look back at this period and have a real sense of how many women were involved in Canadian theatre, in the mainstream and elsewhere, and the range and quality of the work produced.

I had been inspired by Djanet Sears's extraordinary essay, published in 1992, naming black women playwrights—many of whom I had not known. Sears offers a powerful and moving introduction to the work of Black women writing for theatre in Canada and she reminds us, rightly, of the conditions under which this writing is kept from sight. It continues to be important for critical perspectives on feminist theatre in Canada to find strategies for full inclusivity and to ensure, again, that we create an archive for future practitioners and historians both. As Sears described her own motivation, in an interview Joanne Tompkins and I conducted at the 1994 International Women Playwrights Conference in Adelaide: "My bottom line always is 'Does this say what I want it to say so my nieces and people seven generations from now for whom I'm responsible will have a range of texts to choose from?'" (156). This is a responsibility we share—and one we all still have.

Several of the essays included here demonstrate the careful feminist critical work on feminist plays and performance work that has been published. Playwrights Canada Press has, of course, been crucial to ensuring the availability of women's theatre writing for audiences far beyond the performance space; print versions not only preserve (a version of) the work, but enable its dissemination in the classroom and in the university/college/high school theatre. Patricia Badir's essay looks at a range of "monodramas" by women, Ann Wilson at Ann-Marie MacDonald's enormously successful *Goodnight Desdemona*, and Celeste Derksen at Margaret Hollingsworth's *The House That Jack Built*, seeing in it a feminist rewriting of the theatre of the absurd. Each of these essays identifies a particular creativity in addressing, and challenging, the audience for feminist work. Badir writes:

> When she speaks in the first person singular, the solo speaker understands that "I" is always already beyond her control. It is that reality that she documents. From there, direct experience of the monodrama feeds back to revise the spectator's horizon of expectations and to challenge the very conventions and meanings that that "I" represents. (60)

If collective creation has been an important expression of feminist community—with the potential to merge the interests of production and reception—then many women have worked very much alone. Financially, of course, the one-woman show is a pragmatic decision. But Badir's analysis also suggests the effectiveness of direct address. Her broad examination of both English Canadian and Québec women's solo performance provides evidence of its sheer range as well as its imaginative exploration of the genre "monodrama."

Wilson, in a careful reading of MacDonald's playful feminist revision of two Shakespeare plays, astutely observes: "MacDonald's revision is a political act which empowers women through the figure of Constance Ledbelly, who is doubly colonized as a woman and as a Canadian. Her academic project of discovering the two comedies is one which allows her to recognize how Shakespeare colonizes these sources and, in the process, constitutes women as passive subjects, both as characters in the plays and as readers" (73). It is hard, of course, not to see the continuing colonizing force of Shakespeare as at least one reason why *Goodnight Desdemona* has become one of the most successful, most often produced Canadian plays. Derksen's account of Hollingsworth's play pursues a similar revisionist agenda, as she insists "to consider Hollingsworth as absurdist is at once a challenge to the male exclusivity that is a defining feature of absurdism and an argument for revitalizing absurdism as a contemporary critical term" (125). Together, these three essays demonstrate well the challenges for feminist theatre scholars—as well as feminist theatre professionals—to take up institutional space. Traditional avenues of scholarly dissemination have been as exclusionary as mainstream theatre spaces; all institutions are tenaciously resistant to change. But, with that caution in mind, it is important to acknowledge how much feminist critical work has been and continues to be published in Canada.

Any critical perspective on feminist theatre must give appropriate attention and kudos to Nightwood Theatre, Canada's most famous and long-lasting example. Formed in 1979 by Cynthia Grant, Kim Renders, Mary Vingoe, and Maureen White, the history of Nightwood Theatre is illustrative of some of the shifts in feminist theatre and performance over a period now close to thirty years. As Shelley Scott points out in her essay on the changing mandate of Nightwood, the company has been an important venue for the production of women's work, whether single-authored plays or collective creations. It has been important as a touring company, as a collaborator with other companies, as a producer of an annual festival of new works, and, in general, as a mentor organization for women in theatre. Interestingly, the four founding members did not set out to create a feminist theatre company, but found themselves branded as such simply because it was four women running the show. In this context, Cynthia Grant notes of Nightwood, "Over time, we embraced our feminist positioning, as the feminist movement evolved. We also had an obligation to include a more diverse grouping of artists, despite our small size, which led us to process issues of sexual orientation, race, and class" (150). O'Connor's "Still Acting Out After 25 Years" marks the twenty-fifth year of Nightwood Theatre and sketches both the range of productions the company is now doing, as well as the context in which that work is undertaken.

These essays, then, provide a snapshot of critical perspectives on feminist theatre in Canada. Their different approaches and topics show well the range and quality of the work that has been produced over this last thirty or so years. But they also beg a question about the role of the feminist critic. For my own part, I have always considered writing about women in theatre in Canada a political commitment. It is, I believe, crucial that women in theatre studies create the spaces—historical, analytical, theoretical frameworks—that insist on the presence of women's performance work. This is, perhaps surprisingly, still feminist activist work. And I recognize that a significant part of my formation as a scholar was the opportunity to work closely with feminists in the theatre—my years on the Board of Directors of Maenad Theatre in Calgary gave me the opportunity to be in the feminist laboratory, as it were—or, perhaps better put, a feminist rehearsal space. I was actively involved in the incubation, development, and production of new work for the stage by Calgary women writers and I was on the front line in grants writing and other endeavours in support of that work and for the production of feminist work from elsewhere in Canada and the world. Not that this was either easy or necessarily successful. In an essay co-written with Maenad founding member Alexandria Patience, we described the struggles to obtain Canada Council funding in the face of an administrative structure the Council didn't (or didn't want to) understand: "The important elements of our evolving structure and mandate are that Maenad work must be non-hierarchical; collaborative; not sexist, racist, or homophobic; a première of a full production and technically/financially feasible for us to produce" (12). The fact that we named our audience as "women" was always criticized as lacking focus. A 1992 University of Calgary conference, co-organized with my colleague Kathleen Foreman as well as Maenad Theatre, on "women, theatre, and social action" enabled a network of feminist practitioners and scholars who have been in my life in a myriad of different ways ever since. What this all adds up to, for me, is a sustained and sustaining conversation that insists upon feminist theatre in Canada.

Notwithstanding this particular history, I want here to return to that inaugural issue on "feminism and Canadian theatre" (*CTR* 43, Summer 1985) where Margaret Hollingsworth published "Why We Don't Write"—a passionate reclaiming of women's histories in the theatre and a call for much more equitable inclusion of women in the full range of professional theatre activities. At the first International Women Playwrights Conference in Buffalo, New York, in 1988, she commented:

> I wrote an article three years ago, "Why We Don't Write." I had never received any kind of feedback for it, yet I've learned here that many people have read it, and it has helped them in their thinking. If only I'd received one or two letters from somebody, I would have tried to publish it more widely. I would have felt boosted. So, what I'm saying to you all is, please support each other. If you see a play that you enjoy by a woman, let her know she's not alone out there. If you see a play that is badly reviewed, don't sit back and complain about the critics. Write to the critics, tell them what you thought and send a copy to the editor of the newspaper (243-44).

This is a cautionary tale, one that points to the difficulties in forging the very networks and coalitions that feminist theatre and feminist critical practice understand as fundamental to their goals. The intersections and crossovers between feminists in both arenas have always been crucial, but seldom easy—a history that Ann Wilson has described, from her own perspective, in the introduction she prepared for the Winter 1991 special issue of *Canadian Theatre Review* on "Canadian Women Playwrights: (Inter)national Contexts":

> In 1985 [the First International Women Playwrights Conference], I was a little disheartened by what I perceived as the hostility between playwrights and critics. Now the suspicion and wariness in which each group held the other seems to be dissipating .... For me, the mark of this reconciliation was The Second International Women Playwrights Conference which was organized by a group of academics (of which I was one), playwrights, and other theatre professionals. Making the conference an actuality, not just a set of plays, was possible because of the support of the Playwrights Union of Canada, Glendon College, the University of Guelph, the University of Toronto, Company of Sirens (which co-sponsored the two evenings of readings at Theatre Passe Muraille), Factory Theatre and Harbourfront (which each co-sponsored an evening of readings). These organizations had never before worked together and I felt that this co-operation was a particularly important aspect of the conference: in these times when many of us feel besieged by numerous constraints (including financial ones), coalitions are necessary means for achieving ends. (3)

Wilson goes on to express "some sense of regret" (3) that the conference itself was beset by difficulties among different political and identity groups among the attendees. A recent coalition supports the Equity in Canadian Theatre initiative and there are, still, very many reasons why feminists in theatre and feminists in academic theatre studies benefit from alliances and collaborations, whatever the challenges these present. From this vantage point of critical perspectives on feminist theatre, it is perhaps useful to end with a reflection on how this kind of writing does—and might—function. In a recent article about The Women's One World Festival 1980-1981 (held in Manhattan's East Village), "Creating Community, Constructing Criticism," Lara Shalson promotes a rethinking of criticism:

> We are forced to shift our understanding of criticism, to no longer view it as a practice performed by certain qualified individuals, but rather as a site where cultural change is negotiated, and most importantly as a site that performers, spectators, and critics navigate together. We must rethink what criticism is, what work it is doing, and who produces it. To do so is to challenge certain received distinctions such as those between social/political criticism and theatre criticism; it is also to recognize and value the relationship between the kinds of critical work being done by

> artists and performers and that produced by those who write and about theatre and performance (232).

It is in this spirit that this book collects critical perspectives on feminist theatre in Canada. For me, this volume brings together artists and critics in an active demonstration of at least some of the strategies we have used over these last thirty years to spur dialogue, to nourish each other's feminisms, to celebrate women's theatre and performance, and, I hope, to foster one site where cultural change can happen.

(2006)

Works Cited

Bennett, Susan and Alexandria Patience. "Bad Girls Looking for Money." *Canadian Theatre Review* 82 (1995): 10-13.

Bennett, Susan and Joanne Tompkins. "'Making all the white people black': Interview with Djanet Sears." *Performing Women/Performing Feminisms: Interviews with International Women Playwrights.* Ed. Joanne Tompkins and Julie Holledge, Australasian Drama Studies Association Academic Publications 2, 1997. 153-57.

Canning, Charlotte. *Feminist Theaters in the USA*. London: Routledge, 1995.

France, Anna Kay and P.J. Corso. *International Women Playwrights: Voices of Identity and Transformation—Proceedings of the First International Women Playwrights Conference, October 18-23, 1988.* Buffalo, NY: Scarecrow P, 1993.

Fraticelli, Rina. "'Any black crippled woman can!': A feminist's notes from outside the sheltered workshop." *A Room of One's Own* 8.2 (1983): 7-18.

Goodman, Lizbeth. *Contemporary Feminist Theatres: To Each Her Own.* London: Routledge, 1993.

Hollingsworth, Margaret. "Why We Don't Write." *Canadian Theatre Review* 43 (1985): 21-27.

Shalson, Lara. "Creating Community, Constructing Criticism: The Women's One World Festival 1980-1981." *Theatre Topics* (2005): 221-59.

Tait, Peta. *Converging Realities: Feminism in Australian Theatre.* Sydney: Currency P, 1994.

Wallace, Robert. "Feminism and Canadian Theatre: An Introduction." *Canadian Theatre Review* 43 (1985): 4.

Wilson, Ann. "Canadian Women Playwrights: (Inter)national Contexts." *Canadian Theatre Review* 69 (1991): 3-4.

Messages in the Wilderness

by Cindy Cowan

> It is of the nature of Women's Movement that we are on the move. Eventually we find each other's messages that have been deposited in the way stations scattered in the wilderness. (Mary Daly, *Gyn/Ecology* xiv)

Mary Daly, a radical feminist writer as well as an associate professor of theology at Boston College, understands very well the difficulties of women working in fields traditionally dominated by men. Her own experiences have revealed how long it takes feminist ideas to find their way into popular theatre, literature and playwriting. Daly's quote above perfectly reflects the nature of women working in theatre in Nova Scotia.

In this region women's participation in theatre is inconsistent. At best, it can be described as a myriad of "scattered messages" surfacing in isolated pockets throughout the province; at worst, it can be dismissed as non-existent. A lack of communication between these pockets of work has resulted in women having little representation in Nova Scotian theatre, and has condemned their work to anonymity and isolation. If ever there was a group of women who needed to adopt a feminist attitude about their work, it is the women working in Nova Scotia.

In the last 22 years the Neptune Theatre has produced plays that have been written, designed, performed and directed predominantly by men. One hundred and seventy-six mainstage productions have been produced, of which only nine were written by women. Of these, three were co-written with men. Five women have directed for the theatre company; only two, however, directed mainstage productions, the other three being allocated "Lunchtime" and "School" shows. This can be explained by the fact that, like most regional theatres, Neptune has never had a woman artistic director.

Despite these conditions, which obviously are not an incentive for a woman playwright, women have secretly contributed to theatre in this province. Early plays such as *Three Sheets in the Wind* by Dorrie Philips, produced by the Halifax Theatre Company in 1966, *Undercover* by Margaret Armstrong, (which won honourable mention in the 1967 "Women Write for Theatre" competition) and *A True Believer* by Donna E. Smyth, reflect particular female sensibilities and the changing attitudes towards women in Nova Scotian society. And all have as central characters strong, independent women. These plays, however, are relatively unknown by most of the women working in theatre in Nova Scotia. Their writers developed the plays without the support of workshops and other women sympathetic to the play's themes—the contemporary procedure for the development of new work. Instead they worked in isolation, depositing their "messages in the way stations scattered in the wilderness." Although they presumably wrote to communicate to an audience, they have been ignored.

Even if these plays do not appear to be the foundation for a feminist theatre in Nova Scotia, we cannot afford to ignore them. For women concerned with the development of feminist theatre, these plays, as well as many others, reveal the history of women's theatre in Nova Scotia. And what they reveal is that women work in isolation.

Ironically, while women in the theatre have remained scattered and isolated, feminist organizations within the universities have a history of being strong in this province. Most notably, *Atlantis*, a women's journal published at Mount Saint Vincent University, provides an excellent opportunity for communication between women and feminist groups. But although articles on musicians, visual artists and writers of prose and poetry appear in *Atlantis*, articles on women in theatre rarely appear. Sadly, and to the detriment of women's theatre, feminists working in academic fields have had little impact on women working in theatre. Nor have women theatre artists used the feminist organizations to help promote and develop a sympathetic audience for their plays. The reason for this is, at least partially, that the feminist groups work in isolation as well, hidden within the universities and away from the realities of Maritime life.

It is the realities of Maritime life which are the subjects of many of the plays written by and about women here. Usually, women's theatre in Nova Scotia is for and about rural, domestically-inclined women. I believe that because this theatre is about women who bond with men, it is rejected by some feminists as a perpetuation of male mythology. This prejudice within the feminist movement has erected barriers and prevented communication between women. Surely every woman's needs are of concern to feminists and, in return, a strong feminist attitude should be of concern to all types of women.

Unfortunately, the word "feminism" conjures up an image of the white, well-educated, urban elite whose concerns are not those of fishery workers, fishing wives, and the unemployed. Rural women do not relate well to women who nurse openly (if they have children at all), dress differently, eat "peculiar" foods, and say they are actresses, directors, and writers. The reluctance of women theatre artists to label their work feminist comes from a real fear that the term will alienate and inhibit the type of women for whom they choose to write and perform.

Janet Amos, artistic director of Theatre New Brunswick, speculates that there might be a danger in labelling women's work feminist. She says, "The danger is that the work will either be rejected as propaganda, or worse, it will become more important that the work be done by women, than whether or not it is any good."[1]

This statement seems incongruous coming from the first and only woman regional artistic director in Canada. People assume that she must be a feminist. But what Amos's remark reveals about herself and her career is that it is the work which is most important to her. And if you label some work feminist, that implies there is other work by women which isn't. Barriers are erected and women excluded.

If the figures mentioned earlier reveal anything, it is that "our own theatre" is desperately needed. Women need to work, for in working we develop the skills necessary to articulate and dramatize our own theatre.

But is it wanted? It would seem that women, including those who see themselves as feminists, have been attending and supporting year after year theatre that presents women in secondary roles. No matter how good the plays are, I am certain that men would become bored seeing the tedious repetition of only one half the population, if the situation were reversed. It would appear, then, that women care little about what stimulates and sustains their imaginations. Otherwise, women would demand something else. Is it that they see theatre for the conservative institution that it is, without benefit to feminists? If this is the case, why hasn't there been more support and a growth in alternative theatre audiences? Perhaps it is simply that feminism, like the province of Nova Scotia, is conservative in nature, and that feminist women would rather remain isolated in their groups within the universities.

Janet Amos and other women who have succeeded in getting work have essentially done so by rejecting the elements of radical feminism which encourage women to stay away from patriarchal institutions. This attitude springs from a real concern that women's work, when it falls under the scrutiny of men, particularly in any of the non-traditional forms the work might take, will be misunderstood and perhaps compromised. Mary Daly, in an attempt to break down male language usage, describes herself as a 'spinner' or 'weaver' and talks about her work as 'spiralling' and as a 'journey'. While this imagery gives women a sense of their own spirituality and may remind them to keep moving and stay involved, it provides, at the same time, an excuse to be less aggressive, competitive and demanding concerning our needs as women artists.

In large cities this more radical form of feminism is possible since there are more like-minded women who can readily work together and even form their own community, rarely needing to deal with men. But Nova Scotia is too sparsely populated and the theatre profession too small for women to avoid working with men. The reality, whether we like it or not, is that women must work with men or remain isolated. Further complicating women's inclinations towards isolation is the choice to stay and work in Nova Scotia which culturally as well as economically is on the fringe. Halifax is not a major theatre centre compared to either Toronto or Edmonton. Within Canada, the Maritimes *are* very isolated and the women working here are affected by this reality. Perhaps this is why Maritimers, in general, seem to be attracted to a lifestyle that reinforces isolation.

Family is an important element of this lifestyle. Often we find women not only concerned with developing a career but with choosing to raise a family as well. Balancing children and a theatre career may require that their work lose momentum or that they temporarily stop entirely. This is unfortunate. Only women will change the prevailing attitudes towards women, children and work. But to do so they must be directly involved in the work-place, not scattered in way stations throughout the wilderness.

Within Mermaid Theatre this change has already occurred. Comments Sara Lee Lewis, who is the company manager and one of Mermaid's three founding members, along with Evelyn Garbary and Tom Miller: "If one of us has to dash to pick up a child after school we go. No matter who we are in meeting with, if it has to be interrupted for a child, we do so. This includes Graham Whitehead, the company's artistic director." Lee Lewis having raised both Mermaid Theatre and her own five children to a successful maturity has obviously contributed to this company's attitude towards family.

Sara Lee Lewis and Janet Amos are two of the most influential women working in Maritime theatre. Both have resisted becoming isolated in their professions. They work with confidence for they realize they have a great deal to offer the theatre profession. It is essential that other women find the courage to push for jobs as producers, directors, and writers. Only then can women achieve the positions necessary to provide a support system for each other. Feminism can give to women working in Nova Scotian theatre a belief in the value of our work, and this confidence is necessary to get our work produced.

The situation this year is typical: not one script written by a Nova Scotian woman has been sent to Neptune Theatre; three have been submitted from the rest of Canada; and this is out of a total of 26 plays. Neither have scripts been sent to Mermaid, Stage East and the Mulgrave Road Co-op theatres. Although older women are producing some drama for CBC Radio and ATV, there are virtually no young writers pushing for opportunities to have their scripts produced.

The situation of Haligonian director Linda Moore, who is presently associate artistic director at Manitoba Theatre Centre under James Roy, is a very interesting and revealing example of how women actually get work in theatre in the Maritimes. In 1974, Moore, a long-time participant in alternative theatre in Halifax, observed the demise of Pier One Theatre. Pier One was an experimental theatre valiantly attempting to bring less traditional theatre to Halifax audiences. No opportunities were available at Neptune Theatre for a young Nova Scotian woman director, which meant that she had to struggle on her own to continue her career. At the same time, Moore had a two-year-old to take care of. Finally the confidence to be more involved in theatre came with the realization that "No one but myself was stopping me from doing what I wanted. Till then I hadn't admitted, even to myself, that I wanted to direct." Pushing herself, Moore managed to fashion a career locally with the support of Eva Moore (related by marriage), executive director of the Nova Scotia Drama League. Eva saw to it that Linda found work with better amateur theatre groups.

Finally, as a result of her persistence, Linda met James Roy in Victoria, which led to her work at MTC.

Ironically, Linda Moore has found success outside of Nova Scotia and overcome isolation by not staying in the province as much as she would like to. Even more ironic is the situation Moore has found herself in most recently, where in MTC's production of *'Night Mother* she directed two of Nova Scotia's finest actresses, Joan Orenstein and Nicola Lipman. Here were three Nova Scotian women experiencing the rewards of working on a challenging women's play, something they would love to do in Halifax, but they were in Winnipeg.

Remarks Linda Moore: "Eva called me at MTC; 'How can I get this show into Halifax?' And although she failed in getting the show into the city she understood what the play could mean to women working in theatre in Nova Scotia. Women need that alertness and interest in their work."

Communicating, networking, and consciously supporting one another's work would reinforce the work being done in the Maritimes by women. On a small scale, the women members of the Mulgrave Road Co-op Theatre have begun networking their work; in doing so they have provided work for other women in the province and, in some cases, encouraged women who have left the region, like actress and writer Mary Vingoe and musician Marsha Coffey, to return and work with them.

The Mulgrave Road Co-op is a theatre artists' co-operative dedicated to the production of new Nova Scotian plays. In their plays the company looks at the social and political assumptions of the community they live in. Because of this honesty the audiences often leave feeling either unfairly attacked or gratefully identified.

The reason the women in the group have been able to work in the company is the unique way the company is organized. As a co-operative it functions collectively and by consensus. Structurally this is the way many women's organizations are run. Women are more comfortable with decisions that reflect the whole group rather than those of one individual. Within the company, equal opportunity for work is a result of equal creative input. In other words, if someone has an idea for a play and can convince the group of its merit, then she will have an opportunity to have it produced.

What gives strength to the women in the Mulgrave Road Co-op is the attempt they have made to build upon each other's work from year to year. Picking up where the last woman left off, they have incorporated the last "message" or experience and attempted to go one step further in developing plays for women. A direct result is that, unlike individual women they have avoided isolating their work. The company, although located in one of the most isolated areas of Nova Scotia, has broadened its impact by touring extensively throughout the Maritimes and by expanding its artistic membership each year.

Initially, the Mulgrave Road Co-op's plays took the form of the collective, relying on music, humorous vignettes and dramatic monologues. As a result of the needs of the women in the group, however, the company's focus shifted from collective efforts to a policy of commissioning playwrights. Although I say the *needs* of the women, it would be more honest to say the *survival* needs of the women involved. What gets put on stage is the material produced by the most aggressive actors in the collective: initially, therefore, the men prevailed. The subjects of early shows such as *The Coady Co-op Show*, or *Let's Play Fish* reflected the politics of male-dominated community; a single woman was all that was required for a token sister, wife, or secretary. Plays produced by the group's male members were often a reliving or retelling of history through the particular perspective of the time they were produced. And in history, especially the social history of Nova Scotia, men are the characters whose actions and conflicts are recorded.

The roles of women within Nova Scotia communities are much more subtle and, at first glance, not the subjects of exciting drama. Therefore a lot of the women's plays were in the style of "What if?" In such plays, women characters are put on the stage in imaginary situations to illustrate how the characters might respond. Consequently, these plays are more a speculation on what could have occurred based on our own experiences with human nature. The actresses within the company began to write so that they could control what was being presented on stage.

Many plays that have been produced by the Mulgrave Road Co-op Theatre Company have contributed to the development of women's theatre in Nova Scotia. These include *One on the Way*, *Another Story*, *Holy Ghosters* and *Spooks: The Mystery of Caledonia Mills*.

The seeds for *One on the Way* go back to the company's very first production, *The Mulgrave Road Show*. Gay Hauser, alone on stage with an old quilt on her lap, tells in story and song the making of the quilt and how each patch is entwined with her life's memories. The first stitches were made for her trousseau, the rest while her husband was away looking for work. The images of the nights of love under its covers and the eventual children that snuggled with her all weave together to form the final pattern of the quilt. It was a powerful moment of recognition for any woman watching in the audience.

Speaking about *One on the Way*, Gay Hauser, actress and one of the original company members, reflects on her reasons for initiating the play:

> We had been doing a lot of theatre about male heroes. The women I had met in the community were interesting and they deserved to see themselves and their lives on stage. I decided a play with only women would give us a chance to explore the potential for theatre about women.

Problems arose when Hauser, with the rest of the company, Mary Vingoe, Nicola Lipman and director Svetlana Zylin, tried to identify the real drama in the lives of rural women. What they discovered more often than not was that the drama for rural women lay in what they did every day. A new form of heroine emerged from the company, like Bessie, from *One on the Way*:

> If you can feed two children, you can feed seven, and if you can feed seven, you might as well feed 18. You can't let them starve!

Women like Bessie express their hopes, their fears and their disillusionment in the small dramas of every day. These are the same women who are suspicious of the term "feminism" because it suggests careers, to these women that means standing in six inches of water cleaning, gutting, and filleting half frozen fish. From *One on the Way*:

> I've been workin' at the fish plant,
> I've been workin' at the mill,
> I've been workin' at an office for a man I'd like to kill.
> I've been workin' at the cash for the only store in town.
> And I feel I'd like to settle down.

One on the Way was a first step and acted as an incentive to other women who were beginning to join the company to consider their own projects. More importantly, it was an example of how to break down the barriers which keep women working in isolation. First, the production brought women from Toronto, Halifax and Guysborough to do the show, a fact that helped to overcome geographical isolation. Hauser then sought the support of the Mount Saint Vincent's Women's Studies Programme which generously supported a run of the show in Halifax. *One on the Way* toured, like all company shows, to many different rural communities throughout the Maritimes, bringing its message to both men and women. And although none of the actresses had children, Hauser was five months pregnant at the time, thereby setting a precedent for woman and children working with the company and, as it has turned out, for the men as well. Finally, this show indicated what can happen when women work together and support each other's work. Hauser believes this "bonding" was reinforced by her portrayal of the women characters in the show. She suggests, "Rural women aren't aggressive. I admire that. What gives them strength is their friendships, their open dependence on each other, and their community. The result is if they need to mobilize to help each other they can do so quickly."

This statement best reflects my own views on the nature of women working in Nova Scotian theatre; feminism can and must reinforce the above attitude. Women cannot afford to feel or think of themselves as powerless. We achieve power by believing in ourselves and in each other's work. Our power will grow as more women openly depend on one another and bond to form strong theatrical communities. Theatre contributes to this growth because it speaks to our personal lives and can communicate to all women—rural, urban, white, black, educated or otherwise.

Another Story was the next play to deal with a subject related to women in the community. Directed by Jan Kudelka with music by Marsha Coffey, this play set the struggles of the "cardboard cut-out" soap opera stars against those of the rural women of Nova Scotia, women who know only too well the difference between their own lives and the world on television. From the show:

> I lost my husband
> About 10 years ago

I still keep on hoping
He'll walk through that door.
And when Alice lost Steve
It was a comfort of kind
But he's come back to life
While mine's still down the Mine.

Another Story did not confront in the same way as *One on the Way* the patterns of isolation working in Nova Scotia. However, the play did expand the forms and subjects that a play about women can have, revealing that plays about women need not be concerned with children, pregnancy, babies, husbands, boyfriends, and equal rights. *Another Story* presented female characters on stage speaking from their own particular point of view about issues relevant to the whole community. It also led Mary Vingoe to initiate her own production, *Holy Ghosters.*

Holy Ghosters was again a collaboration between Vingoe, Coffey and Kudelka, with Vingoe taking full responsibility as the playwright. Thus was the first play to be produced non-collectively by the company. This play also is an example of the "What if?" type of theatre I mentioned earlier. Vingoe speculates on what the women involved in the broken rebellion against the British military in Nova Scotia's Cumberland County experienced. The play is an interesting view of history from the perspective of three very strong women: Mary Allan, the wife of the rebel leader John Allan; Aboideaux, an old Acadian woman living on the Tantramar Marshes of Cumberland County (both these roles were portrayed with admirable skill and conviction by actress Wanda Graham, artistic director of Stage East); and Martha Maria Delesdernier, wife of John Uniacke. Uniacke was eventually to become prominent in Nova Scotian history as the province's Attorney-General.

Much of the criticism of the play focused on Uniacke and the other male characters who, it was felt, were not strong enough. It is my opinion that they were not meant to be stronger, but were supporting roles; and it was this role reversal that audiences had trouble with. I suppose when you put a famous man on stage and then upstage him with three women you are inviting trouble, but it seems unreasonable to reject a whole play on this basis. No one had criticized the company's earlier plays in which the women were merely supporting roles!

It is interesting that it is the nature of women's plays often to expose unpopular subjects, this making it difficult for the audience to "enjoy" themselves. Often the sensibilities being expressed are those of the underdog who is usually, but not necessarily a woman. In my own play *Spooks* I tried to reveal the true story of a young girl unfairly accused of setting fires in her parents' home. I attempted to show that this girl's story had been manipulated by the media to promote newspaper sales and, in the same way that journalists sought out the "thrills and chills" of the story in 1921, they again sought them in the play. Expecting spine-chilling "ghosts and spooks" they criticized the play for not living up to their expectations.

We all say reviews don't matter, but of course they do. Negative criticism in the media and a lack of understanding of alternative theatre is a serious impediment to the growth of any theatre in this province. The Mulgrave Road Co-op plays have been very successful not only in the rural areas of Nova Scotia but nationally and internationally as well. Yet in Halifax, response to their plays has been mixed despite a small but dedicated group of followers. Indeed the company's continued success and its longevity can be attributed to the theatre's commitment to rural Nova Scotia, and its avoidance of the pressures this conservative city brings to bear on those struggling to develop an alternative theatre.

The support of an alternative theatre audience (which ideally includes the women's community) is essential to the development and expression of women's theatre in Nova Scotia. Feminism can give women working in theatre the confidence to be more vocal and aggressive about jobs and their ability to produce good theatre. But this can only occur if feminists stop working in isolation about the province.

As the example of the women working with the Mulgrave Road Co-op demonstrates, when women playwrights combine with skilled women directors and producers, and when they in turn are supported by the women working in feminist organizations, then we truly see women finding each other's "messages that have been deposited in the way stations scattered in the wilderness," and the resulting awakening of their potential power and position in Nova Scotian theatre.

In the quotation at the beginning of this article, Mary Daly uses the words "eventually we find each other's messages." It could be interpreted that she is implying that fate will take care of us, and that we need not worry about what happens to women in theatre. But I don't believe in fate which, to me, is an accumulation and reflection of social attitudes and prejudices. These attitudes determine how many plays by women are put on the stage, and until our society is educated or told otherwise, it will continue to be very little. "Eventually" our work could become catalogued like the 3000 or so plays written by women before 1967 as merely the base from which all further writing ensued. "Eventually" our work could disappear entirely. Women theatre artists in Nova Scotia cannot afford to wait any longer to start communicating their "messages" to one another.

(1985)

Note

[1] The author does not provide a source for quotations that derive from personal interviews—ed.

Work Cited

Daly, Mary. *Gyn/ecology : The Metaethics of Radical Feminism.* Boston: Beacon Press, 1978.

Fear of Feminism

by Kate Lushington

As part of a recent survey of Miss Teen Canada contestants, the *Toronto Star* asked each young hopeful: Do you consider yourself a feminist? Their answers were even more startling and revealing of the current state of Canadian society than their overwhelming choice of Princess Diana as the most influential woman the world and *The Bible* as the most important book. Almost all answered no. For example:

> *No. I am proud to be a woman.*
> *No. I consider myself to be an independent woman; though it's still nice to have someone open a door for you.*
> *No. I feel that men and women should be equal.*[1]

Wait a minute. That's what I feel too. But I most emphatically *do* consider myself to be a feminist. Aren't we on the same side? What has gone wrong?

Clearly for these young women feminism as popularly depicted has come to imply an imprisoning ideology, fatal to the creative spirit of the free artist and equally hampering to the individual who has "other important goals to achieve" (Miss Teen South Western Quebec). Throughout this issue of *CTR* [vol. 43, 1985] various chance remarks reinforce this view: "women's theatre is 'propaganda';" "I don't want to exclude anybody;" "a strong feminist stance scares people off;" and "I want what's happening to men to get on stage too;" as though male culture were in danger of imminent demise at the hands of the women's movement. At best this all amounts to a serious misconception; at worst we are witnessing "fear of feminism" in epic proportions. What or who do people think feminists are?

A composite picture emerges, like the police artist's impression of a suspected criminal. The Feminist (can't you see the mock centrefold in *National Lampoon*?) is a kind of superior egghead, complete with hammer (for hammering home her points) and welding mask (non-traditional fashion to restrict her field of vision), sporting the latest in iron-clad ideologies. If she happens to be a playwright she writes on domestic issues such as needlepoint or abortion, portraying her female characters as victims who talk about nurturing and relationships.

Such is the Bogeywoman lurking amongst the disclaimers and disavowals expressed by many women in the theatre today. Because of this fabulous beast, any woman who dares to ask for more (work, vision, representation) can be undermined: if she were any good, she wouldn't need to be so fierce; after all, the theatre "speaks the truth about the basic human condition;" doesn't she want to be part of that? Because of this pink peril, any woman who prefers to work with others of like mind outside the male superstructure of the legitimate theatre can be trivialized and her very real fear of marginalisation played on with derogatory references to the "woman's ghetto." The irony is that feminism, which wants to infuse our culture with broader perspectives and greater scope for the stuff of drama, is here reduced to the narrow, petty straitjacket of dogma, making women into their own worst enemy. How has this myth taken hold of our collective subconscious? Whose definition is this? And just how dangerous is it?

> Feminist thinking is really *re*thinking, an examination of the way certain assumptions about women and the female character enter into the fundamental assumptions that organize all our thinking. For instance, assumptions such as the one that makes intuition and reason opposite terms parallel to female and male may have axiomatic force in our culture, but they are precisely what feminists need to question—or be reduced to checking the arithmetic, when the issue lies in the calculus. (Jehlen 75)

This mathematical metaphor is similar to the more 'domestic' one used by Women's Cultural Building member Lynne Fernie in a 1983 interview with Toronto's *Now* newspaper to show how the issues in feminism go beyond the struggle for equal rights. Some women are content, she explained, to fight for a larger slice of the pie; radical feminists wish to change the recipe.[2]

The far-reaching political ramifications of this statement give us another inkling as to why feminism might make Canadian women theatre artists so nervous. Unlike their counterparts in the visual, film and video arts, people in Canadian theatre are not normally linked with the political, let alone artistic, avant-garde. And then there is the question of the systemic powerlessness inherent in the acting profession. Theatre in this country is a young but nevertheless conservative institution, hierarchical in nature, in which people are the commodities exchanged. Actors, especially women, have little or no control over the productions they help to create since, if they want to work, they must please someone, usually a man, who is in a position to hire them. Not once, but again and again and again. No wonder it's hard to rock the boat.

This is true even in the majority of collective creations with which Canadian theatre made its mark in the 1970s: a recurring motif is a cast of several men, and one woman who plays all the female characters. "A clever device," crowed Western author Robert Kroetsch in a *The Globe and Mail* interview, clearly delighted by Paul Thompson's adaptation of his novel *The Studhorse Man* for the Toronto Theatre Festival in 1981. "A clever device in which one actress, Mary Vingoe, portrays the many facets of womanhood."[3] Oh, I get it; we're all the same person, right?

Most women in the theatre bemoan this hidden assumption, but the implications of a feminist analysis are frightening, challenging such comfortably held notions as the universality of artistic qualify, or excellence as the sole criterion for judgement, or even that women are a sub-group of the "basic human condition." "Talent," we are told, "will out." Since at the outset we all believe we are talented, this apparently unbiased attitude proves to be an effective carrot.

> Like a particularly nasty strain of influenza, the persistence of the myth of absolute, unfettered quality is remarkable. Quantum physics aside, the male-centred universe will have none of the relativity of values. And so, with reference to the subject of affirmative action, we are most likely to hear, in horrified tones: "You mean you actually want this ____________ (fill in the blank with one of the following: award, position, salary, grant, commission) to be determined on grounds *other than* pure quality?" We have learned to translate this as: "You mean you want *your* standards and criteria to replace *ours*?" Or, there's the ever-popular: "You mean you *want* to be considered a *woman* artist?" As if we were not. As if there were a choice. As if, by skillful sleight of hand we might succeed in drawing attention away from this fact and actually succeed in "passing" as small, high-pitched, bumpy men. (Fraticelli, "Any Black Crippled Woman Can!" 11-12)

Meanwhile, back to checking the arithmetic. In 1982, Rina Fraticelli saw the release of her report, *The Status of Women in Canadian Theatre*, which established the concept of the Invisibility Factor—the absence of women from significant roles in the work of producing a national culture. As can be seen in her statistical charts and tables, women, who comprise 51% of the Canadian population, and about 60% of the theatre-going public, represent a very small fraction of employed professionals in the Canadian theatre industry. This is especially true for the positions of playwright, director and artistic director, but it also extends to performers, theatre school faculty members, members of (arts council) juries, boards of directors, et cetera.

> Yet women form the vast majority of theatre school graduates as well as the vast majority of amateur (unpaid), volunteer and community theatre workers. That is, where there is low status and little or no money, women are present in great numbers. Elsewhere we are, statistically, nearly invisible. Lack of ability? No. Although we apply in shockingly small numbers, women have exceptional success rates among candidates for individual theatre grants from the Canada Council. And although our graduation seems to mark the end (rather than the beginning) of most of our professional careers, the achievement records of women theatre students offer us absolutely no clue to explain this phenomenon. (Fraticelli, *Status of Women* 9)

That graduation might be an end rather than a beginning to their careers was a thought that never occurred to a group of young women whom I directed recently at a reputable theatre school in this country. Although older and perhaps wiser than Miss Teen Canada, the majority did not consider themselves to be feminists; in fact, one thought the term was synonymous with suffragette. Nor, for that matter, did they feel there was anything about the world today that they would wish to change. When asked how they envisioned their future, and what their idea of success would be, they wanted children, homes in London and Los Angeles, and continual work in film, TV and radio as well as good roles in theatre. Appreciating the undeniable appeal of *People* magazine as food for fantasy, I broke the news as gently as I could. They weren't mad; they smiled at me kindly and their eyes glazed over. I could almost see them thinking, "Those statistics don't apply to me." They wanted to believe in the absolute quality of excellence; they needed to, as much as the test pilots and their families in Tom Wolfe's book needed to believe in "The Right Stuff," a mysterious quality possessed by those who survived, while all around them their buddies were going up in flames. It was not the fault of the system or the technology; those poor guys just didn't have what it takes. "The Right Stuff" lets us off the hook, allows people to maintain that no, they have never themselves experienced discrimination or gender-bias as a woman director or playwright, and that therefore it doesn't exist, despite all evidence to the contrary. Fear of feminism perhaps makes sense in this context; feminists have to accept that "The Right Stuff" is relative, and that people do get burned. How much easier to assume that Queen Bees are the only ones smart enough to run the hive. For if women have the ability and cannot be blamed for the lack of opportunity to exercise it, who can?

> Of course, the scenario is by now familiar to feminists and its roots are broad and complex: social, historical, political, economic....And in the theatre there are further complications resulting from the particularly social, labour-intensive, dependent nature of the art. Theatre is not work which can be accomplished in isolation; on the contrary, theatre artists are dependent for the very conditions, the tools, of our artistic activity on a vast complex of individuals and costly resources. This is the situation which distinguishes the theatre artist from, say, the poet or the visual artist. And this condition of acute dependency afflicts women in a particularly enduring way. For, overwhelmingly, the theatre industry is male-controlled, and the domination of men in each particular area of power and authority greatly increases the likelihood that they will dominate in the next. The preponderance of men on the boards of directors of theatres influences the selection of plays written by men, and the engagement of male directors to direct them. And plays written by men are far more likely to feature roles for male performers. All of this describes an aesthetic which excludes the experience of women. This makes it virtually impossible for women theatre artists to (literally) see ourselves in positions of authority and responsibility, and this formal, objective exclusion becomes internalised. The exclusion of

> women's contribution from the cultural bank negates and undermines the version of reality which is actually lived by the women who comprise the vast majority of Canadian theatre audiences. Thus an internalised, perhaps unconscious, sexism becomes culturally-encoded and institutionalised. This is called systemic discrimination. (Fraticelli, *Status of Women* 9-10)

In arguing for government intervention to reverse the patterns of systemic discrimination, Rina Fraticelli drew a striking analogy between the status of women in the theatre today and that of Canadians a short decade ago:

> There would, arguably, be no Canadian theatre to speak of without the programme of encouragement and subsidy created by governments to promote the production of Canadian works by Canadian companies through those years needed for Canadian audiences to develop an appreciation for their new national theatre. (Fraticelli, *Status of Women*)

The report was devastating in its findings and inspirational in its recommendations. One might have expected a public outcry, demanding that affirmative action and equal opportunity programmes be immediately implemented to redress the serious imbalance in the cultural life of the nation. No such luck. The silence which greeted the release of the report was (and has remained) deafening. Fraticelli now says that she "cannot gauge the effect it may have had on the theatre community, since they in no way supported it, responded to it or even acknowledged its existence." One former member of the Canada Council theatre section did point to a "feminine" flaw in the graphicological presentation of her statistics however. Apparently they are emotionally loaded by being drawn as people instead of columns. In every graph we are confronted with the "poor little woman" and the "big mean man." You better watch it, Rina old girl, those kind of scare tactics will get you nowhere.

It should be remembered that this study was actively solicited by the federal government in anticipation of the Applebaum-Hébert cultural policy review, to help formulate a response to submissions by Canadian women in the arts. Similar studies were also initiated in the fields of visual art, literature, music, film and video. When they were completed, the feds hired someone to summarize their conclusions, to report on the reports, and the individual documents were effectively suppressed. This is a pity, since Fraticelli's Canadian content analogy could do much to alleviate fear of feminism in the Canadian theatre. After all, when incentives to encourage Canadian playwrights were introduced, no one called us "strident colonials and xenophobic separatists;" there was no widespread fear of offending the British by "too strong a nationalist stance;" no one suggested that we should stop sleeping with Americans. Nor did anyone label the Tarragon Theatre "a Canadian ghetto," or worry that its playwrights would write only about awfully decent peace-keeping forces, beaver and moose. Why then are we so apparently terrified to claim our true voice and equal participation in culture *as women*? How has feminism somehow become equated with, instead of opposed to, sexism? Why is feminism seen as anti-life and pro-censorship? No wonder many women prefer to define themselves as "humanists!"

In the ten years since 1975, a period now officially referred to as the International Decade of the Woman, the status of women has not been materially altered in any way. If anything, things are getting worse; rapes are up and wages down. This is no less true in society at large than in the cultural institutions which are supposed to hold a mirror to our times. The failure of feminism and the Canadian theatre during this time is that we have found no way to make accessible to the majority of women across the country the notion that the tools of analysis are available to every individual, rural or urban, middle- or working-class, far from or close to the power centres of culture. These tools are essential if we are to break out of our cultural backwater and join the human race. Yet they are viewed with the utmost suspicion by many otherwise intelligent women theatre workers, in strong contrast to their counterparts in other artforms.

How are we to account for this? It seems to be partly due to the anti-intellectualism intrinsic to the Canadian theatre. Actors are told to trust their instincts and their (male) directors. Heaven forbid they should have a point of view. And it is partly due to clever media manipulation which has made feminism itself the issue instead of debating the issues within feminism. This strategy effectively keeps us busy defending the theory of gender-bias in culture, explaining once again, slowly, the relative quality of quality, and generally reinventing the wheel every time we open our mouths, when we could be busy talking to each other. This is wearisome, time-consuming and deflects our energies from actually developing cultural alternatives. It is small wonder that some convinced feminists, dusty with battle fatigue, are ready to leave the mainstream to its own devices and embrace the "woman's ghetto."

"The theatre may be a place where a woman can work, but it's certainly not a place where a feminist can work; unless she runs the shop."

So muses Rina Fraticelli as she considers her own next step. She would like to start a Woman's Inter Arts Building or Theatre Institute in which women could form a community to learn and teach skills and generate theory and criticism. Women's work will not happen without a permanent, institutionalised context, she observes; it is too easily marginalised, too easily dismissed.

> In dismissing the substance of women's lives as insignificant, inappropriate, uninteresting and bland, the theory of gender discrimination finds its most efficient strategy. The invalidation of the playwright's personal experience sabotages and censors her far more efficiently than any public censorship—which at least comes after the act of creation—could hope to. (Fraticelli, *Status of Women* 13)

As Pol Pelletier has done, Fraticelli feels the need to provide women with the space, time and power to which they don't normally have access. Feminism is not just a matter of doing non-sexist plays or replacing the boys at the top by girls. Feminism, rather, is a search, a constant questioning of accepted beliefs and hidden assumptions.

It's not a state, not an imperative, but a process, a dynamic. It's really not a noun. As Rina reflects,

> A friend once told me of the impact on 20th century theology of the concept that God is not a thing but a tendency—that which we are striving to become. That's my definition of feminism: at once a striving and a becoming. (Fraticelli, *Status of Women*)

So for all us phobics out there, here's the good news: feminism is a verb—**to become**—and an active one at that.

(1985)

Notes

1 The author doesn't identify the *Toronto Star* article she is citing—ed.

2 The author doesn't identify the source of this information—ed.

3 The author doesn't identify *The Globe and Mail* article she is citing—ed.

Works Cited

Fraticelli, Rina. "'Any black crippled woman can!': A feminist's notes from outside the sheltered workshop." *Room of One's Own* 8.2 (1983): 7-18.

———. "The Status of Women in the Canadian Theatre." Unpublished report to Status of Women Canada, June 1982.

Jehlen, Myra. "Archimedes and the Paradox of Feminist Criticism." *Feminisms: An Anthology of Literary Theory and Criticism.* Ed. Robyn R. Warhol and Diane Price Herndl. New Brunswick, NJ: Rutgers UP, 1997. 75-96.

The Body as Spectacle: Women's Theatre in Québec

by Jane Moss

During the last decade, a number of francophone women writers on both sides of the Atlantic have explored new semiotic, linguistic and literary modes in their efforts to "write the body." Leclerc, Irigaray, Cixous and others believe that true liberation begins with the discovery of sexual difference and therefore they must begin at the matrix of their sexuality: the female body. Although theatre has not been a primary medium for partisans of *l'écriture feminine* in France, Québec feminists have seen that on the stage they can focus attention on the female body through words and gestures. [1] They can represent women's bodies by re-presenting them. In collective works, monologues and musical dramas, they have placed the female body at center stage to be exposed, demystified, reclaimed, rehabilitated and reintegrated. These are gynocentric plays in which women authors and performers invite women spectators to see themselves mirrored in the spectacle of the female body. No longer objectified by male writers who used actresses to depict their own phobias or fantasies, the female body becomes the subject, the primary generator of the dramatic text.

Writing the body has been a source of pain as well as pleasure. In the process of overcoming the mutism and prudery of the past, feminist playwrights have dealt with the acts of violence and misogynist attitudes which humiliate and repress women. Often, painful memories must be acted out in pantomime because they cannot find the words to talk about their fear, degradation and frustration. Often the unspoken and unnamed obsessions take the form of hysteria as mad women act out their traumas. [2] When not possessed by their private demons, women take possession of themselves by talking openly about all aspects of their bodies including menstruation, labor pains and menopause as well as by naming and touching breasts, bellies and genitals. Often the female body becomes a source of auto or homoerotic pleasure in explicitly sexual scenes meant to celebrate the female libido rather then excite men.

It is interesting to note that the plays most preoccupied with the body are written by actresses. Tired of portraying women as male playwrights imagine them, tired of the spectator's gaze which judges them by superficial standards, these actresses write because of a deeply-felt need to redefine beauty, to valorize and repossess their bodies. They write plays that will be more faithful mirrors, truer reflections of their bodies and souls. They write to express their difference, that is their female specificity. Sylvie Prégent explained this motivation in an issue of the Québec drama review *Jeu* devoted to women's theatre:

> Si je n'étais pas femme, il me semble que l'urgence qui me pousse a écrire serait moins présente et, si tel était le cas, je n'écrirais pas. Écrire est un acte difficile et exigeant et il me faut, quant à moi, de grandes raisons pour passer à cet acte. Et mes plus grandes raisons sont mon sexe creux et mes seins ronds.
>
> (If I were not a woman, it seems to me that the sense of urgency which compels me to write would be less pressing and, if that were the case, I would not write. Writing is a difficult and demanding act and I, myself, must have good reasons to do it. And my best reasons are my hollow vagina and my round breasts.)[3]

When Marie Savard wrote *Bien à moi* in 1969, Québec theatre was still not ready for the spectacle of a woman talking about and caressing her own body. This poetic monologue, the first Québécois feminist play, presents a lonely woman who talks to herself since no one else hears her complaints about her solitude and frustration. Unsatisfied by conjugal love and tired of being "une statue aux yeux des hommes… statue mal aimée" (24-25, "a statue in the eyes of men…an ill-loved statue"), she finds consolation in auteroticism. The double mirror in her bedroom does not reflect her image but she sees herself:

> Et je me vois enfin dans toute la nudité de mon absence, si loin de moi que je suis. Mais cette distance, cet espace dans le temps qui m'éloigne de moi n'altère en aucune façon la viri…ô pardon…la vivacité de mes sentiments à mon endroit, mon endroit.
>
> L'endroit, c'est moi. (39)
>
> Je jouis. Je n'ai plus à me le cacher, à me refuser à moi pour mieux me réfugier derrière l'immense subterfuge de ma pudeur et de mon savoir vivre. Je redeviens la petite fille de mon miroir, la seule parfaite et unique maîtresse de mes yeux. (40)
>
> Je ferme les yeux
> blottie dans mes bras
> et je me berce doucement pour m'endormir. (41)
>
> (And finally I see myself in all the nudity of my absence, as far from myself as I am. But this distance, this space in time which separates me from myself in no way alters the viri…Oh pardon me... the vivacity of my sentiments toward the place which I occupy, my place.
>
> The place is me.
>
> I come. I no longer have to hide it, to refuse myself the pleasure of myself in order to take refuge behind the immense subterfuge of my modesty and my social tact. I am once again the little girl in my mirror, the one and only perfect mistress of my eyes.

I close my eyes
cuddled in my arms
and I rock myself gently to sleep.)

André Brassard, who directed the production of *Bien à moi* at the Théâtre de Quat'-Sous in February 1970, balked at the masturbation scene and the critics were equally troubled.

By 1976, the Women's Movement had raised the public consciousness to the point where a collective feminist work such as *La Nef des sorcières*[4] could have a successful run at one of Montreal's major theatres, the Theatre du Nouveau Monde, attracting male and female spectators. In the preface to the published text, Nicole Brossard and France Théoret stress the importance of the discourse of the female body to the process of liberation:

> Tout se tient si bien économiquement dans l'exploitation des corps, que lorsque les femmes parlent à partir de leur corps et qu'elles en disent l'exploitation et le refoulé, celles-ci commencent à dégager les toutes premières conditions de l'aliénation foncée en toutes et chacune de nous. (9)
>
> (Everything is tied so well economically to the exploitation of bodies that when women speak from their bodies and when they talk about the exploitation and repression of their bodies, they begin to liberate the very first conditions of forced alienation in each and every one of us.)

The first of the six monologues which make up *La Nef* belongs to Luce Guilbeault, *une actrice en folie*, so dispossessed of her words and body that she is on the verge of madness. Her name, Désirée Desire, suggests that she is both the object and subject of sexual pleasure, she who is desired and she who desires. No longer capable of repeating the words of others or of enduring the spectator's gaze, she seeks her own image in her monologue. This image begins with her sex organs:

Je prends un miroir,
Je le mets entre mes jambes,
Je regarde mon sexe,...
C'est mon autre visage (18)

(I take a mirror,
I put it between my legs,
I look at my genitals,...
My other face)

Shedding the disguised body and personae she projects on stage, the actress affirms herself by affirming her narcissism:

J'aime le corps que j'ai pour moi toute
Seule, dans le miroir de ma chambre,
Toute seule. (19)

(I love my body which is just for me
Alone, in the mirror of my room,
All alone.

In her second monologue, Désirée declares her independence by insisting on her sexuality. Speaking to her father, a representative of the patriarchal system which nullifies female desire, she says:

Papa, je me masturbe.
Papa, je ne suis plus vierge.
Papa, je me suis fait avorter. (51)

(Dad, I masturbate.
Dad, I am no longer a virgin.
Dad, I had an abortion.)

Marthe Blackburn, the menopausal woman uses her newly discovered ability to speak to talk about her body and her blood, that is the menstrual blood which has ceased to flow. She blames the Catholic Church, the medical establishment and Freudian psychiatry for denigrating, repressing and misunderstanding women's bodies:

On ne connaît pas mon corps. On en a toujours eu peur.
Ah! bien sûr on l'a disséqué. Violé, souvent. (23)

(They do not know my body. They have always feared it.
Oh! Of course they have dissected it. Raped it often.)

She rejects the idealization and mythification of women which turn them into passive statues and angrily attacks the commercial sex industry which objectifies and reifies women. For the menopausal woman, the first step toward self-realization consists of reintegrating and reclaiming her body:

Où est-ce qu'elle est ma peau pour que je sois bien dedans!
J'ai l'impression d'n'être plus qu'une écorchée
en tripes et en moelle.
Où est-ce qu'elle est ma peau pour que je lui redonne
sa mesure de dignité
et qu'elle colle à mes veines! (17)

(Where is my body so that I can feel good inside it!
It seems that all that is left of me is a flayed and disembowelled skeleton.
Where is my body so that I can restore its full measure of dignity
And so that my skin will stick to my flesh.)

Pol Pelletier's monologue goes even further in denouncing the humiliation of women's bodies and proclaiming her sexual differences. Her poetic descriptions of lesbian lovemaking and masturbation exalt female desire:

> Ce corps de femme allongé sur son flanc, moi en face allongée sur mon flanc à moi, la sensation d'une peau de femme tout le long de ma peau à moi, les jambes. Oh! mon Dieu, les jambes, longues choses satinées, mêlées, entremêlées, entrelacées, les mains sur des seins, mes mains sur des seins, est-ce possible une invention pareille, merveille....
>
> (UN IMMENSE RIRE ELLE EST RAVIE.)
>
> Les femmes frigides, c'est d'la blague.
> Y a pas une femme sur la terre qui se caresse
> ou se fait caresser le clitoris pendant quelques minutes qui n'a
> pas un orgasme certain. (69)
>
> (This woman's body stretched out on her side, facing her stretched out on my side, the feeling of a woman's skin alongside my skin, the legs. Oh! God, the legs, long satiny things crossed, entangled, interlaced, hands on breasts, my hands on breasts, how is such an invention possible, it's a marvel....
>
> [A TREMENDOUS LAUGH SHE IS ENRAPTURED.]
>
> Frigid women, that's a joke.
> There's not a woman on earth who fondles her clitoris or is fondled by another for a few minutes who is not sure to have an orgasm.)

For Pol Pelletier, lesbianism is an aggressive stance, a slap in the face of male society, and a conscious choice which satisfies, valorizes and liberates her.

La Nef des sorcières marks a double victory for Québécois feminists because it forces the spectator to hear women's speech and see women's bodies from a female perspective. "Jeu de corps autant que jeu de parole" say Brossard and Théoret, "place au corps...place à la parole" (11, "Body play as much as word play...place for the body...place for the word"). In women's plays, the symbolic content and the form of expression are equally important. Writing about French and American feminist plays, Josette Féral insists that the exploded text (multiple voices, nonlinear structure, interruptions, repetitions and blanks) mirrors the fragmentation which women experience in their lives. Fragmented, exposed, manipulated, mistreated, pliant yet triumphant the female body is exposed in these plays through *l'écriture feminine.* While agreeing with Féral, I would add that women's theatrical discourse stresses not only orality but also corporeality. What the actress does with her body on stage, her gestures, caresses and pantomime, are as important as what she says. The orality and physicality of theatre make it an excellent vehicle for women's speech since, according to Luce Irigaray, women tend to articulate their condition physically.

Text or spectacle? The dual nature of *le théâtre au féminin* is underlined by Brossard and Théoret who speak of *La Nef* as at joint effort by writers and actresses (7, 9). The 1978 production of *A ma mère, à ma mère, à ma mère, à ma voisine* was called a "spectacle" by its creators, four women from the Théâtre expérimental de Montréal who later founded the Théâtre expérimental des femmes. *A ma mère* was created primarily for women spectators. In "Notes sur la création du spectacle" appended to the published text, they outline the techniques they employed in the process of collective creation. Although they seem to have favored consciousness-raising discussions and free word association exercises, clearly improvisations yielded the best results. As if reluctant to admit the primacy of the physical in this "spectacle de femmes," they say:

> Nous notons que la parole qui sort des improvisations a très souvent quelque chose de "contingent," d'un peu plat alors que la parole des rêves éveillés est beaucoup plus audacieuse, plus abondante, plus signifiante. Les scènes tirées d'improvisations sont donc beaucoup moins verbales que les autres. Par ailleurs, les éléments physiques et visuels d'une improvisation peuvent être du plus haut intérêt. (56)
>
> (We note that the speech which comes from improvisation is often "contingent," a little dull, whereas the speech of free word association is more audacious, more profuse, signifying more. The scenes derived from improvisations are, therefore, less verbal than the others. In other respects, the physical and visual elements of an improvisation can be highly interesting.)

One of the improvised images is that of La Mère-Momie, the domineering mother figure who reigns over the first tableau. The white cloth which binds her body tightly symbolises the restrictions placed on women in society, restrictions accepted by patriarchal women such as the Reine Mère. The cloth mummifies her, negating her body and her sexuality. She is "reine, mère, vierge, martyre, sainte, pure, intouchée, intouchable, épouse, mère, chrétienne, fidèle" (16, "queen, mother, virgin, martyr, saint, pure, untouched, untouchable, wife, mother, christian, faithful"). The daughters' revolt against the mother is a physical attack, motivated by the need to accept female sexuality. One daughter acts out her refusal to conform by lapsing into madness. La Folle's madness seems caused by her inability to assume her sexuality in ways deemed socially appropriate. Her first words are:

> Ma main est sur mon sexe. Je sais pas ce que ça veut dire ce mot-là. Ma main est sur mon orange. (13)
>
> (My hand is on my genitals. I don't know what that word means. My hand is on my orange.)

A little later she observes:

> Un cul c'est un cul, une tête c'est une tête. Les gens auraient pu cacher leur tête pis montrer leur cul. (16)

> (An ass is an ass, a head is a head. People should be able to hide their heads and bare their asses.)

La Folle's words and actions illustrate her obsession with sex throughout the play. The other daughter channels her sexual energy and aggression into an explosive attack. She drowns out the mother's speech screaming "Jouir! Je peux jouir! Je veux jouir! J'aime jouir!" (20, "Come! I can come! I want to come! I like to come!") and then tears off the mummy's shroud. Exposing her mother's naked body, she forces her to look at her body, to accept her long-repressed sexuality and her maternal nature:

> Regarde-toi! Regarde tes seins! Regarde ton ventre! Regarde tes cuisses! Où est ta vie? Un endroit dans ton corps, un vide inattaqué, un vide plein d'énergie...Parle-moi de ton ventre, ton ventre tapi au fond de ton corps...Montre-moi ton sang, parle-moi de ton sang, du sang dans ton ventre! (20)

> (Look at yourself! Look at your breasts! Look at your belly! Look at your thighs! Where is your life? A place in your body, an unassailable emptiness, an emptiness full of energy...Talk to me about your womb, your womb deep within your body. Show me your blood, talk to me about your blood, the blood in your womb!)

Improvisation also inspired two tableaux in which the daughters act out the conflict between women's true nature and their assigned social roles. Transformed into La Jeune Mariée, La Fille does a pantomime representing her marriage ceremony, the wedding night, marital sex, pregnancy and childbirth. This "normal" sequence of events leads to hysteria, death and disappearance (25-26). La Folle becomes La Femme à la boule, weighed down by the huge rag ball which signifies female nature, the roundness of breasts, bellies and uteruses. As she struggles to free herself from the ball, her anger, distress and exasperation become more evident. Her body movements punctuate the text in which her fear of sexual repression is expressed as fear of clitoridectomy: "Je veux pas qu'on coupe mon clitoris!" (30, "I don't want them to cut off my clitoris!"). Sudden immobility and silence mark her defeat in the struggle against her feminine condition. This defeat is emphasized in the fifth tableau in pathological terms. La Femme a la boule has regressed and become La Petite Fille à l'orange who says that the center of her body is a large fissure, a red and black ravine (32).

Nullified or glorified, the female body remains the primary textual generator of *A ma mère.* The seventh tableau depicts a young girl being trained for womanhood, that is, fashioned into a puppet woman. Inspired by a collective improvisation, this "dressage" scene is performed in pantomime until the trainer breaks out of the training circle crying out her refusal of the reified female body which puts her in the category of domesticated animal. She yells:

> Je veux pas de corps! Je veux pas de ventre! Je veux pas de sexe! Je veux pas des gros seins lourds! Je veux pas des petits seins pointus! Je veux pas des beaux grands yeux! Je veux pas des beaux petits yeux! Je veux pas des

> cheveux blonds, bruns, roux! Je veux pas un gros ventre rondi! Je veux pas un petit ventre platte! Je veux pas de taille, je veux pas de hanche, je veux pas de cul, je veux pas de fesses! (38)
>
> (I don't want a body! I don't want a belly! I don't want genitals! I don't want big heavy breasts! I don't want pointed little breasts! I don't want beautiful big eyes! I don't want beautiful little eyes! I don't want blond, brown, red hair! I don't want a big round belly! I don't want a flat little tummy! I don't want a waist, I don't want hips, I don't want an ass, I don't want buttocks!)

This revolt leads to the battle cry sounded in the final scenic by the Warrior Women, the new Amazons glorified by Monique Wittig's *Les Guérillères.* Despite the burlesque elements of this scene, it is a serious call to arms. The Warriors chant:

> Notre corps nous appartient!...
> Faisons des push-ups!...
> Soyons musclées et solidaires!...
> Nous sommes des amazones!... (41-42)
>
> (Our bodies belong to us!...
> Let's do push-ups!...
> Let's show our muscles and our solidarity!...
> We are Amazons!...

The belligerent words are accompanied by a demonstration of martial arts and feats of strength. Having exorcised the stereotypes of female inferiority, the play ends with the glorification of the new mother, a woman of heroic proportions.

The female body is at the center of a number of other recent plays by Québec and Franco-Ontarian women. The main character of Jocelyne Beaulieu's psychodrama, *J'ai beaucoup changé depuis...* (1980) has been so traumatized by an abortion forced on her by her boyfriend that she ends up in a mental hospital. The straitjacket she wears and the false pregnancy she experiences symbolize the repression of her body, her sexuality and her maternal urge. At the play's end, she casts out her demons and takes possession of her body by giving birth to herself symbolically. Francine Ruel's play *Les Trois Grâces* (1982) presents three circus performers, fat women who display their bodies to a public which considers obesity monstrous. The play is a metaphor for a society that objectifies people and ridicules those who do not conform to its standards of beauty. Despite the grotesque humor of their act, the three fat ladies express their need to be accepted as sensuous, sensual women. They want to be seen and appreciated not just gawked at.

Les Trois Grâces was written at the request of three overweight actresses. Three thinner actresses wrote and performed *Strip* (1980), another play which deals with society's tendency to see women as objects of male sexual desire. Catherine Caron, Brigitte Haentjens and Sylvie Trudel played the parts of three striptease dancers in the original Ottawa production of this low-life musical comedy. No militant feminist stance here, but the nightly experience of stripping in front of an audience made up of lonely horny men and jealous prudish wives, has made the women acutely aware of the importance of sexuality in the search for happiness. They talk openly about their bodies and the dehumanizing effect of current sexual attitudes, yet they continue to fulfill the erotic fantasies of others without satisfying their own. Feeling powerless, degraded and frustrated one stripper laments:

> ...j'ai appris à me laisser regarder, mais de mon regard à moi je sais rien, de mon désir je sais rien, de mon plaisir je sais rien (43).
>
> (...I have learned to let others look at me, but of my own eyes I know nothing, of my desire I know nothing, of my sexual pleasure I know nothing.)

Although there is no triumphal act of self-possession at the end of *Strip*, it does bear witness to the "spectacularization" of the female body in women's plays.

By shining the spotlight on the female body, women's theatre invites actresses and female spectators to talk about, write about and act out the essence of their being, their female sexuality. Denouncing repression, negation, fragmentation and reification, the new body language refuses passivity and encourages psychosexual liberation through the discourse of the female body.

(1986)

Notes

[1] See my article, "Women's Theater in Québec" in *Traditionalism, Nationalism, and Feminism: Women Writers of Québec*, ed. Paula Gilbert Lewis (Westport, Ct: Greenwood Press, 1985). 241-54.

[2] See my article "Les Folles du Québec: The Theme of Madness in Québec Women's Theater," *The French Review* 57.5 (April 1984): 617-24.

[3] This and other English translations are my own.

[4] See [also] Hajdukowski-Ahnmed's excellent analysis of *La Nef des sorcières.*

Works Cited

Beaulieu, Jocelyne. *J'ai beaucoup changé depuis . . .* Montréal: Leméac, 1981.

Brossard, Nicole, France Théoret, et al. *La Nef des sorcières.* Montréal: Quinze, 1976.

Caron, Catherine, Brigitte Haentjens, Sylvie Trudel. *Strip.* Ottawa: Editions Prise de parole, 1983.

Feral, Josette. "Écriture et déplacement: la femme au théâtre." *The French Review* 56.2 (1982): 281-92.

Gagnon, Dominique, Louise Laprade, Nicole Lecavalier, Pol Pelletier. *A ma mère, à ma mère, à ma mère, à ma voisine.* Montréal: les editions du remue-ménage, 1979.

Hajdukowski-Ahnmed, Maroussia. "La Sorcière dans le texte (québecois) au feminine." *The French Review* 58.2 (1984): 264-68.

Irigaray, Luce. "Women's Exile" *Ideology & Consciousness* 1 (1977): 62-76.

Prégent, Sylvie. "Le Théátre au féminin" *Jeu* 16 (1980): 206-07.

Ruel, Francine. *Les Trois Grâces.* Montréal: Leméac, 1982.

Savard, Marie. *Bien à moi* Montréal: Editions de la pleine Lune, 1979.

The Company of Sirens: Popular Feminist Theatre in Canada

by Kym Bird

The Company of Sirens is a popular feminist theatre troupe formed in Toronto in 1985. They are engaged in collaborative theatre whose main objective is to "heal their audiences through humour" and educate them with respect to social and political issues, history, and ideology. *The Working People's Picture Show* and *Foul Play* are performed regularly in union halls, women's shelters, high schools and universities across the country and are adapted to the concerns of particular groups, sometimes with members of these groups helping to create the new scenes. *Mother Tongues* falls into the considerably more esoteric genre of the performance piece but is nevertheless concerned with the same political issues and attitudes that inspire The Sirens's more specifically pedagogical works.

According to Amanda Hale, *The Working People's Picture Show* "evolved in response to demands from unionized workers for popular theatre that reflects their lives and issues."[1] This one-hour show is about women's historical and contemporary relationship to work. It is a joyous and funny collection of satirical skits and popular songs given new, politically conscious lyrics. The opening scene, done to a rap beat, is a paradigm for much of what is to follow. Plain Jane is the product/victim of gender stereotyping at home and school and of sexual manipulation in the work place. After a history of negative socialization, she finally becomes aware and liberates herself by uniting with other women. The individual history of one woman is replaced by the collective history of all women as the focus of the play expands into a historical survey of the types of jobs which women have done. This retrospective glance ends with a piece on World War II, linking women's first *en masse* move into the work force and their untimely return to the home with the end of the war effort. Because these scenes are quick-paced and sweeping, they run the risk of oversimplification. Nevertheless, they give the audience a sense that women have a history, a concept which I don't think we can yet take for granted. They also make the connection between patriarchy, capitalism and imperialism which dictates the working conditions of women in twentieth-century North America, and upon which the rest of the play concentrates.

The Sirens explore the plight of women and work in contemporary North America through a series of colourful characters such as Rosemary Rosedale, an upper-middle class housewife and "true representative of the Canadian economy." Perched atop an enormous princess-style dress, Rosemary represents the large, looming patriarchal ideal of Angel-in-the-house. While she shops for South African diamonds and South American fruit, other characters appear from under her skirts and about her feet to tell of the effect that such naive consumerism has on third world politics, poverty and people. Hanna the housewife, Sarah XJ2, Brain Dead Brenda, and Miss Mendez are just some of the other characters through which the audience confronts issues such as sexual harassment, the effect of technology on traditionally female jobs, wife assault, sexism in hiring practices, female work ghettos, day-care, pay equity, equal opportunity, unions, and collective action.

The play ends on a celebratory note with a compendium of professions into which women have made substantial inroads. I saw *The Working People's Picture Show* at a high school, performed for an audience of young people who will soon be confronting the work-place patriarchal attitudes which the play addresses. Their task will be to carry on the work of liberation that has already begun.

Foul Play borrows scenes and situations from *The Working People's Picture Show* but its specific focus is on sexual harassment and sexual assault. When I went to see the show it played in the Library Sciences building at the University of Toronto under the sponsorship of the university's sexual harassment centre. In a small common room, using only office partitions and two chairs as props, the company staged 40 minutes of entertaining and instructive theatre. In this setting the focus of the play was university students and their dilemma when sexually harassed by professors. Once again, through a series of discrete scenes the play stages various aspects of sexual harassment: what it is—the exploitation of power relations for sexual purposes; who it happens to—usually female but also male students; how it happens; the stereotypical attitudes and myths which fault the often innocent and naive victim; the feelings of guilt and confusion that sexual harassment engenders. And, most importantly for this type of pedagogical theatre, what action a student can take if s/he finds her/himself in this situation. Although The Sirens are careful to point out that anyone of any sex or sexual preference can be a victim of sexual harassment, their focus is upon women and their particularly disadvantaged position given the nature of social relations in our society.

The play opens with Professor Huggems, a middle-aged and dangerously uninformed academic, reciting Freud's long-discredited theory of women as castrated men to a group of young, innocent, first-year students. We see Huggems attempt to seduce a couple of his female students and hear the stories of others who have been sexually harassed. These students are then given information on sexual harassment: humorous descriptions of typical offenders and their victims; a rather pessimistic "weather report" describing the atmosphere of sexism in various universities around Ontario; a "news report" on the prevalence of sexual harassment, undermining the accepted view of it as "harmless fun." Our brash, over-confident Professor Huggems strikes again, only this time he finds that his female student is more informed and threatens to counter his sexual tyranny with court action. If at the beginning of the play the female students are caught in the deceiving web of the professor's sweet talk, at the end they are clear-headed and capable of action. This evening closed with a lively discussion involving the audience, actors and the co-ordinator of the sexual harassment centre, who was able to answer specific questions on university policy and procedures for the filing of complaints.

Mother Tongues played at The Theatre Centre in Toronto last November. Although less specifically pedagogical in its approach, this piece, like The Sirens's other work, remains strong in its political commitment and consistent in the treatment of such thematic concerns as women's history, violence against women, racism, and gender and socialization. Unlike their other two plays, however, this play is not intended for a popular audience. It once again abandons the traditional linear structure of "the well-made play," but instead of replacing it with a series of self-coherent scenes, *Mother Tongues* uses a greater variety of media effects and dramatic approaches: slides, lighting, soundtrack, narrative collage, story, parody, confession, direct address to the audience, simultaneous speeches, song, dance, poetic diction and rhyming verse. Through these techniques it traces the myths and rituals which have patterned women's lives.

The play progresses loosely through childhood and a woman's first sexual stirrings, to adolescence and menstruation, dating, marriage and wifehood in a variety of different cultures. Woven in and amongst these patterns are both patriarchal and matriarchal myths and rituals of a female history; myths of Eve and Ishtar, the rituals of Sutti and the white wedding. The climactic moments of the play juxtapose a *National Enquirer*-esque account of various myths, and the murder of a Black woman in South Africa. This juxtaposition doesn't quite work. Both scenes are strong, perhaps even overstated in their own terms, but when brought together the trivialization on the one hand and melodrama on the other only jar against each other. Cynthia Grant, one of The Sirens's founding members has said, because of its experimental nature and its origin in collective creation, the play runs the risk of moments which don't quite come together. *Mother Tongues* has not been continually polished in the same way as The Sirens's other pieces, and since it does not serve the same agit-prop purposes, it is not likely to be worked on further.

The Company of Sirens has several projects in preproduction which further their political and theatrical work. These include: *Real Wheels Of Fortune*, which will deal with the feminization of poverty; *Les Ms*, a play on the subject of lesbianism; *All The Way*, a piece that The Sirens are creating together with high school students about aspects of gender and sexuality; and *Penelope*, an adaptation of Margaret Atwood's poems on *The Odyssey*. Of course the realization of these works is contingent upon funding, which is never easy to come by.

The most important thing to cherish about The Sirens's theatre is that it manages such important pedagogical work with an ease and lightness of tone which is always delightful. They carry valuable information to audiences which might otherwise have no access to it, and offer that information in such a way that few can refuse their gift.

(1989)

Note

1 The author does not provide sources for her quotations, based presumably on personal interviews—ed.

Getting the Message: The NAAGs of Halifax

by Donna E. Smyth

We were accused of "going too far," of "trivializing war," of being silly, absurd, ridiculous and Communist. From 1983-87, the NAAGs (Never Again Affinity Group) of Halifax performed street theatre and created media events to raise public consciousness about peace issues from a feminist point of view.[1] The original group of seven women, with one exception, had no professional theatre experience.[2] We were scholars, teachers, mothers, writers, artists. We all belonged to the Voice of Women, Canada's oldest national peace group, and we all felt a sense of urgency about the threat of nuclear war and survival of the planet.

Our feelings were shared, of course, by millions of people around the world. These were the early Reagan years with the huge defence buildup in the U.S., the Richard Perle years of playing with the First Strike option, the "evil empire" years. In 1982, during the UN Second Session on Disarmament, New York was the scene of the largest peace demonstration in North America. In response to increased international tension, peace groups sprang up everywhere. Demonstrations, rallies, marches: the people took their protest and concerns into the streets. By 1983, however, the main stream media was already tired of covering these events. They turned marches and demonstrations into numbers games: if there were two thousand, five thousand fewer marchers this year than last, this month than last, then something was wrong with The Peace Movement. The novelty aspect began to wear off for a general public conditioned to the 30-second clip (now "sound bite") of the electronic media.

In this context, the NAAGs group came together to discuss how and if we could make a difference. Our first meetings were like the feminist consciousness-raising groups of the '70s. We talked about the possibility of making the "personal political" and the political personal. We shared our nightmares of nuclear holocaust, our grief and our rage. The overwhelming sense of impending tragedy was mitigated by the sense of trust we developed with each other, by the kind of "gallows" humour that generates black comedy, and by an absurd kind of hope. We experienced the process Camus analyzed in *The Myth of Sisyphus* and *The Rebel*: the movement from existential despair and angst to the refusal of suicide and therefore responsibility for one's existence; the movement from slavery (in this case to nuclearism and militarism) to refusal of enslavement—freedom—and the responsibility, then, of creating conditions where others can be free.

We had a "message": we needed a collective means of expression. Street theatre was an obvious answer. We needed to reach people where they lived and did their shopping; people who ordinarily go neither to a play nor to a peace demonstration. The message had to be in a short and powerful form. Visual images were crucial: someone passing had to get at least a part of the message, carry away with them an image that stuck in the head. The visual impact was also a hook, a means of getting people to stop and listen. We needed a public event to link us to the larger context and we needed a script.

We decided the play would be in the form of a memorial service for nuclear victims. As we talked and shared research and experiences, we came to the conclusion that there were many kinds of nuclear "victims": those in Hiroshima and Nagasaki who had been killed and those who survived—the Hibakasha; uranium miners; nuclear workers; those who lived next to nuclear power plants. We decided that each of us would speak for a particular group of victims—we would be their ghosts come back to speak to the living, to warn them: Never Again! Our costumes would display the ritual signs of grieving: black robes, scarves over heads. White faces, hands; black around the eyes. We had come back from the dead. Against these symbolic images we would juxtapose realistic photographs, those taken of the victims of Hiroshima and Nagasaki showing radiation burns and scars, shock, agony.

As the writer in the group, I worked on the script and found myself haunted by another kind of ghost: W.B. Yeats and his plays based on the Japanese Noh theatre. It was natural to write with a poetic line, to have choral speaking and the counterpoint of voices to weave a collective expression around the individual speakers. We even used a drum to accentuate the rhythm of the playing and to pace us when we walked the streets.

On August 6th, 1983, we performed the play five times on the hot Halifax streets. We were accompanied by a group of people we called "outriders." They wore white with black armbands and handed out pamphlets explaining what we were doing. They also ran interference so that the players did not have to step out of role to argue with spectators. In the next couple of years, this band of "outriders" grew in numbers and they carried huge paper cranes on top of long poles strung with coloured ribbons. This parade-like effect was to contrast with the starkness of the players' costumes.

We played the *Hiroshima Memorial Service* several times and in several locations. Audience reaction was mixed. The solemn and obviously funereal aspects of the play deflected most overt aggression. In 1984, we decided that the last performance of the play for that August 6th should be in a symbolic setting: inside the fortress of Citadel Hill National Park which is located in the middle of Halifax and is run as a military museum. With about 25 outriders, we went in the back entrance and waited until the changing of the guard was over in the main square. Then we marched forth and began to perform. The place was full of tourists, mimic soldiers and security guards who immediately began to blow whistles, yell at us, threaten us. As we left, most of the tourists applauded us but one American man kept yelling: "What about Pearl Harbour? What about Pearl Harbour?"

In the fall of 1983, we were alerted by other peace activists. The NATO exercises of 1984 were to culminate in February with a week-long mock World War III. Nuclear bombs were dropped but only in the computers, and emergency planning services to save top political and military officials were given a trial run. In Canada, the official radiation bunkers (also called Diefenbunkers) were built in the 1950s, one to a province, except in the Maritimes where the Nova Scotian one at Camp Debert, approximately 65 miles from Halifax, served the whole region.

The NAAGs decided on a two-tier strategy (later this became a three-tier event for the group). For inspiration we turned to popular culture forms and black comedy. The result was the *Debert Debunkers Providential Lottery Show*. We printed and distributed lottery tickets: first prize was a Ringside Seat at Ground Zero (guaranteed vaporization); second was a Lifetime Supply of Cyanide Capsules (for the whole family); third was a One Way Ticket to Debert (the bunker). We staged the draw as a TV game show, each played a particular kind of fool: for example, there was the Nurturing Fool, the typical self-sacrificing kind of wife and mother, who had many arms for hugging and was prepared to clean up nuclear "shit" along with other messes; there was the Hope Fool who always hoped for the best and was cheery, cheery, cheerful; the Military Fool, etc. The point of the show was that each fool had to give up her own foolishness in order to "protest and survive."

Again, audience reaction was mixed. Most people seemed to enjoy the comedy and the lottery tickets were much sought after as souvenirs. One onlooker told a friend: "I don't care if they dance on the streets naked, as long as they get their point across." This performance was filmed by the NFB and became a small segment in the Bonnie Klein film *Speaking Our Peace*.

The second tier of the NAAGs' response was designed as a media event to draw public attention to the peace community's protest on February 29 (the leap-day which some mad satirist in the military designated as THE DAY for global nuclear conflict). Emergency Planning Canada had published a document called the Continuity of Government Program which stated that, in the event of a nuclear war, the current government must survive at all costs! The NAAGs developed a new collective identity as an all-female think tank called DD (Debert Debunkers) Research Associates and issued a counterproposal called The Continuity of People Program. Basically, this program suggested that we turn this "survival" exercise around. In the Debert bunker, for example, there were 329 places scheduled to be filled by political and military officials, some civil servants and a handful of media people. Of these 329, only 11 places were to be filled by women. DD Research Associates suggested that all the places be filled by women of "breeding age," with the addition of a sperm bank. We set up and photographed a mock clinic of sperm donors and distributed this documentation to the media. Interviews were done in costume by Dr Mutatis Mutandis and her associate, Dr Amanda Evergood. Media coverage was quite extensive including a newspaper story in Peru that a group of feminists in Canada was proposing to build a new Noah's Ark.

The third tier response was actually a performance piece. A Maritime coalition of women had decided to go to Debert on February 29 and protest the absurdity of the exercise. In this new form of military madness, it would be the women and children who were left exposed while a few men huddled in bunkers where they would probably be sizzled like those in the bomb shelters of Dresden during the fire bombing of that city in World War II.

NAAGs decided that our form of participation would be a Nuclear Victims' Survivors March. We made dummies to carry as the bodies of our dead and dying loved ones. One of our friends was a make-up expert who helped us put on the disfiguring scars and burns of nuclear war survivors. We actually made up in the volunteer fire hall in the town of Debert, about a mile from the bunker. The other women had gone ahead in their march to the gates and would be there to receive us with grief and rage.

We walked through Debert and down the road in the slush and the cold bearing our bodies. We had promised each other: no method acting! But the surreal aspect of what we were doing was very powerful.

As we approached the gates of the military compound, the other women began to keen and grieve. We took the bodies to the gates and knelt with them on either side of the road outside the checkpoint where cars entering with the bunker participants had to stop. We knelt and literally howled with grief while the cars swished in and out. Then, we left our bodies and walked back to the firehall, exhausted and in a state of shock very much resembling that described by Robert Lifton when he analyzed the psychological condition of the survivors of Hiroshima and Nagasaki (see Lifton and Falk).

What had happened was that, on some level, we were no longer "playing." Whereas the ritual aspect of the *Hiroshima Memorial Service* had protected us psychologically and had given profound emotions a structure, the *Nuclear Victims' Survivors March* had taken us past art and into the chaos of "reality." Yet it was a reality that was totally imaginary in the sense that it was based on our identification with a condition we had never experienced. Was it more imaginary than the reality of the men who went into the bunkers that day and other days, saying: It's only an exercise—don't be silly? Or saying: the worst might happen but *we* must survive? Military and nuclear theatre have their own rituals.

From that point on, the NAAGs never again reached for the "lower depths," at least in the tragic sense. We developed the black comedy and satiric aspects of environmental and peace issues. Under the guise of the Ladies of Halifax Auxiliary (LOHA) we staged a *Herbicide Tea Party* and published a cookbook: *New Ways To Cook With Radioactive and Toxic Wastes.* Some people accused us of being in "bad taste" but it wasn't until the *MOGS Action* of May, 1986, that we actually got into trouble.

At that time, the NATO foreign ministers were due to meet in Halifax. NAAGs went back to our think-tank guise and revived DD Research Associates. We came to the conclusion that the arms race was, in part, fuelled by the exploitation of a socially constructed male sexuality manifested in popular culture by such archetypes as Rambo and in political-military culture by the neo-conservatives, the cold warriors, the star warriors and so on. We collected weapons advertisements with an obvious phallic thrust from diverse sources ranging from *Aviation Week* to *NATO 16 Nations.* We looked at language usage; for example, "soft target environment" (human flesh, other flesh and blood); pet names for planes such as "tom cat." We came up with an analysis of a syndrome which we called MOGS, otherwise known as the milito-genital-confusion-dependency syndrome but more popularly called the "dreaded militarization disease." We decided that the syndrome could be cured but that MOGS victims first had to admit their dependency and want to be cured. We created a NATO general, Daniel O'Ratt, a genuine MOGS victim who had come to his senses and was ready to share his story with the world.

About a week before the NATO ministers arrived, NAAGs printed a tabloid, *The NATO Mirror*, which told the story of General O'Ratt and spread the word about the dreaded MOGS carriers (the ministers) coming to town. With the help of about twenty other peace activists, we hit the streets first thing in the morning, dressed as newsboys/girls, handing out the tabloid at street corners, bus stops, at the ferry terminals, wherever there was a rush-hour crowd. Reaction was mixed but tended towards a pattern which we later recognized at other stages of the action: most women and some men found the satire very funny; many men and a few women found it offensive.

The mixed reaction became quite hostile in certain quarters when we moved into the media event sequence. This involved a media kit containing a copy of the case history of General O'Ratt and copies of weapons advertisements. It was media people who accused us of "going too far" and "trivializing war." Some thought we had made up the weapons advertisements. One called the Better Business Bureau to see if DD Research Associates was a registered company. Many now refused to interview our familiar Dr Mutatis.

The night before we were to launch the street theatre part of the action, we discussed our situation. We were wary of more hostile reaction on the street and worried about the nervous condition of the security guards who ringed round the World Trade Centre where the ministers were meeting and where we intended to take our MOGS testing station. These same guards had, the day before, jumped and reached for their guns when the noon-day gun at the Citadel fortress was fired. Authorities had brought in a thousand extra security personnel, the air was swarming with helicopters, sections of the city were blocked to traffic. Halifax was, in effect, occupied. Everyone was talking about terrorists.

We decided that these conditions were the very ones we were trying to illuminate and that we should go ahead with the street theatre. We dressed in white lab coats and wore fantastic headgear, looking very much like clowns. We carried a child's electronic set which made strange noises—this was our testing unit—and a megaphone. We were not only talking about MOGS, we were advertising the peace rally in the evening. We had also printed stickers which certified the bearer had been tested and was MOGS-free. On the streets, we found the same mixed reaction but less actual hostility than the media had expressed a couple of days before. We approached the World Trade Centre very slowly, making sure the guards had plenty of time to observe that we were clowns and not terrorists. As we passed and they heard our patter: "You're doing a good job protecting us from those MOGS carriers inside," etc., the guards began to relax and some even smiled. For a few seconds, the power of laughter threatened to wash away the whole edifice. But then the NATO ministers came racing out, jumped into their waiting cars and sped away to lunch. Maybe one or two noticed some clown doctors cheering them on: there go the MOGS carriers!

The power of laughter and theatre was also clear in our last NAAGs performance in June, 1987. We were asked to participate in an anti-nuclear rally in St John, New Brunswick. The rally was to protest the proposal to build another nuclear reactor, Lepreau 2, next to New Brunswick's first reactor, Lepreau 1. It was timed to coincide with the annual general meeting of the Canadian Nuclear Association who just happened to be holding their AGM at the time when it looked as though the proposal, with the backing of the then-Tory government led by Richard Hatfield, would become a reality.

NAAGs collaborated on a *Nuclear Faith* script featuring a parody of the recent scandal of Jim and Tammy Bakker and the PTL Club. The characters included the Reverend Cobalt Candu and his faithful wife Candy, Dr Heebie-Jeebie who had back-slid from nuclear faith due to a certain nuclear accident and had to be saved again by Candu and Candy, and other broad comic types dressed in bizarre costumes. Johnny Nucleo, for instance, had limbs missing and an eyeball hanging out but he still wanted to set up The Half-Life Cafe in the Nuclear Theme Park our dear little Mrs New Brunswick was proposing for the province. We had also written and printed as handouts, tastefully done, a nuclear parody of the Lord's Prayer.

What began as a peaceful rally almost turned into a riot as counter-demonstrators, mainly construction workers, surged in around the bandstand and attempted to crowd the rally organizers and participants out. In fact, the New Brunswick Federation of Labour had come out against Lepreau 2, but some construction unions had broken away and were protesting in favour of it because of the promised jobs. We participants were jostled and shoved and it looked as though there was sure to be a fight. The NAAGs felt especially conspicuous and therefore vulnerable in our costumes. Fortunately, the police moved in and the union bosses moved their men off the stage. Some of them began to drift away but about 50 stayed to barrack and protest. In this volatile state, the rally began. NAAGs were due to perform in the first ten minutes or so. We had actually blocked ourselves and rehearsed that morning but the blocking was totally ruined because of the situation. We were squeezed onto the platform, it was starting to rain, and the pro-Lepreau guys were very loud.

We pitched our performance to them—were they not adherents of the nuclear faith? When they yelled, we would yell back: Amen, brother! We offered them club memberships, we asked them to join with us in the Nuclear Faith prayer. The script might have been written with them in mind. They could see that we were taking them off but they didn't know how to respond. They even laughed at a couple of the Jim and Tammy jokes. They got quieter. Somehow, the whole mood of the thing changed. We finished our performance; the rally continued with excellent speakers. Some of the pro-nuclear demonstrators stayed to listen and began to talk with anti-nuclear people. Discussion replaced confrontation.

In the next provincial election, the Liberals, who had promised to oppose Lepreau 2, swept the Tories under the table. For the first time in the history of the province, there was no elected opposition. And, for the time being, no more investment in nuclear power.

NAAGs is now on hold: many of the original group moved away and the rest of us have become absorbed in other projects. In some ways, the story of NAAGs is typical of small theatre groups; in others, not. We did not set out "to make a name" for ourselves; we wanted a way to express collectively what we felt individually and we wanted to be of service to the peace and environmental communities of which we were a part. The fact that we were embedded in these communities enabled us to do what we did. We actually refused several invitations to perform as an entertainment group because we did not view ourselves primarily as entertainers and because we had limited time, energy and money. Although we had access to helpful professional theatre people, we learned how to do things by doing them. As a group we tried to remain flexible and, indeed, were forced to be so because of the rapid turnover, after the first two years, of members. New women coming in brought new energy and skills and we, in turn, shared what we had learned.

The limitations of what we did were, in part, the limitations, theatrically speaking, of an amateur group. They were also the limitations of the culture in which we worked. Doing street theatre teaches you things about a city which are not always obvious to those who live there—except to those who live on the streets. There are very few truly public places left in most of our cities. Acres are devoted to commercial private properties where you are not allowed to bring political protest, even in the guise of entertainment. Yet, this is where thousands of people can be reached: in the shopping malls and squares. NAAGs were kicked out of a number of these places. So-called public parks are controlled and patrolled by authorities who also usually object to anything that is considered "political." Citizens have to ask permission to hold certain kinds of events in areas paid for with their own taxes. On the street, you are not allowed to block traffic or entry to stores or buildings: you have to "keep moving." Street people, including prostitutes, are familiar with the problem but ordinary citizens often don't realize exactly how our enjoyment and use of our cities is constrained and restricted, how our role is precisely defined: worker/consumer—and how difficult it is to "act," in every sense of the word, outside these roles.

Theatres and art galleries have restricted access and these "playing spaces" are already occupied by professionals and official culture. Besides, on any given day, there are far more people at the shopping malls than in these places.

Access to the media is perhaps more tightly controlled than any of these other areas. Unless you cast a story in a conventional media frame, forget it. Like the old agitprop theatre, it has to be a simple story with stereotyped characters: the good guys, the bad guys, the confrontation. The environmental theatre of groups like Greenpeace is very effective but hard to manage on that scale by smaller and less well-funded groups. NAAGs and other groups have staged media events to get the "message" across but the odds of good coverage are stacked against any news that is really new; i.e., that would question in some form or the other mainstream institutions, the structures of power and authority in our society, that would challenge what the media views as mainstream values and attitudes.

The feminist grounding of NAAGs informed all our actions. We used our experience as women to play against a male-dominated culture and to comment on our roles within that culture. As the Ladies of Halifax Auxiliary, for example, we donned outrageous hats and gloves, wore pearls and other aspects of respectable ladies' costumes. For one benefit performance, we made judges' wigs out of tampons. We made fools of ourselves in public just as the Raging Grannies groups have done in the past year across the country. In this way we used the power of the Fool, the freedom of the Clown to reach out and touch other people. I think women in particular have this comic gift—once we step out of our conventional roles, we're not afraid to be foolish if that's what it takes to get the message across.

We used the power of theatre to move us beyond ourselves, something more of us are going to have to do if we are to survive as a species with other species living on this planet.

(1989)

Notes

[1] The title of my article is a play on Lucy R. Lippard's *Get the Message?*

[2] The original NAAGs group was: Liz Archibald–Calder, Bonnie Bobryk, Nancy Colpitts, Karen Fairless, Pat Kipping, Kate McKenna, Yvonne Manzer, Wilma Needham, Donna E. Smyth, Gillian Thomas. Ingrid Coenig and Susan McEachern became members while other women participated in specific actions at various times.

Works Cited

Lifton, Robert Jay and Richard Falk. *Indefensible Weapons: The Political and Psychological Case Against Nuclearism.* Toronto: CBC Enterprises, 1982.

Lippard, Lucy R. *Get the Message? A Decade of Art for Social Change.* New York: Dutton, 1984.

Women's Circle: Women's Theatre

by Wendy Philpott

This article is based upon individual interviews conducted by Wendy Philpott with each member of Catalyst Theatre's Women's Circle Collective: Marilyn McLean, Community Co-ordinator for Catalyst Theatre, actresses Patricia Darbasie and Patricia Drake, actress and animator Jane Heather, director Jan Selman, researcher and dramaturge Lise-Ann Johnson and writer Shirley Barrie. The article was written by Jane Heather and Jan Selman with assistance from Lise-Ann Johnson and Wendy Philpott.

Women's Circle is a popular theatre project created by women, for women and about women. We are using theatre in a variety of ways to connect women to other women, and to initiate action for justice. The project has three complementary strands: participatory research, participatory performance, and community workshops. Participatory research uses popular theatre methods in workshops with women. The participatory play will draw a wide variety of women together in order to name, initiate discussion of and explore action around issues which were identified during the participatory research. Follow-up workshops with organized and new women's groups will enable women to explore action and, when appropriate, link together around issues of concern.

> **Selman**: One impulse for the *Women's Circle* Project was my own coming to terms with my position in this kind of theatre. I've done many popular/social action theatre projects with communities that are not my own, and while I feel that there is value and importance in that work, I think popular theatre centred within a community, without outside intervention, is important. There is huge value in working within your own community. So, what is my community? One I very clearly identify with is the community of women.
>
> **Heather**: I'm heading into the '90s and realizing that I don't know any more what a feminist is or what a feminist does. And I used to feel that I was really sure about that. So I came initially to the project feeling that this was something I've been working on all my life, that this was an opportunity to work very closely with all kinds of women.
>
> **Selman**: The other and equally strong impulse was that I wanted to extend and strengthen a form that I believe in a great deal, that still needs a lot of looking at and experimenting with. And that's this

> particular kind of participatory theatre. It is not Boal's Forum Theatre, though it shares some of its objectives; it is work where characters interact directly with the audience to explore issues and skills.

Popular theatre projects have to be situated within a social and political context. We are working with a wide variety of women in urban Canada, specifically Edmonton, in the 1990s. Alberta is a conservative province; our premier thinks that we can improve conditions for families by legislating Family Day and by funding more skating rinks. The activism here is quiet and the links between various agents of change are not strong.

We are also working in the context of the Canadian women's movement. These days the category "women" or "women's issue" often seems too simple to reflect reality. A black twenty-five-year-old working class lesbian feminist smoker may have no basis upon which to *talk* to a white forty-five-year-old middle class heterosexual REAL non-smoker, much less take collective action with her. Women are deeply divided along lines of class, colour, sexual orientation, education, life experience, age and analysis (our own group is by no means homogeneous) and the debates between women at many recent conferences and meetings have been passionate, bitter and perhaps long overdue. So we are struggling with issues of difference, knowing and seeing both the truth of divisions and the truth of alliances. Yes it is contradictory; once you've chosen change and collective action, virtually nothing is straightforward. We're trying to heighten contradiction, not paper it over, to dig into the complexity of the problem and the steps toward the solutions.

> **Barrie**: I don't think there are a lot of easy answers to women's issues at this point in time. There aren't a lot of simple solutions. I think we have to start trying to deal with complexity. In trying to incorporate so many voices this play is trying to be really complex. We're not trying to be obscure but we are trying to be complex.

The project is about change for women. In that spirit we include a wide variety of women at every stage of the creative process. They identify the issues, help create the scenes, characters, metaphors and imagery, investigate the issues during the performances and more. Participation is key. Over and over again decisions are made in this society without the participation of those who are most deeply affected. This project is our way of contributing to righting that imbalance. In that name we struggle for the highest possible level of participation at all stages of process. Our process of research, workshop and play creation grows out of our commitment to work in our own community in an ethical, democratic, inclusive and creative manner. We believe, for example, that the process of research must be of value to the individuals and groups which we interact with. We are not interested in "collecting" other women's stories and translating those into "our" theatre project. Our role is to offer groups another way of achieving their objectives; popular theatre methods can enable groups to find new ways of voicing and analyzing issues and identifying and testing action. It can assist people to acknowledge the emotional aspects of a circumstance and link them to behaviour and action. Conversely, very personal issues can be distanced enough to be examined from new angles.

Identifying the Issues

Early in the process Jan, Marilyn and Jane facilitated research workshops with a wide variety of women's groups. We worked with women in unions, immigrant women, rural women, women from the inner city, survivors of domestic violence and others. We wanted to offer women an opportunity to speak their lives publicly yet safely. We were looking for stories, images and opinions and we wanted to see how women in groups connected to each other and to us. We offered groups our theatre skills and our own stories in return.

We were looking for the answers to these kinds of questions: What's on women's minds these days? What are the key issues or concerns? Where are women getting support? What are women's dreams? What prevents them from realizing their dreams? What are the victories, the great moments in women's lives? Where do women meet? Why do they meet? What do they talk about? What do they do? What should the play be about?

> **Heather**: This kind of project asks you to question everything, assume nothing. The intent, at the very least, is to allow yourself to not create structures for yourself which would make you blind.

Typically a workshop included: a game-based warm-up, the creation of a variety of realistic and representational sculptures and story creation exercises. With groups that we worked with in an on-going way we moved to scene creation as well. Games were an important part of the process. Despite initial reluctance to jump in, such joy and energy was released, such huge bubbles of laughter, that we vowed to include "play" in our play. Again and again we were told how much women needed and wanted to be silly, physical and relaxed together and how rare the opportunities were to do so.

In each group we asked women to create instant and planned body sculptures. Sculpturing is non-intellectual and includes people who are not comfortable with a lot of talking. We used sculpture to begin our list of concerns and issues and for expressing emotional states, dreams, key moments, relationships between people and relationships between women and institutions.

Story-telling plays a significant role in all our work. It is through story that people gain insight into one another's lives. When someone's story is listened to with respect she gains respect for herself. We learn about our common experiences and about how we differ.

> **Heather**: We help to create conditions where women can speak to women through story; it is the exchange of story that helps us name and analyze the situation and form the action.

Stories poured out of women's mouths; funny stories, horrible stories, lyrical stories, more than we could hold in our brains. Some stories may appear in some way in the play but we continually remind ourselves of how the stories were gathered and in what context. It is not the individual story in isolation but the accumulation and exchange of story that is powerful, and empowering.

We often used a "Snap Shot" Story exercise to look at dilemmas or decision points in a woman's life. Participants create a story and tell it back to the larger group using their bodies in frozen positions to form tableaux. Each tableau is examined by the group. Potential points of change are explored. In a workshop with survivors of domestic violence we spent a lot of time looking at events that lead up to the decision to leave an abusive relationship. One night we asked the group to examine a moment of decision or dilemma that might happen after one left an abusive relationship. A group created a frozen picture of a woman and a man at a restaurant. The man was offering the woman a flower. The flower became a symbol of an offer to go home with him. The issue was: how do I decline the request? The group decided that the woman needed to be assertive. One woman who offered to try it was big, energetic and confident and we looked forward to seeing how she would handle this guy. Near to tears she stammered out, "Please could I go home to my own bed, please?" We had to re-examine our assumptions.

Our work with two groups of survivors of violence, and the graphic examples of the need to work with great care, has had and will continue to have significant impact on the play. The effect of violence on women's lives is a key thread in the play and the ethical questions around the effect of the play and workshops will continue to be foregrounded. In virtually all the workshops we asked for positive moments in women's lives and stories and sculptures of women supporting women. Often these incidents were harder to find than crisis points.

We were working with groups of women yet we had an experience in one group where female staff sabotaged female clients; staff stopped women from taking action that they had identified as important. On two occasions smoking was very contentious; one of our members was pregnant and we asked for a non-smoking work area for her. Both times the request was met with caustic hostility. We began to wonder if women *can* support other women.

These early workshops pushed us hard. A picture began to emerge of women needing to have some fun together, wanting to tell their stories and speak of their pain and their triumphs. Women working with other women yet unwilling or unable to support other women. Women working together to find meaning and strength, to change their situations. The questions these workshops raised continue to be central to the project. The disempowerment of women in the name of "help" is scary. We're trying to address these issues, or at least ask the questions which may lead our audiences and ourselves to some new understandings and actions.

Expanding the Circle

In 1990 Jan, Marilyn and Jane were joined by Lise-Ann Johnson, a researcher and dramaturge, actors Patricia Darbasie (Pat) and Patricia Drake (Patty) and playwright Shirley Barrie. Our focus was to move towards realistic scenes which grew out of community research and which left characters at a point of crisis or decision. Our challenge was to find out how to work together collectively, given our differences of age, race, politics, class and experience.

> **Darbasie**: Jane and Jan and Marilyn had been working for two and a half years before Patty and I joined the process so there was already a framework, and in some ways it was totally alien.
>
> **Drake**: When I first came in May, it was really exciting because I had just graduated and I was this hungry actor. And Jan pulls me into her office and talks about the project and everything that's involved, and the only thing in the back of my mind was, "Ha I've got a job, I've got a job, right on!" So there I was in May with all my little theatrical, technical skills and everything I'd learned in school. We came into it the first day, we sat around talking about the project and we got up on our feet. Then Jan moved it to participatory theatre techniques, which was absolutely terrifying, but I'm telling myself, "just trust...you're a professional..." And I was completely baffled, it was terrifying work because you're throwing yourself into the audience.
>
> **Selman**: The project is asking the actors to be workshop leaders and community researchers. I don't think there's a way for the actors to sit back and not do that. They need to be in there with the groups we work with.
>
> **Darbasie**: Coming into a project like this, where it was most important that it was true to women, so that a female audience can say "yes, that's how we think, yes, that's an issue which touches me," was really great.
>
> **Drake**: There is a real frustration which comes along with doing collective theatre.
>
> **Johnson**: Something I like about the process is that it gives everyone a chance, it gives everyone in the Circle a voice. We come together and everybody has different backgrounds: we're actors, and writers, and directors, and researchers, and community resource people. And I don't feel like who I am necessarily limits what I say.
>
> **Drake**: This project and its process is like a relationship. You are in it some days and it's "oh, wow, this is so amazing, this is really what theatre and acting and life is all about." And at other times you're thinking "I hate it, I don't want to be here, I want out."

> **Heather**: I view chaos, I mean "chaos" in the sense of things happening simultaneously and things smashing against one another, some things going forward and some things going backward at the same time, as a normal condition of this kind of project.

> **Barrie**: We have a group of very different people. I think it was really vital that there were younger people there as well as older people. We all looked at life from a different perspective. Rather than one faction saying, "No no no my vision has to get through here" and the other faction saying, "No no no my vision has to get through," we were trying to find a way to take from all sides and come up with something we could all commit to.

> **Selman**: Shirley has a strong sense of what her task is in the group and so knew when to sit back and just listen to everyone else doing all these other things in order that she could down the road do her task. She really has a good sense of self, and that's a very good thing for a writer in a collective; it's hard to be a writer in a collective.

Creating Participatory Scenes

In our form of participatory theatre actors stay in role and interact directly with the audience. Realistic scenes stop when a character is in a moment of crisis; the character must make a difficult decision or discover an action which will allow her to move forward. She turns to the audience in order to discover what she should do next.

The choice to work in participatory theatre is aesthetically and politically motivated. In this age of isolation, theatre offers a rare opportunity for a group of people to come together and share a common experience. When the theatre is good the audience becomes, to some degree, a community. Participatory theatre builds on this communal strength and enables people to start a dialogue and build links right there in the theatre. It shares the power of the stage with the audience; artists become part of the community rather than distanced entertainers. The spontaneity and risk of live theatre is taken to the limit and shared with the audience.

The danger is that we may imply that if the character, and therefore anyone like the character, just solves her personal problems (e.g., learns to communicate better) the world will be okay. While this may be fine if the objective and needs of the audience are to learn a certain skill, the danger is that the underlying message is one of blaming a victim.

> **Heather**: Any time you're doing participation and you're saying the audience is screwed up or they're stupid, you're in trouble because you're not listening to them.

We are trying to create conditions where the forming of the community, made up of audience and performers, enables new discoveries. We are trying to connect images and stories in order to create scenes which link rather than separate issues, which point up contradictions and which ask questions to which neither we nor our audiences have immediate answers.

Scenes come together out of fire. A scene which was very painful to create, but with which we are very happy, is called "The Red Dress." Many threads were wound together during its creation. In workshops women often told stories about image, about "looking good" or "looking awful," about make-up, clothes, nylons, high heels, all the baggage of being sexy or "attractive." We entered the scene development phase with lots of those images in our heads and of course with our own images of "feminine," "female" and "woman." We sculpted images of "how you learned what a woman was." We explored body image and created sculptures of our own perceived "deficiencies." Someone offered an image of "your husband thinks you look sexy in those short shorts but if you leave the house are you providing some stranger with his jollies?" Some of us read a book based on encounters between feminists and sex-trade workers. Women in survivors of violence groups told us that when you're in an abusive relationship nothing you wear is right; if you dress carelessly you get in trouble for looking ugly, if you dress up you must be trying to come on to some other man—either way you get in trouble. We also wanted to weave into the scene how women of different classes meet, how different women can support each other and be friends. We used our own lives and experiences to look for a way to put two dissimilar characters together. I think we were all a little surprised to discover how limited the common ground is for women of different classes. "The Red Dress" is the result.

Testing Scenes

Once we found the basic structure and storyline of a scene, we improvised it for groups who had helped create or spark the scene.

> **Selman**: When we work with a group it's important that we go back to that group and show them what we've done so they can intervene and say, no that's not right, this is what that character would do. When we are truly in process we can truly respond to the offers.

Sometimes we played a scene and asked whether it was "true." Sometimes we asked what might happen next in the characters' lives.

> **Barrie**: I think that the reason the red dress scene worked so well for us was that it constantly kept opening up more questions and every time we played the scene we got different responses or different angles.

> **Darbasie**: Going to specific groups validates what we're doing. With the red dress scene, when we took it to a group of survivors of abuse, women said "hey, this young woman has a problem here." So it validates that information which is sub-textual.

McLean: When we gave the red dress scene a reading at a forum on feminist research and asked the audience what was an issue for them in the scene, they wanted to focus on the power issues between those two women. It wasn't that they didn't see the violence, but for them that wasn't the issue. Their issue was the danger, particularly for feminist women, in laying on their own analysis. The audience really took on the managerial woman's assumptions about the other woman's right to express her own sexuality as she chooses. They were suggesting that she look at her hang-ups about sexuality, and look at the kind of power tripping that she's doing. So, that was a reminder to us to not necessarily focus the participation on the issues that we felt were key, but allow the audience to identify what for them was important.

Experimenting with Participation

Sometimes we, gulp, played a rough scene and entered right into participation with an audience.

Drake: We performed at a conference about mothering and I was one of the actors in a participatory scene and the thing I learned which was so exciting for me, having only dealt with scripted work up until that time, was that it was like parachuting. My chute might open, but it might not, but boy what a thrill knowing that it might not open. Because I was new to it I had to just completely trust the audience and say, "Look, I need help and I don't have any more knowledge than you do." What was exciting was the equality between me and the audience, between actor and audience.

Darbasie: With participation, it's deciding how much you're going to push an audience.

McLean: What was intriguing was the notion of pushing the boundaries of the participatory form. In all of our work we've been trying to move towards an analysis which asks how to effect structural change and then in a theatrical process how do you involve audiences in helping to identify issues of structural change when you are looking at an individual story. From the beginning, one of the objectives was to look at how women could work collectively for change on structures.

Writing the Play

During the summer of 1990 Shirley took the ideas, characters, improvisations and comments and tried to make sense of it all.

Barrie: I had a brief conversation with Jan about my role in the project. She said, "You have to go away and write the play that you want to write."

> And I said, "Well, no, I don't think that in this particular situation that's necessarily my function." That's the Joint Stock way, where it's clear from the very beginning that while the research is done collectively, the play is the writer's. I have never felt that that is my role in this project. I've felt more that it is to somehow try to serve the information and the input that everybody has come up with.

Shirley returned with a first draft of a script in the fall. After workshopping the draft we came to the conclusion that we had several significant holes in our research. Predictably, characters and issues furthest from our own experience needed more development. Before moving to a second draft we determined to return to our process of participatory research and testing with the groups who held those life experiences.

> **Heather**: The project can reflect only as far as we have been able to press our analysis, and overcome our prejudices, such as class divisions. We are as inclusive as we can be.

> **Barrie**: I guess the most frustrating thing is not knowing when or what the end is going to be. Trying to say "just go with the process" is really hard when you're a writer attuned to writing a play that you'd like to have produced at some point.

So, as we move into the next stage of this project we are determined to address a number of issues, including the structure of the participation, the style of the bridges between the major scenes and the nature of the contact between actor and audience. We are exploring how to make the participatory elements of the play theatrical while at the same time allowing the audience to have the time to really dig into the dilemmas and contradictions which the scenes pose.

> **Selman**: The participation has to be on the edge, explosive and charged. It needs to have a couple of agendas. One is to allow the audience to speak amongst themselves and to "strategize" together. And then we must also be there as true animators, which means to challenge the first layer of answers.

Previous work in participation was with homogeneous audiences. With this project we hope to draw a wide variety of women together. The play can act as a bridge, a time when women can talk with women who have very different life experiences than their own. We are also looking for a framework for the scenes which overtly expresses our agenda, our biases, who we are, and which reflects the power of collectivity. Women can change society by working together and apart. When is coalition appropriate?

> **Selman**: We know we have a series of realistic scenes that turn out to the audience. To me, what we haven't got yet is the style of theatre to put between those scenes so that they are brought into relief, giving it a framework that says, "we're looking at these people and also more than these people." I think some of the answers are in choral work because we're talking about many different voices coming together.

This is a long process. There is a lot to work out, question and challenge. But we believe that if we are truly serious about using our theatre skill and artistry to contribute to change for women, then we must find the ways that we can best reach women, best identify movements where change is possible and best offer theatre to that process. A danger is that we lock into the traditionally delivered play because that is how the system works. Perhaps we'll always be in process, creating new pieces based upon our audiences' knowledge and our growing awareness.

> **Johnson**: The project is important because it talks about women. Women don't get a chance to talk about their issues and their experience much. That needs to happen. It's about making sure that women are collectively heard. The project is asking a lot of hard questions: can women work together, is there power in collective femaleness and do we have disagreements that we can work out, or are we too polarized, do cultures make us too different. It's asking all those really hard questions that I don't think are asked very often. I also think it's important because it's a play that reaches out beyond the theatre community, to people who don't go to plays.
>
> **McLean**: The balance that we are trying to achieve is not just representing women as victims or women at points of crisis, but we're also focusing on women's strengths, on celebration, on the wonderful powerful moments that we all experience. Hopefully we'll really find that balance.
>
> **Johnson**: I do believe there's an empowerment in speech that women get when they speak together.
>
> **Selman**: The centre of the whole project is to provide a new style of forum where women can follow their own voice and decide what they want their society to become. That has to be the measuring stick beside all of our work. And that has to be reflected in the way we do all of the work at every stage.

(1991)

Playing Solitaire: Spectatorship and Representation in Canadian Women's Monodrama

by Patricia Badir

In her contribution to *La Nef des sorcières*, Nicole Brossard states: "Au fond, une femme qui parle seule est toujours une femme qui s'attend à quelque chose de nouveau" (74). Expressed in these terms, the private and intimate nature of the monodrama becomes comparable to the solitary yet political acts of journal writing and diary keeping which are forms of personal expression seeking to explore female experiences left out of history, literature and art. I have found that like these prose genres, women's monodramas tend to be autobiographical and intimately connected to the individual bodies that have conceived them as well as to the temporal and spatial context out of which they have grown. The language of the texts is oral and spontaneous, showing remarkable similarity to the entries of diaries. The dramaturgical structures display heavy reliance upon memory as the speakers move freely and frequently imperceptibly between the past and the present. Plots are primarily oriented around the personal process of "getting it straight" with dramatic conflict arising out of a sense of oppositional discourses, as the speaker's story runs perpendicular to that of history, of patriarchy or of the dominant culture.[1] Christl Verduyn explains that because their experience has always been publicly documented by members of the "dominant sex" (if documented at all), women have frequently turned to private and autobiographical forms of writing such as the journal, the memoir, the letter and the monodrama in order to re-inscribe the subjective "I." Verduyn argues that by replacing the written "she" with the first person singular "I," the woman writer accedes to the rank of subject. She leaves behind the status of object suggested by the third person singular as inscribed in historical and literary canons (27).

Monodrama, however, unlike prose forms of personal expression, is conceived with performance in mind. The presence of viewing spectators in the context of a live performance introduces a different set of both aesthetic and political questions as the issue of the representation of the private "I" is brought to the forefront. "In an important sense," says Keir Elam, "it is the spectator who 'initiates' the theatrical communication process through a series of actions at once practical and symbolic, of which the first is the simple act of buying a ticket." Elam elaborates that the audience, by its very presence, "constitutes the one invariable condition of the performance.... It is with the spectator, in brief, that theatrical communication begins and ends" (95-97). The monodrama is a private and intimate endeavour, yet it stands as theatre for public consumption by an observer who, in most cases, has paid for the opportunity to view. The speaker's subjectivity is found to be dependent upon the participation of spectators in an act of semiotic interpretation. The "I" becomes contingent upon a wide range of cultural values and ideological beliefs all of which form, to borrow Susan Bennett"s terminology appropriated from reception theory, the spectator's "horizon of expectations." "The spectator comes to the theatre as a member of an already-constituted interpretive community," argues Bennett, suggesting that the hypotheses which constitute an audience's reading of a particular performance are influenced by and measured against a complex network of extra-performance material (52-54, 149). Sue-Ellen Case also notes that the importance of the author's intent gives way to the composition of the audience in determining the meaning of the theatrical event. In other words, it is the "norms" of a culture that assign meaning to the performance. "For a feminist," says Case, "this means that the dominant notions of gender, class and race compose the meaning of the text of a play, the stage pictures of its production and the audience reception of its meaning" (117). While all this can be said of readership and of the act of reading published diaries or personal correspondence, both Bennett and Case are profoundly aware of the fact that they are concerned with a three-dimensional medium operative on visual and aural senses. In Case's analysis, within the frame of theatrical representation, the female performer is transformed into a kind of cultural courtesan, her physical body standing as a sight for the fulfillment of her spectators'" desires. "The conventions of the stage produce a meaning for the sign "woman," which is based upon their cultural associations with the female gender" (118). Case refers her readers to feminist film theory for elaboration on the problems of three-dimensional representation and the concept of the male gaze. Laura Mulvey describes the process:

> The determining male gaze projects its phantasy on to the female figure which is styled accordingly. In their traditional exhibitionist role women are simultaneously looked at and displayed, with their appearance coded for strong visual and erotic impact so that they can be said to connote to-be-looked-at-ness. (62)

Jill Dolan's feminist analysis of spectatorship suggests that the vast majority of texts occupying a place in the dramatic canon are finally intelligible to an "ideal spectator." Through the conventions of the stage, the performer's address works to construct an "amorphous, anonymous mass" of spectators carved in the likeness of patriarchal culture. Ultimately all material properties of the theatre are manipulated so that the performance is intelligible to the white, middle class, heterosexual male, leaving the performer objectified by his gaze (1).

As the locus of semiotic interpretation, the woman on stage is always already determined and the "I" she defiantly speaks, thrown into question. When a woman playwright chooses monodrama as her medium, it is against these conditions of spectatorship and representation that she must contend. I have selected for study the following examples of women's monodrama because they demonstrate an awareness of these conditions, yet are not weakened by them. I will be arguing in the following pages that Beverley Simons, Pamela Boyd, Janet Feindel, the members of the *La Nef des sorcières* collective, Jovette Marchessault, Marie Savard, and Sharon Pollock have all chosen the monodrama as a vehicle for the expression of a woman's voice, precisely because it aptly inscribes the "I" while recognising that that very act is always already beyond her control.

The conscious theatricality with which Beverley Simons has crafted her monodrama *Preparing* hints at an awareness of the complications implicit in "playing solitaire." The piece depicts the speaker engaged in the act of "preparing" her body for various occasions which are made culturally integral to a woman's experience. The space from which she speaks is established as a private, "off stage" dressing room equipped for the process of adorning make-up, costumes and wigs in preparation for the "stage roles" of daughter, wife, mother and grandmother. The speaker's ritualized dressing of her body becomes an analysis of how women find themselves participating in a life cycle of preparation for a drama that is not their own. "I'm always having to get ready for something," Jeannie says, "As far back as I can remember" (26). Despite her growing sexual awareness, her managerial skills and her stated determination that she will shape her experience herself ("No rituals, no history. I spring, fully developed, out of my own forehead" 29), it is suggested that the speaker's "value" is dependent upon her ability to perform up to her audience's expectations. Her desire is always framed and contained:

> Just once, I wish I could step outside of time where just once I could prepare myself, without being rushed for ....nothing, or ... maybe something ... important ... when I find out what that is. (27)

Simons's understanding of the potential impact of meta-theatrical techniques comes into play as Jeannie's "lookers" become directly associated with the live spectators of the performance. Jeannie recognizes her audience and performs for it. She is overtly theatrical and makes the spectators feel like spectators. As she dons masks and costumes through various stages of her life, the spectator is reminded of how important "being looked at" actually is:

> How shall I make myself appear? What role shall I play today? ... What face shall I put on? (33)

The speaker is overtly aware of the power her public has in the determination of her worth. With this awareness, she similarly condemns all of her spectators as guilty. The collective "you" that she prepares for is defined as hostile and antagonistic from the first lines of the play where she cries "Fuck 'em all" (26). The spectator is recognized as crucial to the cycle of deception and role-playing because it is his or her gaze which sanctions and approves the appearance of the performer. Even though the character is ostensibly alone on the stage, her preparation is played for an audience that has commanded the performance. There is no private space where she remains un-looked-at; in which she is subject alone. As if to question the possibility of subjectivity itself, Jeannie is presented as an actor who, like the actor who represents her, is always already determined by the frame she stands in. "I can't ... make it ...

stop, you see," Jeannie utters, "That's what's so ... unreasonable." Later she remarks: "Maybe they won't notice it's a mask floating over a void" (31-32). Recognizing that traditional theatre is bound to certain representational models, Simons draws attention to the complicity of the spectator which prevents the visioning of the female subject.

In order to disengage both speaker and spectator from a cycle that perpetuates the objectification of the female body, it is possible to propose a revisioning of the traditional patriarchal spectator critiqued by Dolan. In the place of the white, male, heterosexual viewer, the genderless confidant and friend is positioned. If the spectator is conceived as one who listens and participates in a supportive, non-gendered position, then the tendency to objectify or collectivize either party as "other" is, in theory, reduced. The relationship of confidentiality excludes the undressing stare of the male gaze and replaces it with a sense of community and sharing. The speaker is revealed in the simultaneous process of uncovering and exposing herself to individuals whose presence and participation become integral to her discovery. She is established as "very real" as she speaks of her own life and acknowledges the presence and reactions of the audience as supportive. The conventions of the theatrical frame appear to disappear and are replaced by "real life." This effect is enhanced when the author of the piece performs as the speaker, removing the "actor" from her role as mediator between audience and playwright. The "I" of the speaker and that of the author appear to conflate; the playwright performs autobiography. However, the degree to which theory and practise correspond remains a contentious issue. While this kind of performer/spectator dynamic seems to be favoured in the Canadian women's monodrama,[2] I would argue that monodrama written and performed by the same woman frequently bears a conscious awareness that the speaker is no more "real" than the guest on a television talk show who continues to be, despite her "true story" status, framed by the lens of the camera and by the horizon of expectations of her viewers.

Pamela Boyd's monodrama *Inside Out* constructs a woman attempting to manage family, marriage and career whilst juggling answering machines, dinner for four, bottles, diapers and a typewriter. The final act of the piece finds Ellen on the verge of nervous collapse, her monologue seeping into disjointed hysteria:

> But I do *try*. I *try* to keep myself up, show off my attributes, write the odd screenplay. I've written one recently, against great odds, great odds. It's about *hope* and *faith*. Bringing up children in this day and age should be enough, you say. Should be fulfillment. Should be fulfillment. Perhaps I'm a freak. Perhaps we're all freaks. We're all freaks. We're all freaks. We're all freaks. Bringing babies to life doomed to imminent death. Doomed to imminent death. Imminent death. It's animal nature. We're all animals. We're animals. We're animals. Just animals. When faced with extinction propagate in a frenzy. A frenzy. A frenzy. A frenzy. A frenzy. When faced with starvation, eat its young. Eat its young. Eat its young. Eat its young. (134)

Ellen's tirade is broken by her child's off stage cry at which point she lapses into further delirium and picks up an imaginary baby which she lifts to her face. She then reaches for a pillow which she holds to the baby as if to suffocate it. The stage directions to the printed text indicate that she realizes what her hands are doing, withdraws them, and raises her head to the audience and utters a silent scream. Recognizing the onset of madness, Ellen reaches out. The fourth wall is penetrated and the spectator is exposed and invited into Ellen's space. At this moment the boundary that distinguishes "play" from "real life" is approached, and an intimate connection is established between the spectator and the performer. Theoretically, the spectator becomes a responsible confidant, positioned not to "determine" the speaker but instead to acknowledge and respond to her as a real, live subject. When Boyd played Ellen herself, real life and theatre might have been further entwined as the distinctions between author and character were reduced. [3] The problem is, however, that Ellen is not Pamela Boyd. As a character in a play and on a stage, Boyd's body is a text for audience interpretation—she is framed by their expectations and the conditions of the representation. The legacy of motherhood stands dutifully behind her. Boyd, seemingly aware of the impossibility of representing an unmediated "reality," makes use of highly theatrical conventions to underscore her speaker's monologue. The set is made of cardboard cut-outs painted in demented, fantastic colours with a large stopped clock on the wall indicative of how time, in this "mother's world," has come to stand still. Also, Ellen's child is represented by a large stuffed puppet that Boyd obviously manipulates mechanically. The spectator is therefore receiving an interesting mixture of messages. At once he/she is constructed as an intimate confidant—as a participant in Boyd's/Ellen's coming to terms with her life and herself, while at the same time his/her status as "one who expects her to perform as a proper mother should" is underscored as he/she is faced with what is not real life but obvious simulacra. Boyd, like Simons, makes use of theatrical devices in order to consciously subvert her own insights. The speaker reaches out to her audience in order to break down the conventions which contain her and fix her meaning as wife and mother alone; however, ultimately these conditions are highlighted. To her spectators, she remains a representation of motherhood framed by the walls of the doll's house they have confined her to.

Janet Feindel's *A Particular Class of Women*, provides a second example of the interplay that necessarily goes on between the subjectivity of the author/speaker and the nature of theatrical representation. The brash tone and daring confidentiality derived from the personal experience of the author invite the spectator into the glitzy space of the strip-tease nightclub. Sitting in the dressing room with a succession of speakers, played by Feindel herself, the spectator witnesses pre-show preparations. Personal and intimate questions are directed to the spectator in a comfortable and offhand manner, challenging him/her to understand the community of the strip from an insider's perspective:

> Luv: Sometimes I prefer a chick. You compare the difference between a man and a woman in bed. A woman knows what to do. She knows what feels good on herself. Anyone in this room ever sucked puss? (30)

Initially, Feindel's body does not exist in a state of "to-be-looked-at-ness." It stands as an expression of the integrity, intelligence and independence of sex trade workers. At the beginning of Act One, the spectator is introduced to Lil who is describing her experiences with ease and comfort while dancing around her kitchen in a bathrobe making cookies. However, in order to explore the ambivalence of the strip economy, Feindel uses the theatrical devices to remind the spectator that each woman's worth is somehow related to audience estimation. Consider the following stage direction:

> *LIL takes off apron in kitchen area, then moves to the costume rack, and removes dressing gown and wig, to begin change into MARKY, whose hair is in pigtails. MARKY puts on a sparkly jacket over her leotard-type outfit underdressed under LIL's dressing gown. As this change is occurring, the disco ball light goes on and turns, and the spotlight does figure eights around the stage. Circus music plays and the MC's voice comes in as soon as LIL begins the change.* (17)

Initially constructed as a friend or confidant, the spectator is moved from the privacy of the kitchen to the strip where he is redefined as specifically male. The MC's invocation of "Girls! Girls! Girls! Yousa! Yousa! Yousa!" (18) indicates that the spectator's role is to function as the consumer of the commodity on sale within the economy of the strip. As Marky, Feindel dances on a table. As Petal Rose, she teases the audience with her stockings. As Georgia Scott she removes her shorts and her top, changes her bra and then reveals her pubic hair cut in the shape of a heart. The spectator, rendered an active participant in the representation, discovers that the value of the characters is subject to his/her evaluation. As a performer, Feindel becomes an object of lust, fetishized for her potential to satisfy the sexual desires of the spectator, her paying client. Co-existing with Feindel's desire to pay tribute to the women she worked with on the strip, is the realization that the signifiers of her representation are bound by the limitations of sexist interpretation.

Barbara Freedman argues that "to theatricalize one must deconstruct, insert a difference in a term which splits it, mimics it, then displaces or usurps it. 'A woman writing like a woman writing like a woman' is never the same woman" (75). Simons, Boyd and Feindel each develop speakers who remain overtly conscious of the fact that they are "looked upon"—a fact which displaces, confuses and challenges the gaze of the spectator. But is it politically expedient to replay Catch-22 representations of women which always seem to re-enclose a fragmented subjectivity in a structure of sexist oppression? Jill Dolan intervenes in the post-structuralist assumption that the "I" is always bound by representation by arguing that desire, far from being a "fixed, male-owned commodity," can be "exchanged, with a much different meaning, between women" (80). Experiments such as *La Nef des sorcières* and Jovette Marchessault"s *Les Vaches de nuit* attempt precisely such a project. The spectators constructed by these plays are exclusively female and respond to an aesthetic that does not seek, at any point, to objectify or commodify the represented women. The monologues *of La Nef*—a collection of one-woman pieces to be performed in succession—individually mark out and address women who stand outside of the speakers' private spaces. The speaker of Odette Gagnon's "La Fille" piece calls out women's names and reaches out to make contact:

> J'ense aux filles, j'pense à: la femme d'en avant … celle qui a des enfants, la fille d'à côté, celle qui est pas mariée … la femme d'en bas … celle qu'on dit qu'a travaille pas … la fille d'en haut qui tape des lettres dans un bureau … la femme d'en arrière qui est bonne couturière … qui aurait bien aimé devenir infirmière. (49-50)

She goes on to list more women who, like herself, are isolated in their own spaces and who are uncovering their own monologues. As her thoughts go out to other women, the walls existing between speaker and female spectator disintegrate and contact is made. [4] Similarly, Marie-Claire Blais's "Marcelle" initiates the female spectator to lesbian desire. In the subsequent "Marcelle II," Pol Pelletier trades in the accusatory "vous" for the more communal "nous," thereby inviting the female spectator into her lesbian space: "Nous formons à nous toutes une société secrete" (70). Nicole Brossard's "Écrivain" concludes the performance by speaking of a political pact amongst women: "… je ne veux plus faire cela toute seule. Je nous veux. Faire craquer, grincer, grincher l'histoire" (75).

These women, isolated in their monologues, either consciously or unconsciously transcend the restrictions of their spaces and make contact with the female spectator. Though each woman remains in her room, her story escapes through the walls and is given a public hearing. Yvonne Mathews-Klein and Ann Pearson, spectators of the performance, gave this account:

> The terrible isolation in which each speaker stands and, indeed, in which each appears to rejoice, is disturbing. Yet, each time I saw the play, the connections were made nevertheless, between the actors and every woman in the audience who seemed to hear herself speaking out loud for the first time. (19)

The dynamic is even stronger in Marchessault's *Les Vaches de nuit*, which audaciously dares to imagine a community of women flourishing outside the restrictions of "l'ordre des castrants." The representation, which presents a young cow in the process of explaining her nocturnal liberation into a uniquely female space, is developed around a particularly female aesthetic closely associated with the imagining of difference through memory and within the female body. The delightful association of the heretofore derogatory cow with the female body indicates that the piece is not concerned with providing an in for everybody:

> Beauté! Le grand fleuve de lait, la terre de l'enfance où mères et filles sont enfin réunies. Beauté! Beauté! Canaux de lait fleuris de nénuphars. Ivressée lactée, fluidité blanche, liquide astral, le fruit des entrailles de nos mères se répand dans le temps frais du ciel. (87)

Women alone are invited to participate in the celebration:

> Entre les dames comeilles et les mammiares, à chaque fois c'est la fête, la joie des retrouvailles, tous les embrassements possibles du corps et de la mémoire. (91)

As the speaker describes female animals gathering around their mothers, so female spectators gathered around Pol Pelletier at the Théâtre du Nouveau Monde on the evening of 5 March 1979, on the occasion of International Women's Day.[5] Together female speaker and spectators attempt to transform the theatre into a common space for their mutual subjectivity. Women, in Marchessault's words, "ne peu[ven]t qu'apprendre à se rappeler, chacune à son tour" (92). A communion is created and celebrated.

Though effectively surmounting problems of representation with exclusive female spectatorship, *La Nef* and *Les Vaches* are no longer monodramas. The isolation of private monologue has been gleefully abandoned in favour of a political dialogue between women. The recognition of the female spectator, and her inclusion into the process of the drama, effectively establish a situation where the term monodrama no longer applies. It is the "we" and not the "I" that becomes the subject of the representation. Without devaluing the importance of the communities created and celebrated in these two plays, I return inevitably to my initial query. Can there be monologue for women? Should there be? Is there a public space where the first person singular is tolerated in the hope of finding something new? Do the pitfalls of representation and the desperate need for the establishment of a feminist community render the monologue both practically and politically problematic?

Marie Savard and Sharon Pollock address these questions by circumventing traditional theatrical representation and indulging in what is more closely allied with performance art. The only listener actually recognized by Savard, in her piece *Bien à moi,* is the speaker, La Marquise. The piece, about one woman's creative act of self-discovery, is implicitly linked with the solitary/private act of masturbation. It is clear that the speaker engages in acts of auto-eroticism at specific points in the play:

> Il est vrai que je viens. Je viens du fond de ma jeunesse …sainte!…. Il est vraie que je vis. Je jouis. Je n'ai plus à me le cacher, à me refuser à moi pour mieux me réfugier derrière l'immense subterfuge de ma pudeur et de mon savoir vivre. (40)

Under such conditions, the spectator is outside of the speaker's private space yet given special access. Unlike in *A Particular Class of Women* where the performance text arouses the voyeur/spectator's consumerist gaze, here the focus is internal and rests upon la Marquise's self-exploration. The speaker is active, as opposed to acted upon. By positing the speaker's desire as the subject and form of the representation, the piece, in theory, subverts any possibility of an objectifying gaze. Again, theoretically, there is no opportunity to satisfy any desire other than la Marquise's for all other viewpoints (in a very political reversal of fortune) are left silent and unrepresented. This kind of deliberate exclusion of the objectifying gaze of the spectator, for the purposes of "playing solitaire" was not well met by the critics. Reviews of *Bien à moi* reduced La

Marquise's delightful self-indulgence to evidence of a nervous condition. The character was written off as inarticulate, "décousu, farfelu et souvent absolument abeffant" (Dassylva 27). While a reviewer's opinion is not necessarily representative of all spectators' experiences, it does stand as the testimony of one, proving the inability of a performance text to fully release the representation from sexist stereotyping. While a specific look may be inscribed by a performance text, the possibility of aberrant receptions by individuals or the collective is always a potential reality (Bennett 164).

Sharon Pollock's *Getting it Straight*, about a schizophrenic who finds herself beneath the bleachers of a rodeo once the crowd has all gone home, has suffered much of the same criticism. The content of this recent monodrama consists primarily of the speaker's (Eme) grappling with the images of a postmodern world in an attempt to "get it all straight." Naturally, the structure is violently fragmented leaving the spectator with thoroughly disjointed images of personal and social breakdown:

> I dream, I dream ... I lie on my back in a field full of yellow mustard at midnight ... I look deep into time for the nearest stars are tens of thousands of years closer than the stars that are distant and far, time being space, being time, my room, is square, one second by one second when I run screaming, rushing, hit the wall, pressing in-small, seven seconds by seven, square measured walk, drift ... in a dream ... slow ... space stretches ... like vowels, rooom ... groows, I see ... the milky way holding back the night so that fragments of darkness are unable to fall, crushing me, and the mustard, and a very small egg that I, hold, in my hand, it, could crush, you too, like an egg ... they say ... I say, nothing ... I whisper, I am not certain if I dream it or ... if it dreams me .... [6]

Like *Bien à moi*, *Getting it Straight* makes no attempt to define a place for the male gaze; neither does it recognize the spectator as a confidant or friend; instead complete self-indulgence dictates content and form. Like *Bien à moi*, Eme's digressions were panned by the critics as a contrived exercise succeeding only in venting the playwright's personal despair:

> As with many writers, Pollock has apparently arrived at a moment when the unending news of famine, atrocity, war and ever more degrading consumerism is simply too much. She doubts the point of being a writer, of trying to create sanity. But instead of enduring the crisis quietly, she has made the mistake of foisting her chaos onto a mad character. She is in short, using Eme as an excuse for 80 minutes of free association. (Conlogue)

Manfred Pfister says that "in the real world ... talking alone for too long is generally thought to be a pathological deviation from the norm and those who are not pathologically disturbed generally restrict their thinking aloud to brief exclamations" (131-32). In theatre, Pfister continues, the familiar conventions of the soliloquy and the monologue re-establish speaking alone and aloud as normative forms of self-expression. But la Marquise and Eme, like real life "deviants," can be diagnosed as pathologically disturbed. Their discourse is not necessarily sanctioned and their subjectivity re-centred within established theatrical conventions. Ultimately the signifier of the woman's body does not exclude from the range of signifieds: hysteria, madness and deviant sexuality.

It is my contention that the act of "playing solitaire" sets into motion the very subversion of the "I" that it wishes to articulate; however, I do not conclude that monodrama and theatre in general are inaccessible to feminist concerns. Freedman argues that the paradox of avant-garde theatre is that in seeking to stage a moment outside of representation, one cannot evade the gaze of the spectator that constitutes that representation. She notes: "Theatre has always suggested a funhouse of mirrors we never escape, a precession of simulacra which remind us we can never reach a body outside of representation" (72). The women's monodrama, in its very struggle to surmount the pitfalls of representation, is a documentation of the struggle to control one's look:

> Theatre calls the spectatorial gaze into play by exhibiting a purloined gaze, a gaze that announces that it has always been presented to our eyes; is designed only to be taken up by them.... Theatre's masks announce that the "I" is always already another; its characters assure us of their displacement, announcing, "I am already taken," as in "this seat is taken".... (Freedman 74)

Theatre, the monodrama in particular, is the appropriate medium for the dislodgement of the spectatorial gaze and the re-dressing of representation. When she speaks in the first person singular, the solo speaker understands that "I" is always already beyond her control. It is that reality that she documents. From there, direct experience of the monodrama feeds back to revise the spectator's horizon of expectations and to challenge the very conventions and meanings that that "I" represents. In the words of Nicole Brossard and France Théoret: "l'isolement provisoire et stratégique du monologue permet à la fois de ne pas tout égaliser et de ne pas tout réduire" (13).

(1992)

Notes

[1] Each of these structural claims merits further individual exploration. I have treated them all to some extent in my MA thesis at the University of Alberta (1991).

[2] Joan Macleod's *Jewel*, Wendy Lill's *The Occupation of Heather Rose* or Louisette Dussault's *Moman* are a few examples, other than the ones discussed here, of pieces which develop particular moments in which the speakers, performed by the playwrights themselves, make direct contact with the spectators.

[3] I am here referring to the Tarragon Extra Space production of the play in Toronto in March 1986.

[4] It should be noted that "Actrice," "La Fille" and "Marcelle II" were all performed by the women who wrote them. The particular dynamic of "self-performance" noted in Feindel's and Boyd's plays is also applicable here.

[5] Reviewers Jean Royer and Andrée Lebel both document that the audience was made up mostly of women.

[6] This is taken from Sharon Pollock's *Getting It Straight* (unpublished manuscript 1989, 8). I would like to thank Ms. Pollock for making this manuscript available to me.

Works Cited

Bennett, Susan. *Theatre Audiences: A Theory of Production and Reception.* London: Routledge, 1990.

Boyd, Pamela. "Inside Out." *NeWest Plays by Women.* Ed. Diane Bessai and Don Kerr. Edmonton: NeWest P, 1987.

Brossard, Nicole. "L'Ecrivain." *La nef des sorcières* Ed. Brossard et al. Montreal: Quinze, 1976.

Case, Sue-Ellen. *Feminism and Theatre.* London: MacMillan, 1988.

Conlogue, Ray. *The Globe and Mail* 12 January 1990, C7.

Dassylva, Martial. Review. *La Presse* 9 fév 1970: 27.

Dolan, Jill. *The Feminist Spectator as Critic.* Ann Arbor: UMI Research P, 1988.

Elam, Keir. *The Semiotics of Theatre and Drama.* London: Methuen, 1989.

Feindel, Janet. *A Particular Class of Women.* Vancouver: Lazarus Publications, 1989.

Freedman, Barbara. "Frame-Up: Feminism, Psychoanalysis, Theatre." *Performing Feminisms: Feminist Critical Theory and Theatre.* Ed. Sue-Ellen Case. London & Baltimore: Johns Hopkins UP, 1990. 54-76.

Lebel, Andrée. "Un spectacle beau par sa simplicité." *La Presse* 6 mars 1979: 67.

Mathews-Klein, Yvonne and Ann Pearson. "A Stage of Seven Women." *Branching Out* 3 (September/October 1976): 17-19.

Marchessault, Jovette. *Les vaches de nuit.* Montreal: Editions de la pleine lune, 1980.

Mulvey, Laura. "Visual Pleasure and Narrative Cinema." *Screen* 16.3 (1975): 6-18.

Pfister, Manfred. *The Theory and Analysis of Drama.* Cambridge: Cambridge UP, 1988.

Royer, Jean. "Le théâtre au féminin de la fête." *Le Devoir* 7 mars 1979: 6.

Savard, Marie. *Bien à Moi.* Montreal: Editions de la pleine lune, 1979.

Simons, Beverley. *Preparing.* Vancouver: Talonbooks, 1975.

Verduyn, Christl. "Écrire le moi au feminine." *Journal of Canadian Studies* 20.2 (1985). 18-29

Naming Names: Black Women Playwrights in Canada

by Djanet Sears

> ...Someday somebody'll
> Stand up and talk about me,
> And write about me—
> Black and beautiful—
> And sing about me,
> And put on plays about me!
> I reckon it'll be
> Me myself!
>
> Yes, it'll be me.
> (Langston Hughes, "Note on Commercial Theatre" 90)

Black women playwrights in Canada may be one group I can presume, albeit tentatively, to speak on behalf of. Tentatively, for as the colour of our skin varies in shades of Black, so do our visions, aspirations, experiences and sexual preferences. However, we have continued to write for the theatre, and we continue to offer creative defiance to a world in need of our particular vision, by virtue of a unique vantage point of race and gender.

By and large Black women writers have not written for money or recognition. We "write for [ourselves] as a means of maintaining emotional and intellectual clarity, of sustaining self-development and instruction. Each [Black woman playwright] writes because she is driven to do so, regardless of whether there is a publisher, an audience, or neither" (Tate xviii). Our scripts, and here I speak from personal experience, can be found anywhere in our worlds, from the hard drives of our computers, the bureau drawers among our bras and panties, to the floors of our closets right beside our corporate shoes. It is important to note that while I intend to identify some of the obstacles with which we are faced within the theatre industry, and to examine some of the issues that appear in the works of Black women playwrights in Canada, I also hope to record the names and plays of those Black women playwrights whom I am aware of, for their ingenuity in getting around or over those hurdles in order to write.[1]

Lillian Allen:
One Bedroom ... With Dignity

One of the most popular perceptions of Canadian culture is that Black women rarely write for the stage. Supported by the limited number of plays by Black women playwrights ever produced, proponents of this theory are further encouraged by the paucity of plays by Black women that actually arrive on the desks of artistic directors across Canada.

Janice Banigan:
Free't Be

In fact, far from providing a significant rationale for the lack of Black women's plays produced in Canada, this argument merely overlooks several serious and complex issues. As Black women we learn from an early age that our work, whatever the context, may not be recognized or valued. "Many of us experiment only to find that such work receives absolutely no attention. Or we are told by gatekeepers, usually white, often male, that it will be better for us to write and think in a more conventional way" (hooks, *Talking Back* 129).

> Fundamentally ... the core of racism in the arts remains constant: the refusal to treat as valid the cultural experience, knowledge or expertise of the artist coming from a non-European culture, wedded to the belief that Eurocentric values are in and of themselves better. (Philip, "Gut" 20)

While the message is often subliminal, we rarely have the opportunity to see ourselves on the Canadian stage and even when our images are included, they remain marginal, stereotypical or clichéd. It's as if the dominant culture is not open to cultural contexts it does not know or understand and would rather dismiss a piece that does not adhere to European mythology, European standards for high art and a Western narrative structure as its foundation, and so it refers to other cultural forms as amateurish or undeveloped.

Diana Braithwaite:
The Wonder of Man
Do Not Adjust Your Set
Living With Irma
Cherry & the Ginger Wine
Martha and Elvira
Nutshells
Time to Forget
The Lost Picture Show

This type of bias is also prevalent on a gender level within the dominant culture. Take the standard plot, for instance. A closer look at the traditional narrative structure will reveal its resemblance to a male orgasm: an intense and struggle-filled rising action, producing a climax and a quick resolution. Since an important aspect of maintaining dominance involves the belief that whatever the dominant has is, in and of itself, better, I propose that perhaps if men had female-type orgasms, the accepted standard narrative structure would involve a more complex form. It would more than likely involve a multiple of endless rising actions, climaxes and resolutions.

Deborah Castello:
What Goes Around

Further analysis of the theatre industry will also give us clues as to the systemic nature of the racism and sexism within it.

> The preponderance of men [read: White men] on the boards of directors of theatres influences … the selection of plays written by men, and the engagement of male directors to direct them. And plays written by men are far more likely to feature roles for male performers. (Fraticelli 9)

Not only are we excluded, but we in turn often tend to internalize this exclusion and in many ways agree with it. Especially since it's women who form the majority of cultural consumers.

Pat Dillon:
Servant's Nite Out

Another misconception in the mainstream culture is that the literary works of Black women are being produced, published and promoted at such a rate that it wouldn't be difficult to say that cultural racism is now extinct. Or at worst that the level of marginalization of Black women is at least equal to that of White women's. Some even go so far as to say that a kind of reverse racism is taking place.

Bernadette Dyer:
Fiction, Fantasy & Tabix

Such a perception is thoroughly misguided, as most readers would be hard-pressed to name more than one or two Black woman playwrights in Canada, if that. Such an argument merely brings into question the motives of its proponents. Marlene Nourbese Philip refers to this mode of thinking as one of "binary opposition," the "either/or conundrum":

> My life or your death. My well-being or your lack of well-being; my wealth or your poverty. Closely tied to this is the concept of scarcity, real or contrived, which is essential to the proper functioning of capitalist societies. We are continually encouraged by various means, to believe that the satisfaction of one person's needs automatically means the non-fulfillment of another's. White middle-class female writers, therefore, come to believe that the publication of works by black and non-European writers automatically means the non-publication of their works. Scarcity wedded to binary oppositional thought becomes a deadly combination. ("Gut" 25)

Amah Harris:
Anasi and Cooyah
Anasi and Rescue in the Kingdom
Anasi and the Return of the Stories

Binary opposition is often camouflaged beneath a type of political correctness in both dominant and alternative progressive culture. It can be a mask behind which those in this society who do not personally "own" certain human rights' issues hide: racism in feminist organizations or communities and sexism in Black organizations or communities, for a Black woman can never be a politically correct issue. She experiences racism and sexism every day, sometimes simultaneously. To her they are "gut" issues (Philip, "Gut" 13).

Bianca Jacobs:
Man You Mus'

In addition, there are no facts to support this "extinction of cultural racism" theory:

> …figures released by the Playwrights Union of Canada in 1988 show that of all new plays produced in the 87/88 season, still only 17 per cent were by women. Even fewer were directed by women, and the Women's Committee at Canadian Actors' Equity Association can show how few roles there were for women actors that same season. This is "The Invisibility Factor" as termed by Rina Fraticelli in her landmark report on the Status of Women in the Canadian Theatre… [T]he Invisibility Factor increases exponentially when the woman in question is not white. (Lushington 20-21)

Anastasia Kaunda:
Breathing Space

However, in the face of such daunting realities, many of us remain prolific. We write in order to define ourselves, by ourselves, and create stories to keep that definition within the limits of our own controls. Otherwise we find ourselves framed in foreign, inimical contexts, appearing as exotic slices of life and local colour or, even worse, featured as "ghettorized [sic] irrelevancies" (Wideman vi). So we tell our stories as a way of "extracting meaning from chaos, a handful of water we scoop up to recall an ocean" (Wideman x).

Vernita Leece:
Ain't That a Shame Trip to the Library

Claudia Tate writes about Black women playwrights that,

> They project their vision of the world, society, community, family, their lovers, even themselves, most often through the eyes of black female characters and poetic personae. Their angle of vision allows them to see what white people, especially males, seldom see. With one penetrating glance they cut through layers of institutionalized racism and sexism and uncover a core of social contradictions and intimate dilemmas which plague all of us, regardless of our race or gender. Through their art they share their vision of possible resolution with those who cannot see. (Tate xvi)

Heather Lord & Junia Mason:
Third Floor Women's Where?

Examining the themes of "protest and resistance, conformity and imitation, regeneration and celebration" (mandiela vii), ahdri zhina mandiela's *dark diaspora ... in dub* ran to both popular and critical acclaim at the 1991 Toronto Fringe Festival. In creating *dark diaspora ...* mandiela aimed to expand the literary tradition of dub poems and to present a totally new stage experience: dub theatre: "dramatised stage presentation comprised of varying performance components, including an indispensable/uniquely tailored dance language threading thru oral/choral work proliferating with endemic musical elements" (xii).

ahdri zhina mandiela:
dark diaspora ... in dub
t.v. again!?!
solid gold

The play explores the psyche of the Black diaspora, the "scatterlings of the world's descendants of afrikan origin," who "regardless of international location ... share history, memories and desires moulded by various events, circumstances, and phenomena, among them: *racism, colonization, emigration, segregation, assimilation, domination, denigration, ghettoization and denial*" (mandiela vii). Traversing some thirty years during the life of the play, the central voice in *dark diaspora ...* records the psychological journey of a woman of African descent, via the Caribbean, living in Canada in the 1990s.

Claude Moise:
Chronicles of a Free Fall

dark diaspora ... falls into a category of writing that I call autobio-mythography, the fictionalization of autobiographical events. Autobio-mythography often takes the form of a healing, in that the "longing to tell one's story and the process of telling is symbolically a gesture of longing to recover the past in such a way that one experiences both a sense of reunion and a sense of release" (hooks, *Talking Back* 158).

Masani Montague:
Up on Eglinton

Afrika Solo, one of my works, is also autobio-mythographical. A play loosely based upon a year-long journey that I took across Africa. A journey that not only changed my perception of the world, but my perception of myself in the world (Sears 95). The play tells us of a young Black woman's journey of self-discovery, beginning in a world where Black people are presented through the media as savage cannibals, slaves, or domestics.

Pauline Peters:
Mavis Rising

As we follow the central character through the body of the play, we watch her slowly deconstruct Western perceptions of Africa and Africans, and hence her own self-image as a woman of African descent. In one instance early on in the play she flashes back to a major revelation she had experienced as a child:

> Harry Belafonte and Dorothy Dandridge in "Carmen Jones." It was so fantastic! Harry Belafonte, so handsome and Dorothy Dandridge, so beautiful. She is the most beautiful woman I've seen on TV … I mean, she looks just like Jean Harlow. Dorothy Dandridge looks exactly like Jean Harlow—'cept she's black! (26)

Later, when she finds herself in the midst of a fiery debate with the Masai people about why Westerners wear clothes that hold in their farts, she begins to realize that she has internalized many Eurocentric precepts about female beauty. As she points out, "[Masai] women stretch their ear lobes and the closer her ear lobe is to her shoulder the more beautiful she is. Like I mean, Dorothy Dandridge would not have made it here" (64).

Itah Sadu:
Ms. McDoon of McDoonville

Afrika Solo also examines the question of the need for a home or homeland, a central question in the minds of many displaced people. Being born in Britain, for this Black woman, did not mean she belonged there. Her parents are from two different countries in the Caribbean: does that mean she is Caribbean, even though she has never lived there? And which country should she choose, anyhow? The common denominator is Africa, but which country in Africa? And what does all that have to do with carrying a Canadian passport?

Alison Sealy-Smith:
Home Away from Home (co-author)
No Problems Here (co-author)

Stylistically, *Afrika Solo* belongs to a traditional West African genre that I call the "sundiata form." This form involves a fusion of music, poetry, song, movement and dance to tell a story. We here in the diaspora have only begun to experiment with the fullness of this form.

Djanet Sears:
Afrika Solo
Sangoma: The Mother Project (contributor)
Double Trouble
Shakes a Pear Tree

The Wonder of Man along with *Do Not Adjust Your Set, Martha and Elvira* and *Time to Forget* make up the collection of plays by Diana Braithwaite known as *The Wonder Quartet*, first produced by Toronto's Nightwood Theatre and performed in repertory at the Poor Alex Theatre in Toronto in the winter of 1992. *The Wonder of Man* utilizes several elements of the sundiata form—narrative, music, songs, praise-singing (choruses), and movement—to explore Black male/female relationships in Canada. Braithwaite also pulls together elements of Western theatrical forms to create a hybrid form of musical theatre: a po-mo-afro-woma (post-modern afro-centric womanist) cabaret.

Carol Thames:
(In)visible

Subtitled "a Black woman's trip through the galaxy," *The Wonder of Man* is about a woman called Hope, an articulate, womancentric, (probably) celibate, and successful, visual artist, who has put her life in turmoil by accepting an invitation to dinner from a Black man with whom she is quite taken. The invitation instigates a journey into the "galaxy" of her mind, where she has to "look to the past for a path" and to confront several archetypal aspects of herself—Desperate Lady, Woman in the Veil, Barefoot and Pregnant, and Her Self—in order to "make a new road for the future" (Braithwaite). The play argues that slavery was directly responsible for the destruction of the African family in the diaspora, and that the Black male/female relationships you see around you today are the remnants of that past. The play reminds us that slavery was abolished a mere one hundred years ago. For four hundred years before its abolition Africans in the Americas were the victims of horrendous human atrocities. We lived in a world where our bodies were the property of our white owners, where marriage, or even the suggestion of union, was forbidden, and where mating was permitted solely for breeding purposes.

Morancie Webb:
All in a Day

Implicit in the works of Black women playwrights in Canada is a perspective that crosses two points of intersection as a result of being Black and female in a White male-dominated society: "where Western culture cuts across vestiges of African heritage, and … where male-female attitudes are either harmoniously parallel, subtly divergent, or in violent collision" (Tate xvi). But, "despite limited production opportunities," Black women playwrights "continue to speak with authority on the many questions which trouble human beings as individuals and as citizens" (Wilkerson xxiv). We have created our own theatre from a language that was forced upon us, and we season it with our own sense of rhythm, ritual and music. Not a song and dance, but a heightened language and ritual. I endorse the use of the following step by step guide: "Slip mouth over the syllable; moisten with tongue the work. / Suck Slide Play Caress Blow—Love it, but if the word/gags, does not nourish, bite it off—at its source— / Spit it out. / Start again" (Philip, *She tries* 67).

(1992)

Note

[1] The author has continued and updated her project of naming the names of African Canadian playwrights male and female in her Spring 2004 co-edited edition of *Canadian Theatre Review*—ed.

Works Cited

Braithwaite, Diana. *The Wonder of Man.* Manuscript for the production at Nightwood Theatre [1992].

Fraticelli, Rina. "'Any black crippled woman can!': A feminist's notes from outside the sheltered workshop." *Room of One's Own* 8.2 (1983): 7-18.

hooks, bell. *Talking Back.* Toronto: Between the Lines, 1988.

———. *Yearnings: Race, Gender and Cultural Politics.* Toronto: Between the Lines, 1990.

Hughes, Langston. "Note on the Commercial Theatre." *Selected Poems of Langston Hughes.* New York: Random House, 1974. 90.

Lushington, Kate. "The changing body of women's work" *Broadside* 10.5 (1989): 20-21.

mandiela, ahdri zhina. "preface." *dark diaspora … in dub.* Toronto: Sister Vision, 1991.

Philip, Marlene Nourbese. *She tries her tongue, her silence softly breaks.* Charlottetown: Ragweed Press, 1989.

———. "Gut issues in Babylon" *Fuse* 12 (1989): 12-20.

Sears, Djanet. "Afterword." *Afrika Solo.* Toronto. Sister Vision, 1990. 95-101.

Sears, Djanet and Ric Knowles, ed. *African Canadian Theatre: Honouring the Word. Canadian Theatre Review* 118 (2004).

Tate, Claudia. "Preface." *Black Women Writers at Work.* Ed. Claudia Tate. New York: Continuum, 1983. xv-xxvi.

Wideman, John Edgar. "Preface." *Breaking Ice: An anthology of contemporary African-American Fiction,* ed. Terry McMillan. New York: Viking, 1990. v-x.

Wilkerson, Margaret B. "Introduction." *9 Plays by Black Women.* Ed. Margaret B. Wilkerson. New York: Mentor Books, 1986. xiii-xxv.

Critical Revisions: Ann-Marie MacDonald's *Goodnight Desdemona (Good Morning Juliet)*

by Ann Wilson

> Comedy is a "bad girl" thing to do. Poking fun at institutions is iconoclastic and girls are not supposed to be rebels.
>
> Good going, boys, but get your fucking metaphors off of my body! Ann-Marie MacDonald ("Interview" 136, 143)

A commonplace of feminist criticism is that Western culture accepts woman to be, by nature, secondary to man. Within this paradigm of gender, woman is man's antithesis: he is active, she is passive; his realm is the public sphere, hers is the private; his accomplishments are seen, hers are hidden. In the words of Laura Mulvey,

> Woman ... stands in patriarchal culture as a signifier for the male other, bound by a symbolic order in which man can live out his fantasies and obsessions through linguistic command by imposing them on the silent image of woman still tied to her place as bearer, not maker, of meaning. (15)

This perspective on gender is the point of departure for Ann-Marie MacDonald's *Goodnight Desdemona (Good Morning Juliet)*. MacDonald revises *Othello* and *Romeo and Juliet*, transforming two of Shakespeare's most familiar romantic tragedies into comedies. In so doing, she shows that Shakespearean tragedy is predicated on a hierarchy of gender which can only accommodate a passive woman. By refusing this construction of gender, she opens a new position for the woman reader.

The premise of *Goodnight Desdemona (Good Morning Juliet)* is that Shakespeare emended his source texts, comedies which featured strong, independent heroines. He radically revised these characters so that they became supporting figures in the dramatic action which focusses on the male protagonists. This thesis, tantamount to literary heresy, is the subject of Constance Ledbelly's doctoral dissertation, titled "*Romeo and Juliet* and *Othello*: The Seeds of Corruption and Comedy." Constance is employed as an assistant professor in the English Department of Queen's University, one of English Canada's oldest and most established academic institutions. Whatever license MacDonald may take with her depiction of the life of a young woman professor, it rings with a certain truth. Taking her cue from stereotypes of the absent-minded professor, she shows Constance as blissfully unaware of how she presents herself to the world. Early in Act I, for example, she enters her office,

> *absently humming and occasionally singing, "Fairy Tales Can Come True." She wears a coat, boots and a bright red woolen toque with a pom-pom at the end. She is laden with a bookbag, a "Complete Works of Shakespeare" and a stack of dog-eared loose-leaf foolscap ... She removes her coat, under which she wears a crumpled tweedy skirt and jacket suit. She forgets to remove her toque and wears it throughout the scene.* (14)

The primary focus of Constance's life is academic work, particularly her dissertation which absorbs her imaginatively and intellectually. Because Constance seems imperfectly socialized, oblivious to the dominant social codes, she is vulnerable to the ridicule and exploitation of those who are more adept at negotiating the university structure. Women, like the female student who comments snidely that she likes Constance's hair which is hidden under the toque, seem contemptuous of her; men, like Claude Night, her colleague who is "perfectly groomed and brogued, speaks with an Oxford accent," use her shamelessly, as if her role were to serve (22). That Constance seems pathetic is precisely MacDonald's point: like Shakespeare's heroines, Constance's passion and verve are effaced by the social position of women. Indeed, the identification of Constance with Desdemona and Juliet is made during the Dumbshow which opens the play. Three vignettes play simultaneously: Desdemona being smothered by Othello; Juliet awakening in the crypt to find the dead Romeo and stabbing herself; Constance throwing away her plumed pen and an ancient manuscript (13). The inclusion of Constance throwing away the symbols of her academic passion suggests that her abandonment of her quest for the source comedies of Shakespeare's tragedies is a form of death.

The precise terms of this "death" are important because they depend on a series of binary relations which are gendered. Constance enjoys less professional success than Claude Night, who recently has been appointed as a full professor at Oxford. He is widely published, whereas she is still caught in her speculations about Shakespeare's sources and so is unable to complete her dissertation. He is concerned with publicly appearing to be successful whereas she finds great satisfaction in retreating to the private world of imagination. That Claude appears to be successful is crucial because all his work has been ghost-written by Constance who, because she is in love with him, is willing to allow herself to be exploited in the hope that he might reciprocate her affection.

Within a Canadian context, MacDonald's representation of Claude Night as a tweedy Brit is not innocently comic, but serves as a reminder of Canada's history as a colony which Great Britain dominated culturally and exploited economically. The relationship between a Canadian woman and a British man sets into play a complex set of colonial relations which is further complicated by Constance's academic focus on the tragedies of Shakespeare, whose work is represented as the apex of British cultural achievement and consequently is central to humanist studies of English literature. To quote Allan Bloom, "men live more truly and fully in reading ...

Shakespeare than at any other time, because then they are participating in essential being and are forgetting their accidental lives," (qtd. in Hodgdon 106).

What is effaced by Bloom's remark is the politics of English literary study. The study of the text from a humanist perspective involves the search for a unified meaning which presents "universal human" truths. That these "truths" often represented the values of the colonial power, and hence frequently were incompatible with those of the colonized, meant a devaluing of the colonized culture. The intersection of English literary studies and colonization occurs on several registers, including as part of the imperialist efforts of Britain in the nineteenth century, when the study of English literature was used, according to Gauri Viswanathan, to maintain "control of the natives under the guise of a liberal education" (qtd. in Ashcroft, Griffiths & Tiffin 3); and as part of humanism's project which equates "human" with being male, white and middleclass and so "colonizes" woman, denying her a position as reading subject.

Indeed, the politics of colonization are reinforced by critical readings of tragedy itself. In Aristotle's *Poetics*, still the seminal theory of tragedy against which others are read, we are advised that the tragic hero should be "good," and that "there can be goodness in every class of person; for instance, a woman or a slave may be good, though the one is possibly an inferior being and the other in general an insignificant one" (51). Tragedy is compatible with, and indeed reinforces, the social position of the hero, a man who enjoys power and privilege within his society. Given this politic, it is not surprising that humanist critics have tended to value Shakespeare's tragedies over his comedies because the ideology of tragedy is compatible with that of humanism—and, indeed, with that of imperialism. Read in the context of this tradition, MacDonald's revision is a political act which empowers women through the figure of Constance Ledbelly, who is doubly colonized as a woman and as a Canadian. Her academic project of discovering the two comedies is one which allows her to recognize how Shakespeare colonizes these sources and, in the process, constitutes women as passive subjects, both as characters in the plays and as readers.

The clue to Constance's search for the missing comedies is the Gustav manuscript which "when finally decoded, will prove the prior existence of two comedies by an unknown author; comedies that Shakespeare plundered and made over into ersatz tragedies" (21). Constance has been able to decode the inscription to the manuscript, which reads:

> You who possess the eyes to see
> this strange and wondrous alchemy,
> where words transform to vision'ry,
> where one plus two makes one, not three;
> open this book if you agree
> to be illusion's refugee,
> and of return no guarantee—
> unless you find your true identity.

And discover who the Author be.
(27-28)

When she reads the inscription, she is drawn into the world of the source for *Othello* where she immediately overhears Othello telling Iago of his plan to murder Desdemona. Shocked, Constance intervenes, telling him that he's about "to make a terrible mistake" (30). She instantly regrets acting on this impulse, exclaiming, "Omigod, what have I done … I've wrecked a masterpiece. I've ruined the play, / I've turned Shakespeare's *Othello* to a farce" (30).

But whatever Constance's skepticism about her action, it is received with awe by Othello, who believes that her ability to see the future is evidence that she is an oracle. When Desdemona approaches, Constance introduces herself, saying, "I'm Constance Ledbelly. I am an academic. / I come from Queen's" which Desdemona hears as "Constance, Queen of Academe" (33). What were liabilities to Constance at Queen's—for example, that she is unmarried—become signs of her greatness: she is "a virgin oracle," a "brave ag'ed maid" (33). Unused to celebrity, and still plagued by her sense of inferiority, Constance, in what is a typically feminine (to say nothing of Canadian) response to praise, immediately denies that she is worthy of the attention. Asked by Desdemona about her life, Constance responds, "There isn't much to tell. It's very dull. / I'm certain your life's much more exciting" (33). To Desdemona, Constance's reticence is humility, a further indication that she is a great emissary from another world, "Academe … [R]uled by mighty Queens, / a race of Amazons who brook no men" (34).

Were that academe were so; nevertheless what is established in this section of the play is the importance of the reader in constituting the meaning of the text which is raised thematically in *Othello* when the Moor sees Cassio with the strawberry handkerchief and, cued by Iago's innuendoes about Desdemona, concludes that she and Cassio are having an affair. In *Goodnight Desdemona (Good Morning Juliet)*, MacDonald parodies this scene by having Desdemona, in the company of Iago, witness Othello showing Constance a diamond necklace which he intends for his wife. Like Othello in Shakespeare's play, Desdemona in MacDonald's misreads the scene and assumes that the gift is for her spouse's lover. Enraged by the prospect of infidelity, Desdemona is on the verge of murdering Constance, who is saved because she is magically spirited into the world of the *ur*-text for *Romeo and Juliet.*

The crux of the first act is the irony of Desdemona's reading of Constance which conversely parallels Shakespeare's reading of her: as Desdemona empowers the timid, submissive Constance by insisting that she is strong and powerful, so Shakespeare tames the fiery, independent Desdemona, representing her as the passive embodiment of goodness. Through Desdemona's response, Constance sees herself in a new light, one which overturns the world of Night. When Desdemona asks, "But tell me more of life in Academe. / If there be *cannibals that each other eat, / and men whose heads do grow beneath their shoulders?* / These things to hear, I seriously incline" (41). To which Constance explains that universities are "dog eat dog," that she has

slaved for years to get my doctorate,
but in a field like mine that's so well trod,
you run the risk of contradicting men
who've risen to the rank of sacred cow,
and dying on the horns of those who rule
the pasture with an iron cud.
Not that I'm some kind of feminist.
....
and after years spent as a laughingstock,
I finally came to think that it was true.
But, Desdemona, now that I've met you,
I want to stand out in that field and cry, "Bullshit!"
(41)

In response to this spirited cry to rally, Desdemona is prompted to ask what "bullshit" means. Constance explains that it is a "kind of lie. For instance, Academe / believes that you're a doomed and helpless victim" (41). Incredulous, Desdemona, asking rhetorical questions, reminds us of her independence:

Did I not flee my father, here to dwell
beneath the sword Hephaestus forged for Mars?
Will I not dive into Sargasso Sea, to serve abreast the Amazons abroad?
Will I not butcher any cow that dares
low lies to call me tame, ay that I will!
So raise now the battle cry, *Bullshit!!*
(42)

The affinity between the two women occurs because they recognize that they are both dismissed by the male-dominated academy: until recently, critics have denied Desdemona's independence by insisting that she is an almost allegorical figure who personifies goodness (Kernan xxx); Constance's scholarship is dismissed as the work of a crackpot, yet the work which she has written, but which is attributed to Claude Night, brings him great acclaim. For Constance, meeting Desdemona, whom she admires and with whom she identifies, is empowering because it allows her to see her own strength and to realize that she was the perfect victim because she had so internalized her own sense of inadequacy that she had victimized herself (49).[1]

Constance leaves the world of *Othello* to enter that of *Romeo and Juliet's* source to discover herself watching a fight between Mercutio and Tybalt. When her presence is acknowledged by Romeo, who likewise is an onlooker, he assumes that she is a boy. Constance does not disabuse him of this perception. MacDonald plays with the homosocial ambience of *Romeo and Juliet*, pushing the homoerotic undercurrents to the surface. The boys invite Constance to the baths, saying, "Greekling, splash with us" (54). Afraid of the consequences of her deception being exposed in the change rooms of the baths, Constance declines the invitation, commenting that

> Those guys remind me of the Stratford shows I've seen,
> where each production has a Roman bath:
> the scene might be a conference of state,
> but the steam will rise and billow from the wings,
> while full-grown men in Velcro loin-cloths speak,
> while snapping towels at each other.
> Why is it Juliet's scenes with her Nurse
> are never in a sauna. Or "King Lear":
> imagine Goneril and Regan, steaming
> as they plot the downfall of their Dad,
> while tearing hot wax from each other's legs;
> Ophelia, drowning in a whirlpool full
> of naked women. Portia, pumping iron—
> (55)

Constance's musing on the productions of the Stratford Festival raises the question: why are women not shown in eroticized situations with other women? The implied answer is that as long as woman is understood only in relation to man, a lesbian erotic is unimaginable. MacDonald's project in Act II is to subvert the theatrical codes which cannot accommodate woman's desire. She begins by establishing the marriage between Romeo and Juliet as one which is sanctioned by both families. The problem with their union is not their defiance of paternal authority but, given their bickering over their pet turtle and the threats they make to squeal to daddy when they're annoyed, it is their immaturity. Juliet, who seems not so much interested in love as in sex, is utterly miserable because she feels that marriage will deny her the thrill of meeting new boys and becoming infatuated. She is consoled only by the prospect of seeing handsome young men at the masked ball being given in honour of the marriage.

Like Romeo in Shakespeare's play, Constance intercepts the servant delivering the invitations to the ball. Still maintaining her guise as the Greek boy, she attends the party where both Romeo and Juliet independently declare their love for her. Juliet is particularly enamoured with Constance whom she believes to be homosexual and so, to appeal to her beloved, she disguises herself as Romeo. After the ball, she sneaks into the garden of Constance's lodgings where she woos her beloved who is standing on the balcony. This scene, rife with confused identities (most notable sexual—two women are disguised as men) has Juliet offering to initiate Constance's "budding taste of woman's dewy rose" (69).

The gleefully chaotic sexuality of this act is reminiscent of *As You Like It*, in which Rosalind, disguised as the boy Gannymede, teaches Orlando to love her. Here, however, homosexual encounters do not disguise heterosexuality but lesbianism. When Juliet finally discovers that Constance is not a boy but a woman, she isn't disappointed. On the contrary, the social prohibition of lesbian desire is attractive to her because its illicitness romantically dooms the lovers. Juliet emotes:

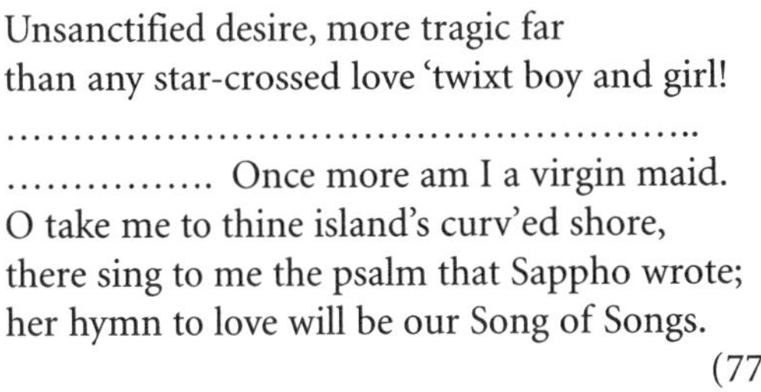

Unsanctified desire, more tragic far
than any star-crossed love 'twixt boy and girl!
……………………………………………..
……………. Once more am I a virgin maid.
O take me to thine island's curv'ed shore,
there sing to me the psalm that Sappho wrote;
her hymn to love will be our Song of Songs.
(77)

Juliet lures Constance to her bed by promising that, in exchange for a kiss, she will tell Constance the identity of the author whom she seeks. She provides Constance with directions to their rendezvous which send Constance to the graveyard, where she meets a ghost who is wearing her red toque. The appearance of the Ghost, something of a second grade vaudevillian intent on telling tired jokes rather than a menacing harbinger, causes Constance to ask, "A ghostly fool? A jester from the grave? / Are you— ? You couldn't be. What play is this? / Could you be …Yorick?!" To which the Ghost replies, "Na-a-ay. You're it" (73). Pressing the Ghost for information, Constance asks if he knows who the author of the Gustav manuscript is. "A lass," he replies (73).

Constance isn't able to solve the Ghost's riddle. She escapes from the graveyard for her tryst with Juliet, the identity of the author still eluding her. When she is with Juliet, she presses her for the promised information:

CONSTANCE. … Now who's the Author?
JULIET. I did lie.
(76)

It is then that Juliet professes her love for Constance, enraptured by the tragic possibilities of the unsanctioned lesbian love. She proposes that they commit suicide, "having loved each other perfectly, / our deaths proclaim one night, eternity" (78). When Constance reaches into Juliet's shirt to take the vial of poison which she has hidden in her bosom, she finds another page of the Gustav manuscript which reads:

Thy demons rest not till they've eaten thee.
Get Desdemon and merge this trinity,
or never live to see another Birthdy.
(78)

With that, the identity of the author becomes clear: it is Constance herself. Desdemona comes through a time warp, joining the two women and the Ghost, who is present as a voice telling Constance, "You're it." "I'm it? … I'm it. *I'm* the Fool! … 'The Fool and the Author are one and the same'…" remembers Constance (86).

Amidst the bad puns and the general atmosphere of fun somewhat akin to an all-girl pajama party,[2] MacDonald offers insight into the relation of the author and the reader. As a woman, as a lesbian, as a Canadian, MacDonald's experience is one of being colonized by the hegemonic narratives of gender, sexuality and nation which dominate English-language culture. Historically, readings of Shakespeare have been ideologically compatible with, indeed justified, the privilege of the dominant culture. These readings have buttressed the imperialist enterprises of Britain by entrenching a sense of the inferiority of the colonized culture. Nowhere is this more evident than in Canada where the Stratford Festival receives huge grants from the various levels of government while small theatre companies struggle to mount productions on budgets which would barely cover the cost of one costume made for a single Stratford production. MacDonald's comment about the Stratford Festival isn't a gratuitous swipe at the Festival but suggests that the celebration of manliness, particularly in the context of Shakespeare, isn't an apolitical aesthetic but one which is compatible with the humanist tradition. "Men live more truly and fully" reading Shakespeare, as Allan Bloom claims.

But not all of us are men, and not all men want to adhere to humanist agendas. What is pernicious about humanist readings is the failure to query what investment the readers have in them. MacDonald theatrically explores what is by now a commonplace of literary criticism: it is the reader who constitutes the meaning of the text. By refusing to accept the conventional readings of Desdemona and Juliet as the women who, through their patience and goodness, teach men to love and thereby bring them to full manhood, she begins to explore the conventions of tragedy which cannot accommodate women, except in roles which support men. As MacDonald commented in an interview with Rita Much, the kind of roles which are available to women often requires that they serve as "emotional barometers and the representatives of vulnerability and instability in general" (MacDonald 129).

If Constance is the figure of the reader, then reading is empowering through the process of identification which allows us to become part of the drama where we, like Constance, can explore ourselves. The text is a sort of Arden (in the case of Shakespeare, literally) where, free from the demands of the actual world, we can live imaginatively. In this sense every reading is autobiographical because the reader invests herself in the text as she produces its meaning. For me, a Canadian woman, *Goodnight Desdemona (Good Morning Juliet)* is a post-colonial drama of empowerment which through comedy up-ends the ideology of humanism. I want to join Desdemona, Juliet and Constance and be one of the girls who swears "To live by questions, not their solution. / To trade our certainties, for thy confusion" (85).

(1992)

Notes

1 In Margaret Atwood's *Survival: A Thematic Guide to Canadian Literature* (1972) Atwood suggests that Canada as a nation is a collective victim and outlines four basic victim positions. See *Survival* 36-39. That Constance allows herself to be victimized may not be simply an aspect of her individual character but may be an aspect of her Canadian-ness.

2 Bañuta Rubess, in her introduction to the Coach House Press edition of the play, recalls, "It began with a joke. On a tour of England in 1985 with *This Is For You, Anna*, Ann-Marie MacDonald crammed a pillow on my face and with great hilarity pronounced: 'Goodnight, Desdemona!'" (7).

Works Cited

Aristotle. *Poetics. Classical Literary Criticism.* trans. T.S. Dorsch. Baltimore: Penguin, 1965.

Ashcroft, Bill, Gareth Griffiths and Helen Tiffin. *The Empire Writes Back: Theory and Practice in Post-colonial Literatures.* London: Routledge, 1989.

Atwood, Margaret. *Survival: A Thematic Guide to Canadian Literature.* Toronto: Anansi, 1972.

Hodgdon, Barbara. "The Prosper-ing of the American mind, or culture in the ma(s)king." *Essays in Theatre* 9.2 (1991): 105-19.

Kernan, Alvin, ed. "Introduction." *Othello.* By William Shakespeare. New York: Signet, 1963.

Mulvey, Laura. *Visual and Other Pleasures.* Bloomington: Indiana UP, 1989.

MacDonald, Ann-Marie. *Goodnight Desdemona (Good Morning Juliet).* Toronto: Coach House, 1990.

———. "Interview." *Fair Play: 12 Women Speak (Conversations With Canadian Playwrights).* Ed. Judith Rudakoff and Rita Much. Toronto: Simon and Pierre, 1990.

Making it Happen: A Commercial Model for Self-Production

by Shawna Dempsey with Lorri Millan

Lorri Millan and I became friends in 1986. I arrived at the first day of rehearsal for *Michi's Blood* (a Crow's Theatre Production), and found her, the stage manager, knee deep in water in Harbord Street's Ohm Performance Space. Flooding was a new foible to Ohm, but neither of us were particularly surprised, and together, stoically, bailed it out.

I had begun my professional work in theatre in 1984, stage managing for D.D. Kugler, and acting as summer administrator for Nightwood Theatre. In both of these capacities, my duties included countless tasks that one would not usually consider part of these job descriptions. This was to be the case during my six years as a worker in alternative and children's theatre. Everybody did everything because we had to. Lorri's career was not dissimilar. At the age of sixteen she learned to run a lighting board one afternoon, so that she could operate it that evening for one of the first annual *Rhubarb!* festivals. Through these do-or-die situations we both acquired a tremendous number of skills, all of which enabled the presentation of live art. Mopping the floor of Ohm was yet another adventure in how to make theatre happen.

At the same time we began to develop our own work as artists, outside the theatre system. For Lorri, this took the form of photographs, drawing, film making, and song writing; for me, performance art. Each of us also began to critique the theatrical model: its preoccupation with character psychology rather than ideas; the formal conventions of its presentation; the tremendous amount of unseen labour that goes into its execution; and the seemingly unavoidable hierarchy circumscribing the roles of its workers. We concluded that even within alternative theatre, the weight of theatre history sets up expectations in both the audience and artists. It is these expectations that we wanted to attempt to dissolve.

We began our collaboration on feminist, costume-based performance art in 1989, and have been supporting ourselves full-time with it since 1991. This self-created label, "Feminist, Costume-based Performance Art," roughly translates into a set of ideals and practices that fuels our process. Performance art, by its experimental nature, is difficult to define. We have come to call it: "live presentation in which artists use their bodies to communicate ideas in a visual manner, while not adhering to traditional narrative conventions."

Each performance artist approaches their work in a different way, be it through dance, music, text, or sculpture, and there are as many types of performance art, as there are types of theatre.

For us the work begins with a costume. We conceive, design, and build this wearable object together. We often spend up to a year, after its construction, looking at it and unravelling its meanings. I then write, and Lorri then re-writes the texts that will animate it. I perform the finished piece, and Lorri acts as outside eye and technical coordinator. Despite this loose division of labour, we share ownership of all aspects of the work. After the first public performance of a piece, we will often work for two more years, re-writing and refining it. In addition to writing, this process might include the creation of video pieces, film, slide and sound components, and music. Sometimes the finished performance bears little resemblance to its original incarnation. Occasionally it remains virtually unchanged. No matter which path the development takes, the final product is truly ours, and where her ideas leave off and mine begin is indecipherable.

Finally, the philosophical passion behind the work is feminism. It is our hope to change the way people see themselves and the social constructs around them. This critique of patriarchal systems means that the content of our pieces is not what one usually thinks of as populist entertainment.

> It has been said of all mad women, witches, bitches and whores, "She is not well groomed. She does not fit the hit and bridle of a do-good, feel-good, don't-rock-the-boat-baby world." (*The Thin Skin of Normal*, 1993)

Because our work combines marginal content with a marginal form, venues are an issue. We do not have a performance space, or a "season" with subscribers, or even work that fits into the standard two-act-with-intermission framework (most of our pieces are five minutes long). We have realized that our unique position requires unique solutions to the problem of where to present.

The first strategy has been to take our work to where people already are. This has meant that we have opened for bands in bars, performed in classrooms as part of women's studies programs, or entertained participants of a United Church conference. Although these venues are usually not very lucrative, they take us to people who would not necessarily see our performance art, or be exposed to our way of thinking. The most interesting discussions often arise after these performances, discussions that can be instrumental in the development of the work by exposing us to ideas we have not considered and by forcing us to become increasingly lucid about the ones we have. As well as conferences, bars, and universities, we have found limited access to comedy clubs, restaurants, political rallies, union meetings, poetry readings, and folk clubs, And of course there is no shortage of "benefits" to perform at. We have had to be aggressive and inventive in our quest for audiences, and to think of all gatherings of people as a potential gig.

The other spaces we find ourselves in most often are art galleries, or in venues billed as visual arts events, presented by an arts service organization or an art school. We find that in these contexts the audience is less hampered by theatrical expectations we cannot fulfill. (While performing at Factory Theatre's Studio Theatre, a patron called the box office and asked if our piece had a happy ending. In truth, the piece did not have an ending, in the theatrical sense, at all.) In an art setting, the audience seems more willing to "read" us like a painting, a collection of ideas and images that can be personally interpreted by each viewer according to their own experiences. Art galleries are also flexible about what should constitute "an evening of entertainment." Rarely are we asked to sign contracts demanding one, play-length piece, and are able to do a variety of short pieces and show some of our video and film work (for example). The structure of the evening is less preordained, and allows us to present our work in a way that serves that particular piece or pieces best. In soliciting this type of venue, we approach artist-run centres, regional art galleries, arts service organizations, universities with visual arts programs, and university student associations.

It should be noted that these organizations pay us artists' fees: we are not dependent on moneys garnered at the door of these events. Generally the organization applies for funding to cover our expenses and fees, and then judges accordingly what they need their ticket price to be, in order to cover their out-of-pocket expenses. As a result, our performances are often quite inexpensive to attend, and are occasionally even free. This is definitely our preference. We believe strongly in accessibility, as demonstrated by our varied choice of venues. Because we are not dependent on the gate, we can afford to take risks with form, content and new material that perhaps, in another arrangement, we might need to reconsider out of financial necessity. In our experience, the more an audience pays, the less willing they are to participate in something experimental.

> I can't get enough of this dirt. Frankly it's just not dirty enough for me. But I'm trying to make do, trying to make out, tiny specks that have fallen between my cracks, that I can come to on my hands and knees, and rub and scrub until I slip in the grease of my own elbows. (*Arborite Housedress*, 1994)

About half of the opportunities to perform come to us, unsolicited. The other half we have to search out. And performances only account for about 40% of our joint, annual, gross income. Our other source of revenue is grants to individual artists, offered by three levels of government, and special project grants offered by arts service organizations. One of our many mottoes is, "Never miss a deadline." This, and the constant pursuit of venues, means we spend a tremendous amount of our time (at least half) doing the business of our art. With the decrease in public funding for the arts, our time investment in the business aspect is increasing. Not only is funding for individual artists shrinking, but so is funding to organizations (women's and art) that have sponsored our work in the past (i.e., visiting artist funds used to produce our work are fast disappearing everywhere). We are increasingly looking towards self-production.

Using a commercial model for our unconventional material might be foolhardy, but it seems we will need to find a commercially viable way to access audiences outside the places they are used to finding us. Perhaps concert style productions are the way to proceed at this terrifying juncture. Our experience suggests that there is an audience anxious for different sorts of live performance, especially work that reflects their realities. One idea has been to produce a Feminist Revue—a mixed evening of music and performance—pooling the resources of artists in similar situations. A venture like this was undertaken in the fall of 1988, by LEAF (Legal Education Action Fund), to the delight of audiences across the country. We must also look to expanding our audience to the United States, Asia, and Europe. Screenings of our work in other media (film, art video and TV) fortunately seems to pique interest in our live work, as does the wide distribution of our T-shirts and postcard projects.

Of course the ugly reality of this is that commercial self-production will only eat further into our already precious creative time. As things stand, all of our administrative work goes on while we are conceiving, building, writing, performing, and teaching our pieces. Despite the exhaustion level this entails, we would never step back into the system of live art production that we left in the late '80s. We have taken the model of theatrical production in which we collectively invested fourteen years, and have downsized it as far as it will go. In the process we have taken responsibility and credit for all phases of production, and have created a space in which we can explore the parameters of live art in different ways.

> I've got a challenging job, a stunning apartment, and a retirement plan that's nothing to sneeze at. I love stress. And stress loves me. In fact working eighteen hours a day, six days a week just isn't enough. I also play racket ball, tournament chess, and Russian roulette. (*Mary Medusa* 1992-93)

It is unclear whether, if arts funding does collapse in this country, we will be able to survive as commercial art producers. And one must wonder if there will be too great an artistic and political cost attached to participating in the commercial world. On the other hand, we are certainly not going to stop producing art because of financial considerations. Years of building a diverse audience and the leanness of our operation perhaps gives us a chance, should we enter that world. Naturally economic factors other than government grants available to artists impact on us as well. The recession of the early 1990s seems to have left live performance audiences permanently shrunken. The strategy of taking ourselves to where audiences are, and luring them to new, live art venues has worked for us so far, but the search for creative solutions continues, on the long, hungry road ahead.

(1995)

Diversity and Voice: A Celebration of Canadian Women Writing for Performance

by Susan Bennett

This article can start with a happy and certain fact: there are now more women involved in producing more theatre than at any time previous in the history of Canadian theatre. Canadian women playwrights (the latter word a term I want to use in the broadest sense, to include all kinds of writers for performance) are seeing and making their work on all kinds of stages across the country and, indeed, in many venues far from the national borders. Because of the strength and number of women's performances, I cannot hope, far less claim, to offer a comprehensive account of their contributions to contemporary Canadian theatre; what I want instead to chronicle is something of their emergent history and to suggest a multiple trajectory of interest which finds particular expression in this historical moment.

As other histories of women's theatre have indicated,[1] the post-1968 growth of the Women's Movement provided a context for the development of much more work by, for and about women (some feminist, some ambivalently so, some not, some resolutely not) on both mainstream and alternative stages. It is the last twenty-five years or so, as a more or less global phenomenon, that has brought into both stage production and academic focus a subgenre under the umbrella of theatre recognized as something specific to women.[2] In Canada, the organization of such work is perhaps complicated by the particularities of specific regional interests which concentrate the arts, like so many aspects of the apparently Canadian cultural experience, in the provinces of Ontario and Québec.[3] It is nonetheless true that a contemporary history of women's dramatic writing in Canada can locate performances across the map and, when the focus is narrowed to more local geographies, they can be located both within and without theatre buildings in every region. And those maps are not just the literal ones produced by the cartographer; there are also those which might chart the diversity of identity positions that represent Canadian women across race, class, ethnicity, sexuality, age and other positionalities. At the interstices of identity and place, the strength of Canadian women's writing for performance finds both voice and presence.

But before celebrating the diversity of such work, it is perhaps worth re-marking this contemporary history onto a more conventional (linear) record of playwriting in this country. In other words, it is important to remember the foresisters to women writing today. Yvonne Hodkinson has pointed out in her useful introduction to

Female Parts: The Art and Politics of Female Playwrights, the many, largely unsung and unremembered women who contributed to the emergence of drama and theatre in Canada. Nineteenth-century playwrights Eliza Lanesford Cushing and Sarah Anne Curzon wrote resisting, transgressive plays, subtly reworking the melodrama form to speak of their own cultural experience. [4] In the earlier part of the twentieth century such different women as Dora Mavor Moore (whose labours established a professional theatre in Toronto) [5] and Gwen Pharis Ringwood (whose writing for and work with the little theatre movement in the West brought women-centred theatre to all kinds of new stages) [6] provided a model history of how women in Canada have made it happen—not always or not often on the main stage of existing theatres, but by inventing forms and creating theatres where their work might develop and explore an aesthetic which engaged with the lives that they found themselves living. Moreover, as the pageants and performances around women's suffrage issues ably demonstrate, [7] women have also long known the efficacy and necessity of entering their creative work into the political arena so as to bring visibility to their hopes, concerns and oppressions. If the contributions of these many gifted women are only now beginning to be documented and analyzed, and names such as Elizabeth Sterling Haynes and Elsie Park Gowan [8] remain woefully unfamiliar, it is nonetheless important to locate contemporary energies in a continuum of activity, to see (in Canada as elsewhere) a women's dramatic tradition.

The 1970s, however, brought an intensity of interest in women's theatre and many women playwrights who might now be thought of as the senior, accomplished representatives in the field were then trying to find theatres and other performance spaces interested in producing their work—or, at the least, agreeable to them producing their own work. Writers such as Sharon Pollock, Joanna Glass, Margaret Hollingsworth and Carol Bolt created works with perspectives that challenged notions of what Canadian theatre and drama was and could be, even as some of this earlier work now seems tentative in its interest in what might be termed a feminine aesthetic. [9] At the same time, the first spaces which would proactively encourage women's dramatic writings were coming into existence, although and once again it should be noted that their commitment to a women's project was not always obviously foregrounded. Catalyst Theatre in Edmonton, for example, has consistently produced scripts for and with women, and had key artistic direction provided by women (Jan Selman, Jane Heather, Ruth Smilie among others); [10] yet its primary commitment is to a broader field of social action theatre. Furthermore, as Cynthia Grant's account of Nightwood Theatre makes evident, "[w]hen we established the company in 1978 we were very anxious that people not consider Nightwood a 'women's theatre.' Personally, I wished to have a career as a director, *not* as a woman director. Although I was already clearly defined as a feminist, I knew the derogatory, second-class implications of such terms" (45). Nightwood, of course, went on to become Canada's most significant producer of women's theatre, has been proactively feminist, and the venue where so many of the contemporary writers considered here had some of their first work produced.

With these frames in mind, I want to impose three categoric designations on contemporary writing for performance by women and to gesture towards the kind(s) of diversity that such multivalent writing produces, and is produced by. Most obviously in what I have suggested is a tradition in women's writing in Canada, I want to examine some contemporary plays, texts that both retain and examine the possibilities of the conventional form. Beyond that, I will examine the emergence of a performance art tradition (even if that seems something of a contradiction in its terms) as well as the development of collective theatre writing and performance.

Plays and Playwrights

The merest glance at the membership list for the Playwrights Union of Canada indicates just how many women are writing and, moreover, how prolific so many of them are. It is still the case, even with all the achievements of those women writers and practitioners in the 1970s and through the 1980s, that only a small percentage of women writing for theatre see their work professionally produced. Full productions of new works by women remain noteworthy simply by their occurrence. While many more plays by women are receiving attention, so many of these scripts are not supported beyond the workshop or staged reading. With that caveat in mind, it is not unreasonable to name Judith Thompson as one of Canada's foremost playwrights—female or male. Her plays (including *The Crackwalker*, *White Biting Dog*, *I Am Yours*, and *Lion in the Streets*) have not always enjoyed critical enthusiasm or, indeed, respect, but her gripping creations of what one critic describes as "a surreal day-dream or nightmare spill[ing] into a naturalistic picture" (Adam 22) have brought her Governor General's Awards for Drama, productions of her texts both across and outside Canada, and considerable academic attention. Thompson's representation of people who struggle to articulate themselves, along with situations that impinge on that articulation, bring to theatre audiences a compelling dramatization of aspects of the world that we (as a hegemonically white and middle-class realization of the gaze) are otherwise efficiently trained to screen out. Robert Nunn suggests that Thompson's plays "are increasingly bold journeys into the abyss of the unconscious" (27)—and these are apparently journeys that audiences and academic readers are anxious to make. Her remarkable contribution is to provide an innovative and provocative aesthetic which attempts to account for generally invisible aspects of contemporary Canadian life.

Yet if Thompson's plays flatten out aspects of gender difference in order to explore a universalized psychic debilitation, then many other contemporary women playwrights have brought on to the stage their relationship to dramatic tradition precisely in terms of the gendered body. Many of their plays insist on entering into visibility the specificities of women's histories. Writers such as Jackie Crossland (*Collateral Damage*), Deborah Porter (*No More Medea*) and Ann-Marie MacDonald (*Goodnight Desdemona (Good Morning, Juliet)*) have turned to the canonical texts of dramatic literature and insisted on their own precisely female, re-readings. Others have taken as their subjects women little known and less recognized in history and brought the women's stories to the stage: specifically Canadian are Mary Vingoe's *Living Curiosities: A Story of Anna Swan* (which imagines the world inhabited by Anna Swan, a seven-feet-ten-inches tall, nineteenth-century Maritime woman who by virtue of her amazing height found herself at the age of seventeen one of Barnum's exhibits in New York City) and Wendy Lill's *The Fighting Days* (which explores the friendship of Frances Beynon with well-known suffrage activist Nellie McClung). Bañuta Rubess's plays have also often turned to women's obscurity in history. A short radio play fantasizes the life of Isabelle Eberhardt, the nineteenth-century, Swiss-born writer and adventurer. Her *Tango Lugano* tells the story of Aspazija Rainis, a Latvian political revolutionary—a play which Rubess produced in Riga after the dissolution of the Soviet Empire (see Much and Rudakoff 51-52).

That Rubess returns to the experience of her Latvian background (her parents came to Toronto in the 1950s) is indicative of many contemporary women playwrights' particular interest in the cultural formation of their identities. Monique Mojica's powerful *Princess Pocahontas and the Blue Spots* counterpoints popular received images of Native women (always inaccurate, inevitably abusive) with the stories that Native women have always told and which have provided a non-linear but sustaining history. The high farce of Princess Buttered-on-Both-Sides not only draws a white audience's attention to Hollywood and other misrepresentations of Native peoples, but at the same time marks our on-going complicity in the maintenance of these images/stories. And an unmistakable part of her critique is directed at the white feminist who has insisted on a univocal feminism. As the Contemporary Woman #1 in Mojica's play describes it, "So many years of trying to fit into feminist shoes. O.K., I'm trying on the shoes; but they're not the same as the shoes in the display case. The shoes I'm trying on must be crafted to fit these wide, square, brown feet. I must be able to feel the earth through their soles" (58). The play claims a strong, but heterogeneous Native identity. If nothing else—and there *is* much else—*Princess Pocahontas* demonstrates how rare it is, still, for women of colour to see their realities on any stage and, as part of that, celebrates a recognition of the power of diversity in/as identity.

Djanet Sears, who directed the first workshop production and dramaturged the first full production of Mojica's *Princess Pocahontas*, raises her own complicated series of questions concerning identity. A one-woman show, *Afrika Solo*, explores the cultural condition of hegemonic whiteness. Djanet (raised in the United Kingdom and Canada of Jamaican and Guyanese parents), irrespective of that background and her own skin colour, discovers that she was "white" in the way she perceived the world. The play takes the form and the story of a quest, Djanet's own discovery of her roots and, as a result, her coming to terms with (her) identity. As Joanne Tompkins rightly suggests, "*Afrika Solo* does not occupy the usual colonial split of enunciation (of imperial centre and colony), rather it focuses on a multi-vectored site of enunciation, all violence of which must be accounted for in the construction of Djanet's 'Canadian' cultural heritage" (36-37). Once again, H/history is invoked not only to expose the fractures around gendered positionality, but to remark the colonial imperative of our Canadian heritage which hovers, yet, to restrict expressions of identity and selfhood.

And Audrey Butler's *Black Friday?* (in *Radical Perversions* 13-65) collapses labour history in Cape Breton into a classic coming-out story of lesbian identity. As Butler herself writes in the introduction of *Black Friday?* "[m]any people have asked: why the question mark?...Through the process of writing the play I began to perceive one of the characters as Black. Why? For me there was a clear connection between homophobia, racism, and the system that destroyed Terry's father. The title transcends a real historical event (my intention when I started the play) and encompasses issues I have been struggling with as a white working-class dyke" *(Radical Perversions* 12). As with *Princess Pocahontas*, part of the attraction to *Black Friday?* resides simply in making visible the otherwise invisible through the focus of a dramatic text.

The plays mentioned here represent only a few of the many exciting and innovative works women are producing for the Canadian stage. But they represent an active assertion of women's (counter)history, of the making and remaking of an aesthetic which asks new questions of the art form known as drama, and solicits new processes by and through which audiences recognize the form. And if these writers have transgressed, in the most productive sense, the container of the play, other women have sought other less text-based expressions for their ideas and concerns.

Performing Women

As Lenora Champagne explains, "[t]he performance-art form has subversive origins and tendencies....Contemporary performance has precedents in the avant-garde movements of the early twentieth century that challenged established standards and definitions of art and sought to shake up social conventions with shocking, outrageous behaviour in public appearances" (xi). [11] It is hardly surprising, then, that this is a form that many women have chosen seemingly instead of conventional theatre. Given the history of exclusion in mainstream theatre, it must have often seemed easier to invent a new form and to pursue new venues for radical work. Moreover, women have often made it an explicit aspect of their performance strategy to seek out non-traditional audiences. Both *Princess Pocahontas* and *Afrika Solo* were Nightwood Theatre "plays" and both, to differing extents, divert their energies from the conventions of theatre and drama, to explore form(s) that will more readily realize the complex ideas they are endeavouring to stage. Yet both, I think, retain some connection with conventions of the play, the shape of that performance. ahdri zhina mandiela's *dark diaspora ... in dub* was likewise first produced by Nightwood Theatre, but this text bears far less resemblance to the kind(s) of structures we generally identify as a play. *dark diaspora* was developed with a collective choreography and mandiela's dub poems were performed by seven women representing internal Voice, shape and sound. [12] The work has also been performed as a solo show, with and without live musicians, and is available as a print text and as an audio recording. mandiela's performance poetry is full of rage, calls to empowerment, and celebration for women of colour. *dark diaspora* performs a strong and pointed challenge to the conventionality of both form and subject matter in others' (play) texts. The writer states in the prefatory material to the published text of *dark diaspora ... in dub* that she envisages her work performed by up to fifty women. Even if only as fantasy, this possibility gives testament to the remarkable sight/site a theatre stage occupied by so many women (of colour) would undoubtedly be.

Margo Kane's *Moonlodge* looks "to explore and mine the stories from within my [Kane's] experience" (Kane 26) and so, like Mojica's *Princess Pocahontas*, it records a history that has carried orally but which has in so many ways been denied by "Canada." *Moonlodge* has been performed in venues such as Native Earth Performing Arts in Toronto, the Banff Centre for the Arts in Alberta and the Vancouver East Cultural Centre, but it is important to note that it has also been seen by Native and Inuit communities across Canada. I offer here a long description by Kane of that experience, but one I think worth repeating for its sense of the community in/as performance:

> I join my relations in their evening circles over tea and bannock smeared with red, red jam. As mosquitoes and flies vie for our attention, the young and old alike sing, with hand drums and crickets as accompaniment. Babies swing in hammocks. Dogs wander in and out, sometimes curling at our feet, then sneaking off together to chase down the night animals beyond our circle of light. Poetry, songs, memories and stories are shared. It is a place to give a first reading of a new poem, to receive encouragement for a new piece of progress. Sometimes I am coaxed to participate; other times I bring out material to be read aloud by those gathered. I need to hear it spoken by them. I want their impressions and advice. Often I just want to give something of myself....
>
> It is at times like these that I feel a strong sense of belonging. For all my wanderings, in and out of urban cities and towns, here the connection to tribal family and nation is reaffirmed. It is where my relations gather and my ancestors smile at me through their faces. (26)

Notions of land and place are so crucial to Native beliefs and practice, and Kane's *Moonlodge* marks those connections as a powerful performative, one that is offered as a gift to her nation. For the non-Native audience, as with Mojica's play, there is the invitation to listen—a contract from which we might learn much.

Other performance work draws more specifically on a visual arts context in which to frame issues by, for and about women. Such a context has, as Champagne suggested, its roots in the provocative "acting out" of the so-called avant-garde movements in this century. An example of such "acting out" is *Lies About Betty and The Truth about Zucchini*, a multimedia performance piece by Lori Weidenhammer.[13] In this work, Weidenhammer stages a plethora of domestic rituals, emphasizing through comic exaggeration the often ridiculous logic enforcing women's quotidian experience. The video segment of *Lies About Betty* imagines a "holiday from misogyny" and, like her earlier work *The Saskatchewan Lawn Ornament Opera*, suggests a serious social critique behind the melodramatic farce of her performance elements.

Shawna Dempsey and Lorri Millan, performance collaborators based in Winnipeg, have created the kinds of revisionist feminist histories that were highlighted in the plays of some of the more conventional writers. Dempsey and Millan, however, do not start with a written text but instead create the object which they eventually animate. The object functions, they suggest, as "a visual metaphor for the paradox we find ourselves in politically" (Bennett and Patience 9). *Mary Medusa* worked from the construction of a wig of snakes to articulate the imagination and assumptions of a contemporary corporate woman whose body carries the legacy of the Medusa myth. More recently, they have created a series of unlikely dresses—an arborite housewife's dress, a stained glass window dress of the Virgin Mary, a Saran Wrap dress for the contemporary feminist and so on—through which to explore questions of identity as an embodied practice. As I have discussed at some length elsewhere, all of Dempsey and Millan's work "explores and exposes those systems of exchange in which the female body has functioned as the currency for its Other's power and as the material evidence for a stability of reference to the so-called objective world" (Bennett, "Radical" 37).

The performance of a counter-currency for female bodies—one of lesbian eroticism and desire—has brought much attention to the work of the Vancouver-based collective Kiss & Tell. *True Inversions*, a live performance incorporating video and audiotapes, slides and music, explores "the view that sex and the world are intricately complicated....Sexual pleasure is interrupted by, framed by and simultaneous with concerns about AIDS and safer sex, sexual abuse, male violence, pleasure, sexism, friendship, love, racism, state control of our bodies and our art, political disagreement, television, coming out to our families...all of these things are part of our sexuality. And still there is joy which we affirm alongside our pain" (Publicity material, first set of ellipses indicating omitted material; second set of ellipses in the original). A development of their well-received interactive "photo-event" "Drawing the Line,"[14] *True Inversions* both celebrates lesbian identity *and* re-marks the diffuse and complicated territory of its possible constructions.

While Weidenhammer, Dempsey and Millan, and Kiss & Tell use a multi-media approach to performance through which to interrogate the assumptions of more traditional, linear arrangements of enacted text, Karen Hines has chosen another marginalized dramatic genre—clowning—on which to script a performance of her female body. In *Pochsy's Lips*, Hines as Pochsy performs a part-spoken, part-sung monologue which explores the dilemma (to quote the first two lines she sings): "falling apart,/But everyone's falling in love" (38). Like Weidenhammer's transformation of the domestic into artistic ritual, Hines/Pochsy manipulates the hospital bed and I.V. unit to play partner to her enactment of a "sick world." And in the story she tells, Pochsy is wildly funny, but always in that potentially sad and tragic mode of clowning. And the performance ending brings not the usual resolution: for a comedy where women fall in love usually bespeaks marriage; in *Pochsy's Lips* she simply cannot be saved by love or anything else and dies.

The performance work of these Canadian women, above all else, has its emphasis on the body as the bearer of culture's scripts. With diverse and often contradictory strategies for its realization, women's performance art makes explicit the spectator's gaze and poses the crucial question: how do I look?[15] At a time when visibility politics has consumed much of the energy of feminism(s), the prevalence and directness of these women's performance speaks to "an effort to recover, or postulate, a prediscursive body, a critical effort to free the female body from its overdeterminations as a body saturated with sex, site of pleasure for (an)other, subjected and devoid of subjectivity" (Hart in Hart and Phelan 5).

Collective Creation

A third and important aspect of this map of contemporary women's writing for performance in Canada is the work of women's collectives. As Lynda Hart has noted, "[c]ollective authorship was an extremely important concept in early feminist companies of the 1970s and 1980s" (Hart and Phelan 6). While some earlier collectives no longer exist, others have developed and broadened the notion of "collective" to encompass a number of performance and writing strategies which address particular community and women's issues. Kiss & Tell, whose *True Inversions* I have already mentioned, are one such example: alongside a core group of three members, the collective has added other women as their various projects dictate which, it would seem, allows both a freedom and a renewal of energy. While Kiss & Tell's work has been focussed on lesbian visibility, collective performance by women in Canada has addressed a multiplicity of social and artistic concerns.

Perhaps the most notable and, indeed, successful of these is Toronto's The Company of Sirens. This company started in the mid-1980s and involved many women who had previously been associated with Nightwood Theatre. Much of their work is produced as the result of commissions (such as *The Working People's Picture Show* for a convention for the tenth anniversary of Organized Working Women; *Shelter from Assault* for the Ontario Ministry of Education Family Violence Prevention Initiative Programme; *Whenever I feel Afraid* on violence against women for Metropolitan Toronto high school audiences).[16] A measure of the company's success is its recent division into a main company and one directed at productions for young audiences, as is the fact that they have been performing more than three hundred shows a year. Using the presentational style common to much popular, touring theatre and engaging/empowering audiences in post-performance discussions, the Sirens's work is often seen—and engaged—by many more spectators than number the usual audiences for plays and, particularly, for more performance-oriented art. In this way at least, it is interesting to consider that the Company of Sirens might well be Canada's most significant women writers/performers.

But I want to end this incomplete survey of women's theatre work in Canada in the city where I live and work. Calgary, a city of less than one million people, has had for some seven years a women's theatre collective in the name of Maenad. This group came into existence to produce the work of one of their founding members, Rose Scollard,[17] but has since that time staged each season two full productions of new plays by women and a three-week "New Voices/FemFest." Many of Maenad's playwrights (who devote a minimum of six weeks to participation in the rehearsal and production process) have been found in Calgary though others have been drawn from across Canada. The festival has showcased many different types of local performance work, alongside presentations by women from England, Germany, Japan and the United States. And this company's history is, in effect, a microcosm of what I have charted here. Maenad's history, in a sense typical of the complex trajectory that I have tried to suggest, characterizes contemporary Canadian women's writing for the stage.

Among Maenad's work there is *Aphra*, co-written by founding members Rose Scollard, Nancy Cullen and Alexandria Patience, a play which retrieves Aphra Behn from the margins of (theatre) history; *Dance Me Born*, written by Alice Lee and co-produced with Sweetgrass which was in 1993 the first full-length script by a Native woman to be produced in Calgary—an all the more remarkable fact when it is remembered that the city is almost entirely enclosed by Native land. The 1994-95 season opener, Gisele Villeneuve's *Oldest Woman in the World*, brings to the spotlight a woman whose age would usually mean that there is literally no role for her, on the stage or anywhere else.

And this is what Canadian women writing for performance are doing in/as the theatre. These women have rewritten the parameters for the cultural experience of "theatre;" they have, in short, reinvented the term. Many wonderful playwrights whose work I have not considered here—all the ground-breakers from the 1970s along with "newer" names like Pamela Boyd, Yvette Nolan, Sally Clark, Joan MacLeod, Janis Spence, Colleen Craig, Cindy Cowan and others—make Canadian theatre stronger and more diverse than ever before. Other artists, some of whom I have mentioned here, use more visual arts, cabaret settings, fringe festivals, women's festivals to reimagine women's bodies and the way(s) that we might see them. In so many communities, inside and outside of Canada's major urban centres, women are claiming their own performance spaces, some of which they name as theatres and some not. We can celebrate that seeing the work of Canadian women playwrights is, in the 1990s, an easier task. More of it gets done (though even more of it should) and it doesn't always mean paying at least $35 for a seat.

Writing for performance by Canadian women is not only strong and diverse; it is in more places and spaces than ever before. A cause for celebration, indeed, and—I hope—a cause, too, for some optimism for where it will surely lead us.

(1996)

Notes

1 See, for example, Wandor, Goodman, and Canning.

2 To some extent, to speak of women's theatre is to echo the tenets of cultural feminism, and an effect of that is to bring together a disparate collection of writers whose only commonality might in fact be their biological make-up. It is possible, too—or at least this article takes as one of its assumptions that it is—to celebrate a diversity of positionality which speaks to an inclusive, diverse and contradictory women's theatre. The relationship between a category defined as women's theatre and one defined as feminist theatre is both complicated and problematic. In either case, production of histories seems to me to pose questions that theatre historians have not yet grappled with in an entirely satisfactory way. For an account of some of the historiographical problems in accounting for feminist theatre, see my "Feminist (Theatre) Historiography/Canadian (Feminist) Theatre."

3 Theatre work in Québec is discussed in another article in this collection [Glaap with Althof]. Here I'd like to make two notes. One is that women's theatre in Québec has had a particularly rich and interesting history, drawing on French feminisms and European avant-garde performance styles that give, I think, a different shape and expression to much of the work Québecois women have produced. The second is an emphasis of the first: while much of the work I include here has commonalities with work produced in Québec, the difference—or, to pick up on the most common adjective summoned in support of Québec's sovereignty—its distinct nature makes its inclusion in my own discussion both too complicated and, indeed, inappropriate. I should also record this article's restriction to writing in English, a fact which excludes contributions as important as Antonine Maillet's long and brilliant career in the Maritimes and works by Native women which primarily utilize their own languages to tell their stories.

4 Heather Jones's "Feminism and Nationalism in Domestic Melodrama" provides helpful prolegomena to this area.

5 An important biographical account of Dora Mavor Moore's huge contribution to the development of professional theatre in Toronto which emphasizes her experience precisely as a woman has been written by Paula Sperdakos.

6 Anton Wagner's "Gwen Pharis Ringwood Rediscovered" offers an interesting account.

7 See Kym Bird's "Performing Politics: Propaganda, Parody and a Women's Parliament."

8 See Hodkinson's introduction as well as Moira Day and Marilyn Potts's "Elizabeth Sterling Haynes," Anton Wagner's "Elsie Park Gowan," and Moira Day's "Elsie Park Gowan's (Re)-Building of Canada (1937-1938)" for accounts of both women's contributions to Canadian theatre.

[9] The possibilities of a feminine (or, more explicitly, a feminist) aesthetics constitute a fraught, if interesting, debate among contemporary theorists. It would seem to me that many Canadian women now writing for performance quite deliberately construct a counter-aesthetic which is absolutely committed to the engagement of an interested spectator. Yet the risk that such an identification always already contributes to women's marginalization is an argument that cannot be too easily dismissed. See Rita Felski's persuasive account in *Beyond Feminist Aesthetics.*

[10] The Women's Circle project of Catalyst Theatre is recorded in Philpott.

[11] Despite the usefulness of Champagne's definition, the distinction between a play and a work of performance is often hard to draw. For the most part, the publication of a script appropriates it for the category of a play, although a text like Monique Mojica's *Princess Pocahontas* is not legible in terms of conventional dramatic structure. Other work I have tended to organize as performance. An exception here is ahdri zhina mandiela's *dark diaspora*; my inclination, despite its publication, is to retain the category "performance" to describe this work in its flexibility—mandiela performs it with and without a supporting cast, with and without live music, and it exists not only as a published script but also as recorded music.

[12] See Bennett, Review.

[13] Performance art is generally thought of as a marginalized form—yet paradoxically most of it is produced very much in the centre: New York, London, Los Angeles, Montreal. Lori Weidenhammer extends the marginality to include geography and, indeed, to stage geography since much of her work addresses precisely her coming from Cactus Lake, Saskatchewan where she still resides. Shawna Dempsey and Lorri Millan, discussed later in this article, started in Toronto, but now live and work in Winnipeg. It is tempting to suggest that Canadian women performance artists—some of them at least—have made the most of what Lynda Hart suggests is "certain advantage that is produced alongside their marginalized status. In that sense they are in limited but important ways 'unbound,' achieving a fluidity of movement simultaneously inside and outside dominant discourses" (Hart and Phelan 6).

[14] For an interesting and thoughtful review/analysis of "Drawing the Line" see Bociurkiw.

[15] I am indebted to the anthology *How Do I Look?* and especially Teresa de Lauretis's article "Film and the Visible" (see especially page 233) in that anthology for drawing attention to the significance of this question. See Bad Object Choices.

[16] See Bird, "The Company of Sirens," for a fuller discussion of some of their performance strategies. Also, Maria DiCenzo's interview with Cynthia Grant (DiCenzo and Bennett), one of the company's Artistic Directors, brings to attention many important issues.

[17] Susan Stone-Blackburn's interview with the founding members is useful for its charting of the group's mandate and history.

Works Cited

Adam, Julie. "The Implicated Audience: Judith Thompson's Anti-Naturalism in *The Crackwalker, White Biting Dog, I Am Yours,* and *Lion in the Streets.*" Much 21-29.

Bad Object Choices, ed. *How Do I Look? Queer Film and Video.* Seattle: Bay Press, 1991.

Bennett, Susan. "Feminist (Theatre) Historiography/Canadian (Feminist) Theatre: A Reading of some Practices and Theories." *Theatre Research* in *Canada* 13.1/2 (1992): 144-51.

———. "Radical (Self-)Direction and the Body: Shawna Dempsey and Lorri Millan's Performance Art." *Canadian Theatre Review* 76 (Fall 1993): 37-41.

———. Review of ahdri zhina mandiela, *dark diaspora ... in dub*; Monique Mojica, *Princess Pocahontas and the Blue Spots;* Robert More, *Patches;* and Wendy Lill, *Sisters. Canadian Theatre Review* 75 (1993): 82-83.

Bennett, Susan and Alexandria Patience. "A Dialogue on the Expression of Sex and Self in the Political Theatre of the Body." *i.e.: a magazine of contemporary culture* (December 1992): 9-10.

Bird, Kym. "The Company of Sirens: Popular Feminist Theatre in Canada." *Canadian Theatre Review* 59 (Summer 1989): 35-37.

———. "Performing Politics: Propaganda, Parody and a Women's Parliament." *Theatre Research in Canada* 13.1/2 (1992): 168-93.

Bociurkiw, Marusia. "The Transgressive Camera." *Afterimage* 16.6 (January 1989): 17, 19.

Butler, Audrey. *Radical Perversions: Two Dyke Plays.* Toronto: Women's Press, 1990.

Canning, Charlotte. *Feminist Theatres in the USA.* London: Routledge, 1995.

Champagne, Lenora. *Out from Under: Texts by Women Performance Artists.* New York: Theatre Communications Group, 1990.

Crossland, Jackie. *Collateral Damage.* Vancouver: Press Gang, 1992.

Day, Moira. "Elsie Park Gowan's (Re)-Building of Canada (1937-1938): Revisioning the Historical Radio Series through Feminist Eyes." *Theatre Research in Canada* 14.1 (1993): 3-19.

Day, Moira and Marilyn Potts. "Elizabeth Sterling Haynes: Initiator of Alberta Theatre." *Theatre History in Canada* 8.1 (1987): 8-35.

Dempsey, Shawna and Lorri Millan. *Mary Medusa. Canadian Theatre Review* 76 (Fall 1993): 42-57.

DiCenzo, Maria and Susan Bennett. "Women, Popular Theatre, and Social Action: Interviews with Cynthia Grant and the Sistren Theatre Collective." *ARIEL* 23.1 (January 1992): 73-96.

Felski, Rita. *Beyond Feminist Aesthetics: Feminist Literature and Social Change.* Cambridge, MA: Harvard UP, 1989.

Glaap, Albert-Reiner with Rolf Althof, ed. *On-Stage and Off-Stage: English Canadian Drama In Discourse.* St. John's: Breakwater, 1996.

Goodman. Lizbeth. *Contemporary Feminist Theatres: To Each Her Own*, London: Routledge, 1993.

Grant, Cynthia. "Notes from the Front Line." *Canadian Theatre Review* 43 (Summer 1985): 44-51.

Hart, Lynda and Peggy Phelan, ed. *Acting Out: Feminist Performances.* Ann Arbor: U of Michigan P, 1993.

Hines, Karen. *Pochsy's Lips. Canadian Theatre Review* 75 (Summer 1993): 36-46.

Hodkinson, Yvonne. *Female Parts: The Art and Politics of Female Playwrights.* Montreal: Black Rose Books, 1991.

Jansen, Ann (ed). *Adventures for (Big) Girls: Seven Radio Plays.* Winnipeg: Blizzard, 1993.

Jones, Heather. "Feminism and Nationalism in Domestic Melodrama: Gender, Genre and Canadian Identity." *Essays in Theatre,* 8.1 (1989): 5-14.

Kane, Margo. "From the Centre of the Circle the Story Emerges." *Canadian Theatre Review* 68 (Fall 1991): 26-29.

Lill, Wendy. *The Fighting Days.* Vancouver: Talonbooks, 1985.

MacDonald, Ann-Marie. *Goodnight Desdemona (Good Morning Juliet).* Toronto: Coach House, 1989.

mandiela, ahdri zhina. *dark diaspora ... in dub.* Toronto: Sister Vision, 1991.

Mojica, Monique. *Princess Pocahontas and the Blue Spots.* Toronto: Women's Press, 1990.

Much, Rita. *Women on the Canadian Stage: The Legacy of Hrotsvit.* Winnipeg: Blizzard, 1992.

Nunn, Robert. "Spatial Metaphor in the Plays of Judith Thompson." *Theatre History in Canada* 10.1 (Spring 1989): 3-29.

Philpott, Wendy. "Women's Circle, Women's Theatre." *Canadian Theatre Review* 69 (1991): 5-14.

Rubess, Bañuta. *Oblivion: A Story of Isabelle Eberhardt.* Jansen 1-24.

Rudakoff, Judith and Rita Much. *Fair Play: 12 Women Speak. Conversations with Canadian Playwrights.* Toronto: Simon & Pierre, 1990.

Scollard, Rose, Alexandria Patience and Nancy Cullen. *Aphra. Theatrum* (September/October): 1991.

Sears, Djanet. *Afrika Solo.* Toronto: Sister Vision, 1990.

Sperdakos, Paula. *Dora Mavor Moore: Pioneer of the Canadian Theatre.* Toronto: ECW, 1995.

Stone-Blackburn, Susan. "Maenadic Rites on Stage in Calgary." *Canadian Theatre Review* 69 (Winter 1991): 28-33.

Thompson, Judith. *The Other Side of the Dark.* Toronto: Coach House, 1989.

Tompkins, Joanne. "Infinitely Rehearsing Performance and Identity." *Canadian Theatre Review* 74 (Spring 1993): 35-39.

Vingoe, Mary. *Living Curiosities: A Story of Anna Swan.* Jansen 25-50.

Wagner, Anton. "Elsie Park Gowan: 'Distinctively Canadian'." *Theatre History in Canada* 8.1 (1987): 62-82

———. "Gwen Pharis Ringwood Rediscovered." *Canadian Theatre Review* 5 (Winter 1975): 63-69.

Wandor, Micheline. *Carry on, Understudies.* London: Routledge, 1986.

A Clash of Symbols[1]: When I Put on What I Want to Put on

by Louise H. Forsyth

> Et puis tous les moyens sont bons pour me rejoindre. Et si je n'viens pas à moi, c'est moi qui irai à moi. (And anyway all means to connect with myself are good. And if I don't come to me, it's me who will go to me.)[2]
>
> (Marie Savard, *Bien à moi* 43)

> Le monologue était une caractéristique du théâtre de femmes à ses debuts. Quoique les gens moins gentils ne disaient même pas « monologue », ils disaient « témoignage ». « Le theatre de femmes, ce n'est pas de l'art, c'est du témoignage: un paquet de femmes qui racontent leur vie.» (The monologue was a characteristic of women's theatre in its beginnings. Although less nice people did not even say "monologue," they said "testimony." "Women's theatre, it's not art, it's testimony: a pack of women telling their life story.")
>
> (Pol Pelletier, *Joie* 22)

Marie Savard's *Bien à moi* was created with Michel Tremblay's *La Duchesse de Langeais* at the Théâtre de Quat'Sous in Montreal in February 1970. The almost universal reaction to Savard's extraordinary monologue was that the character was deranged, incoherent and uninteresting. Savard later said, "C'était une feministe qui s'ignorait et heureusement d'ailleurs. Elle se serait sentie bien trop seule à cette époque" (11, "She was a feminist without knowing it, and in any case this was fortunate. She would have felt herself much too alone at that time.").[3]

Bien à moi is a delightfully bold, playful, satiric, and poetic text. It functions dialogically to create many hilarious moments of unexpected distancing. In each episode of the monologue the character sends and reads love letters to herself as she works her way through a process to *enterrer une vie de femme mariée* and establish her sense of humour, self, and community without relying on the traditional roles of wife, mistress, and mother. Savard created a strong, irreverent, and beer-drinking character fed up and positioning herself and her reflection in the space of her choosing, freeing her emotions and getting in touch with her body's desires, daring to face a situation of vulnerability, and affirming her right to take action on her own behalf. Savard wanted the character to wear either jeans or a wedding dress, the latter marked ironically.

André Brassard was the director of both *Bien à moi* and *La Duchesse de Langeais.* Savard says that Brassard assumed an attitude of *patience passive* toward *Bien à moi.* He expressed his discomfort with the play by saying, "[I]l était impuissant à mettre en scène une femme se masturbant...et que de le faire serait pour lui de la fausse representation" (Savard 11, "[H]e was impotent to put a woman masturbating on stage ... and to do it would be a false representation for him."). While this directorial hands-off approach, reflecting an unwillingness to grapple with personal bias or discriminatory social taboos and theatrical conventions, allowed creative freedom for Savard and actor Dyne Mousso, it also deprived them of directorial support, to the point of their losing legitimacy in theatre space and their withdrawing for most rehearsals to Savard's home. They found they preferred it there, where they felt more secure and free to create. An additional negative result of Brassard's failure to assume directorial responsibility for the show was the authority which passed to designer Jean-Paul Mousseau, who appears to have aggressively refused to understand Savard's dramatic creation, seeing the Marquise instead as a frustrated old woman who has lost her man:

> Jean-Paul avait dans son idée que la Marquise était...une vieille femme frustrée d'une quarantaine d'années...il y avait erreur sur la personne dans sa conception des femmes. Il faut dire que Jean-Paul était un homme qui concevait plus qu'il ne percevait...Jean-Paul avait prévu un décor en fonction de sa conception...Il avait prévu des accrocs, de fausses loques, dans la robe de chambre de la Marquise.
>
> (Jean Paul had it in his head that the Marquise was...a frustrated old woman of about forty...his conception of women caused him to make an error in his conception of this person. It must be said that Jean-Paul was a man who conceived more than he perceived. [...] Jean Paul designed a set that matched his conception...He envisaged the Marquise in a tattered and torn dressing gown.)

For purposes of his design, Mousseau could see the Marquise only in domestic space, not public space, with a stylized gilded mailbox and a ripped dressing gown. Mousseau's design choices signal that an hysterical woman is being positioned and confined in the master's house, where she finds needed protection and is available to provide sexual services if and when the master returns. In terms of costume, she was not allowed to put on the clothes her creator wanted her to put on. The lively character Savard wanted to create and present to the public was seriously distorted.

The story of difficulties in mounting *Bien à moi* provides a telling example of censorship of women's writing, justified on the basis of unexamined societal and theatrical conventions and norms. Freedom of expression for author, actor, and character was constrained in this case by dominant discourses, ideologies, and technologies imposed by men who held greater power and who either did not listen to them or got their stories wrong. At the same time, when author, actor, and character moved to acquire the necessary technologies—space, costumes, tools, objects, and props, whereby they might control their representations, share their narratives and assume agency—they were denied access to them.

Québec feminist playwrights and actors reacted strongly in the 1970s against attitudes, images, stories, sets, costumes, props, styles of acting, and roles based on tenacious gender stereotypes. They wished to make them disappear so as to free fresh sources of creative energy and vision, listen to silenced voices, and represent still untold experiences. They sought new communicative relations with each other and with spectators.

One can only muse about and take regretful note at the tenacity with which assumptions regarding gender can blind the most perceptive of people. I am astonished by André Brassard's detachment from the production of *Bien à moi* and his inability to perceive the theatrical coherence of a character exploring the basis for autonomous action and representing this exploration on stage in a scene of *jouissance* where she touches her body and *comes.* Brassard has demonstrated throughout his career bold creativity in delicate areas involving sexual taboos. Equally disconcerting is Jean-Paul Mousseau's inability to understand *Bien à moi* at any level, whether artistic, personal, or cultural. As a member of the *Refus global* group, a radically innovative artist with enormous energy for democratizing art and making it accessible to all classes in public places, and a pioneer in the cultural renaissance of Québec, he could be expected to share and enjoy the fresh creative direction chosen by Savard.

Gender stereotypes are still far from having disappeared in social, theatrical and critical practice, despite the energy of the women's movement in the 1970s and 1980s. Women continue to be excluded. Traditional male voices and discourses of authority and legitimacy remain strong; material and symbolic places for autonomous women are hard to represent in the theatre; women's stories are too often viewed as narcissistic or lacking dramatic interest and shape; women who position themselves in theatrical space as autonomous agents find that all elements of design—setting, costumes, props, and movement—still form integral parts of representational systems in which they are seen to be absent, powerless, or silenced. To overcome this serious problem, feminist women of theatre in Québec have, on many occasions over the past thirty years, taken as their starting point emptiness, whiteness, silence, and immobility. They have also found that it is necessary to disturb in flagrant ways the assumptions brought by spectators to the theatre, frequently by materially altering the configurations of stage and house. While this move to break down or displace old constructs is an important first step, all the plays discussed here present in a variety of forms a second step: that of creating in the void which remains. The writer is an important figure in the monologues, as is the storyteller, the mythmaker, and, in the case of Pol Pelletier's *Joie*, the maker of both myth and theatre. Having detached themselves, at least partially, from the patriarchal dreams and fantasies that held them captive for so long, they are now in the process of giving form and movement to dreams and myths of their own.

Pol Pelletier—actor, writer, and woman of the theatre—has been an extraordinary presence and animating spirit in the experimentation and exploration occurring since the mid-seventies. For Savard, Pelletier, and many others, monologues and innovative modifications thereof have proved to be a fertile medium for new growth and discovery. These are not monologues designed to attract an admiring gaze, tell a *real* story, reveal the psychological essence of individuals, or provide a soapbox for authors seeking a captive audience for their ideas. The monologues which interest me here all structure themselves dialogically and allow many voices to be heard, including the multiple voices likely to resonate in the spectator. They offer multiple spaces and temporalities, and they explore human problems and opportunities polyvocally, leaving spectators to put the various pieces together for themselves as they see fit.

Unlike the pathetic, monolithic creature which Mousseau wanted to see permanently ensconced in the boudoir awaiting the master's return, Savard's Marquise does not have a unitary and timeless nature. She is a fragmented, playful, and inconsistent character, whose words and actions frequently appear anomalous. She answers to two names: Marie and Marquise; she sees two reflections of herself in the mirror and experiences her body in strange fragments. She is an historicized and poeticized fictional creation who, having severed her ties with socially dictated roles, has chosen to bounce her desires off the memory of these roles and to situate herself in a place where the many facets of her presumed existence can be represented or reflected.

Shortly after Savard's *Bien à moi* was mounted, Antonine Maillet created her well-known monologue *La Sagouine*, first for radio, then for publication and stage performance. Unlike Savard's Marquise, Maillet's La Sagouine claims to be *real* and seeks neither autonomy nor *jouissance*. Still, there are several interesting similarities between the two monologues. Both characters are marginalized, older women dressed in rags, victims of dominant values, ideologies, and discourse, representatives of groups whose voices are almost never heard on the public stage. Both plays are bold and witty satires that confront the audience dialogically. In order to disturb spectators' assumptions, Maillet and Viola Léger had the character circulate among the public in the foyer and work as a cleaning woman before she moved to the stage. Spectators were forced to acknowledge their spontaneous resistance to the unexpected presence of this woman from a class not usually seen among theatre audiences. The set for the play was minimal. In the modesty of her costume and of the props, as well as the absence of stage interlocutors, La Sagouine had only her scrub pail, her broom and her rags. Her dialogue was carried on with the dirty water of her pail, with her absent husband Gapi, and with the audience, while an omnipresent *nous* created a strong impression of a silent and absent community, *L'Acadie*, named in this theatrical event but excluded by it.

Six women's monologues comprise *La Nef des sorcières*, presented at the Théâtre du Nouveau Monde in 1976. Once again, an innovative use of monologue succeeded in representing those whose lives enjoy no place or image on the stages of public culture, whose stories remain untold, and whose experiences are manipulated and distorted by technologies and ideologies over which they have little or no control. The play was perceived by many as marking a radical new departure in Québec women's theatre. Each character had a story to tell: an actress, a woman who has gone through menopause, a garment worker, a *fille* (she is a call girl, but the word also means daughter, suggesting that her family conditioning as a girl/sister/daughter taught her to prostitute herself), a lesbian, and a writer. On stage together, there was no direct communication among them. Nevertheless, one had the clear impression that the dramatic monologue gave them permission to connect with their own bodies and to say things aloud that authors, actors, characters, and spectators had been thinking but not daring to express openly, not even to themselves.

As in *Bien à moi*, the characters were isolated and alienated. They sought a sense of place, self, and community in situations where roles of daughter, wife, mistress, and mother had proven dangerously unsatisfactory. The collapse of dominant discourse and traditional roles for them was dramatized in the first monologue where the actress had a loss of memory while playing the classical theatre of Molière. In the painful silence when she was unable to continue with the memorized role, she desperately searched for alternate discursive forms and finally had to confront her own sense of self, her words, her fears, her memories, and her dreams in a theme explored throughout the six monologues: *la vie privée est politique.*

Created in Québec's largest establishment theatre, the Théâtre du Nouveau Monde, the sorcières of *La Nef des sorcières* boldly occupied theatrical space on their own terms, assumed the legitimacy of their subject position and their acts, and confronted an audience which they constructed as sexist, misogynist, and attached to elitist sociocultural values. Within this structural configuration, the play radically disturbed the presumed ideological position of spectators as well as theatrical convention, according to which spectators, regardless of how they respond mentally to the dramatic action, are allowed to remain silent observers in a darkened hall. Here they were challenged to respond to the actors, to themselves, and to society. The dialogue and dramatic action were intended to take place between the actor/character and the spectator: "Point de spectateur à l'abri : le drame se joue entre la salle et six femmes."[4] ("No spectator has safe cover: the drama is played out between the house and six women.") This structure was profoundly subversive: whereas women and actresses have almost all been conditioned and trained to be seductive and to seek to please, the actors of *La Nef des sorcières* chose to anger and to confront.

This sustained disturbance of expectations was perceived by many spectators in at least some of the monologues; that of Pol Pelletier, for example, as an aggressive, in-your-face disruption. It produced strong reactions and a dismissal on the part of critics who said this was not theatre. However, at least one well-known male writer, Pierre Vallières, in an article entitled "'La nef des sorcières' met un point final à l'ère brailliarde des 'belles-soeurs'," welcomed the play enthusiastically, calling it "l'un des spectacles politiques les plus solides qu'il m'ait été donné de voir." ("*La Nef des sorcières* puts an end to the bawling era of 'Les belles soeurs'"; "one of the most solid political spectacles which I have had the privilege of seeing."). Louisette Dussault, creator of *Moman*, has said that *La Nef des sorcières* and Denise Boucher's *Les Fées ont soif*, in both of which she played, mark for her a major breakthrough in theatre because of their success in setting aside many of the patriarchally driven technologies standing between women's experiences and the conventional representations of these experiences. However, Dussault knew that such lucidity does not come without pain:

> J'ai toujours eu l'impression de jouer derrière des écrans jusqu'au moment où il y a eu *La Nef des sorcières* et *Les Fées ont soif*: enfin des femmes qui faisaient des femmes au théâtre! Il était temps! Ces experiences-la ont été déterminantes pour moi, très douloureuses aussi, parce que les personnages dans ce qu'ils charriaient me confrontaient profondément dans ce que j'étais, à l'idée que je me faisais de moi-méme. (24)
>
> (I always had the impression of playing behind screens until the moment when there was *La Nef des sorcières* and *Les Fees ont soif*: finally women were creating women in theatre! It was about time! These experiences/experiments were determining for me, also very painful because the characters, in what they contained, confronted me profoundly in what I was, in the ideas I had about myself.)

Jovette Marchessault's monologue *Les Vaches de nuit*, performed by Pol Pelletier in 1979 during the second collage of texts *au féminin* sponsored by the TNM, *Célébrations*, resonated on the Québec and Canadian stage with an impact that has not yet disappeared. Like the monologues already discussed, it is a bold, playful, and poetic satire functioning dialogically through the voices of a character and an actor whose identity is fragmented. It is also, and above all, an epic narrative succeeding in forging powerful new mythic structures and characters, *Les Vaches de nuit* took as its implicit point of departure the many forms of violence against women, their alienation, silencing, and disempowerment. In the final part of the text crows addressed the suffering in women's lives:

> Après le temps des mères, tout nest qu'extermination, massacres, chantages, longue marche des femelles vers les abattoirs, les buchers, les cimetières de l'anonymat, les chambres nuptiales de la torture. Tout n'est que viols, tueries, mainmise des couteaux et de la vengeance sur la gorge de la misère. (93)
>
> (After the time of the mother, all is but extermination, massacres, blackmails, long walk of the females toward the slaughter houses, stakes, cemeteries of anonymity, nuptial chambers of torture. All is but rapes, killings, the holding of knives and vengeance to the throat of misery.)

However, *Les Vaches de nuit* is predominantly and forcefully celebratory, rather than angry or fearful, Pelletier performed powerfully on a starkly simple, symbolic set. She wore a costume from which all signs of the images and roles of women in patriarchal society had been removed and which imposed no constraints on her body's energy and movement. She placed on her head with ceremonial gestures a large mask of a cow's head. Control of the theatrical event was entirely in the hands of the actor, without interference from authoritative voices of an alien theatrical tradition, as was the case with the staging of *Bien à moi.* The mask, the body's movement and the voice formed a magnificent synthesis representing the power and legitimacy of a woman's vision.

Once again, but in a way different from the aggression of *La Nef des sorcières*, audience expectations were disturbed and displaced. In *Les Vaches de nuit*, the displacement occurs in the surprising first line of the play: "Ma mère est une vache. Avec moi, ça fait deux." ("My mother is a cow. With me, that makes two.") In view of the denigrated image borne by cows in dominant representation systems, spectators had to wonder what kind of interesting dramatic story could possibly be told after such a beginning. The rest of the monologue played to great effect on this reversal, on the surprisingly exciting identification of women with cows, and on the ambiguities resulting from them, all the better to shed entirely new light on female sensuality, sexuality, and the meaning of motherhood. All the better as well to move out of domestic space and into the vastness of the milky way. *Les Vaches de nuit* works on the assumption of a deep complicity among author, actor, character, and spectators. On this basis, the theatrical experience of a mythic journey is transformed magically into a vast, collective, sensual ritual:

> Voici que nous sommes toutes nues dans nos robes, dans la chair de nos robes de nuit, dans l'embrasement de nos poils...Et nous partons! Et nous volons vers notre rendez-vous dans la voie lactée.
>
> Beaté! Le grand fleuve de lait, la terre de l'enfance où les mères et filles sont enfin réunies. Beauté! Beauté! Canaux de lait fleuris de nenuphars. Ivresse lactée, fluidité blanche, liquide astral, le fruit des entrailles de nos mères se répand dans le temps frais du ciel. Toutes les mammifères de la création sont au rendez-vous! (87)
>
> (Here we are completely nude in our robes, in the flesh of our night robes, in the conflagration of our fur...And we depart! And we fly toward our rendez-vous in the milky way.
>
> Beauty! The great river of milk the land of childhood where mothers and daughters are finally reunited. Beauty! Beauty! Channels of milk flowering with water lilies. Milky intoxication, white fluidity astral liquid the fruit of the entrails of our mothers flows in the cool surrounding sky. All breasted creatures are at the rendez-vous!)

Anne-Marie Alonzo's *Veille*, produced in 1981 by Mona Latif-Ghattas, was among the first shows put on at the Théâtre Expérimental des Femmes. The compelling poetic text gives voice to the urgent, complex, and contradictory longings of a woman in a state of simultaneous reverie and heightened wakefulness. Like *Bien à moi* and *Les Vaches de nuit*, *Veille* explored a sense of urgent need for emotional fulfillment, connections, and myth. Without them, the *moi* of the monologue was at risk of dissolution. Like Savard's Marquise, Alonzo's character affirmed several times that writing allowed her to make some sense of her conflicting pulsions:

> Je t'aime et t'écris.
>
> Je t'aime et te crie les mots m'écorchent je ne guéris pas je m'éteins et m'éteins encore. Les jours se fanent et moi et déjà moi!
>
> (I love you and write to you.
>
> I love you and cry to you words rub me raw I do not heal I fade away and fade away again. The days wither and I and already I!)

Her words formed a disconnected dialogue with *toi*, whose identity appeared unstable. Always a passionately desired woman, the character's interlocutor remained mysteriously elusive and in constant metamorphosis, responding at times to the character's desires, while at other times becoming emotionally or physically distanced. Initially she was the mother, associated with the rich fluidity of the sea and the sky: "J'ai la mère rouge et toute passion l'emporte. J'ai la mère femme (et j'écris car j'écris pour elle)...J'ai la reine mère et cheveux d'étoiles...J'ai la mermour" (11-12, "I have a red mother and all passion carries her away. I have a woman mother (and I write for I write for her) I have a queen mother and hair of stars...I have la mermour.").[5] In subsequent scenes the desired woman who held the key to love, meaning, power, and mythic truths appears to be a friend or lover. Without the spiritual and emotional security which sustained connections would bring, the character remained in a precarious state. Her fragmentation, precariousness, and confinement were represented on a bare stage in the presence of a shadowy second woman whose back was turned. The character speaking was clothed in a stylized full-body suit, within which only limited motion would be possible.

Pol Pelletier's *Joie*, the final versions of which were created in 1993 by the Compagnie Pol Pelletier, tells a dramatic story—in words, song, dance, music, and gesture—of the many Québec plays *au féminin* created and produced by Pol Pelletier during the 1970s and 1980s. Its storyline parallels, then, the narrative thread which I have woven in this discussion around monologues by Pelletier and others. It is a story of anger and resistance to devastating misogynist social practices and ideologies. It is also a story of vision and courage in the opening of theatre spaces and the creation of theatre forms and languages drawn from the powerful emotions and the dynamic body of a woman who has made a full commitment to theatre. Pelletier was one of the first to recognize that changes in deeply rooted conventions can't be produced with words alone. She said in 1982, "L'invention du théâtre 'autre' est une question de forme. Et le premier élément formel au théâtre est le corps de la comédienne."[6] ("The mention of other theatre is a question of form. And the first formal element in the theatre is the body of the actress.") It's necessary to engage the body, no matter how fragile, impermeable to fetishization, as a site for struggle, creation, myth, and passion. This is what theatre is all about for Pelletier.

The starting point for *Joie* was the combined theme of *les femmes, l'art et la joie.* The theme of *Joie* is retained in the title, in the isolated first word of the play, "joie," resonating like a powerful challenge to any spectator tempted by an attitude of *patience passive*, and echoed throughout the first poetic scene with rollicking repetitions of the phoneme written in French as *oi* [wa]. This includes the words used to evoke the most dominant material presence of the play and the driving force of the narrative, memory, "l'oiseau noir de la mémoire," represented by the character's left hand clad in a black glove. The tenacious commitment to the theme of *Joie* finds its counterpoint throughout the play in all that has threatened *les femmes, l'art et la joie* throughout the years in Québec theatre and society: *Les femmes, l'art et* ***la peur*** (Pelletier 22), *Les femmes, l'art et* ***les problèmes*** (63), *Les femmes, l'art et* ***la culture*** (81).

There was considerable slippage in the monologue between the *moi* who is a fictional character and the *moi* who is the *real* Pol Pelletier. The character played consistently on this ambiguity and difference as she multiplied levels of reference, moved among many language registers, and added additional voices. By introducing into the play extracts from many of the plays she had done over the years, while also reflecting on them and their reception, she drew spectators into a dazzling array of emotions and experiences where distinctions between fiction and reality became blurred. Time and space splintered and whirled in the dance. Music of the people from several countries introduced other dimensions. The play became a powerful ritual to undo all the constraints imposed by social and theatrical tradition, to put on neglected earlier plays and new visions, to feel anger about problems remaining, and to share love. Pelletier achieved public participation in this by reconfiguring the space of the theatre so that spectators were seated on the stage, with the character turning her back to the house. Spectators had in their line of vision the empty seats, the walls, the balcony, the doors—everything that usually remains invisible to the audience:

> Quand les gens viennent au théâtre
> Ils doivent en ressortir avec leur vie transformée.
> CHANGER LE MONDE.
> Oui, j'ai cette prétention. (95)
>
> (When people come to the theatre
> They must leave again with their lives transformed.
> CHANGE THE WORLD.
> Yes I have that pretension.)

I know of no one who has been more successful than Pol Pelletier in changing the world of theatre. Working alone and with many colleagues, she has discovered new sources of physical and spiritual energy, broken down tenacious traditions, claimed ownership to a range of technologies both traditional and startlingly innovative, and created myths and stories of incredible power. At the same time, as *Joie* has shown, neither the theatre as a whole nor the world has yet been changed. Much remains to be done, and, unfortunately, the momentum which brought forth so many exciting feminist plays in Québec in the 1970s and 1980s seems much less strong in the 1990s. Pelletier addresses this phenomenon in the following terms in *Joie*:

> Mais tu sais pas le pire!
>
> Depuis que les femmes occupent des postes de pouvoir, elles ne montent que des pièces d'hommes, avec des distributions majoritairement masculines, avec des contenus misogynes. Exactement comme avant, même pire…Tous les jeunes génies misogynes, cruels, cyniques.
>
> Comment ça se fait que l'histoire que je vous raconte est tombée dans l'oubli?…
>
> Tu sais ce que je pense? Je pense que nous, les femmes nous nous sentons collectivement COUPABLES d'avoir crié haut et fort dans les années 70, même les jeunes femmes qui n'étaient pas là, et qui s'imaginent que tout est réglé, elles aussi sont coupables, la culpabilité est partout, dans l'air, dans nos os. Je pense que nous nous sommes fait très peur et que nous n'osons plus rien dire.
>
> Et que nous voulons nous faire pardonner…? En oubliant, en occultant, en effaçant ce qui s'est passé? (91)
>
> (But you don't know the worst!
>
> Ever since women have held positions of power, they put on only men's plays with casts which are majority masculine, with misogynist content. Exactly as before, even worse…All the young cynical, cruel, misogynist geniuses.
>
> How has it happened that the story I am telling you has been forgotten?
>
> Do you know what I think? I think that we women we feel ourselves collectively GUILTY for having shouted loud and strong in the 1970s, even the young women who weren't there, and who imagine that all has been fixed, they too are guilty, guilt is everywhere in the air, in our bones. I think that we really frightened ourselves and that we no longer dare say anything. And that we want to be pardoned…? By forgetting, by concealing, by erasing what has happened?)

(1997)

Notes

[1] *A Clash of Symbols* is the title given by Linda Gaboriau to her translation of the six monologues of *La Nef des sorcières.*

[2] All translations are my own.

[3] A bilingual edition of *Bien à moi* (*Mine Sincerely*) will be published in 1998 by Les Éditions Trois, containing all material originally published, my translation, and new introductions by Marie Savard and me.

[4] The author does not provide a source for this quotation.

[5] Among the many playful connotations deriving from the sounds of this neologism, one discerns: mother, sea, love, murmur, death.

[6] The author does not provide a source for this quotation.

Works Cited

Alonzo, Anne-Marie. *Veille.* Paris: Editions des Femmes, 1982.

Boucher, Denise. *Les Fées ont soif.* Montréal: Editions Intermède, 1978.

Dussault, Louisette. *Moman,* précédé d'"Itinéraire pour une moman." Montréal: Boréal Express, 1981.

Maillet, Antonine. *La Sagouine.* Montréal: Leméac, 1971.

Marchessault, Jovette. *Les Vaches de nuit. Tryptique lesbien* Montréal: Éditions de la Pleine Lune, 1980.

Pelletier, Pol. *Joie.* Montréal: Éditions du Remue-Ménage, 1995.

Savard, Marie. *Bien à moi.* Montréal: Éditions de la Pleine Lune, 1979.

Vallieres, Pierre. "'La nef des sorcières' met un point final à l'ère braillarde des 'belles-soeurs.'" *Le Jour* 12 mars 1976: 24.

Collective Creation and the Changing Mandate of Nightwood Theatre

by Shelley Scott

Nightwood Theatre is the longest running feminist theatre company in Canada and "the most influential feminist theatre company in Toronto" (Forsyth 206). In her review of the 1990 collection *Fair Play: Twelve Women Speak: Conversations with Canadian Playwrights*, Maria DiCenzo writes "it becomes clear from reading this collection that Nightwood has played a critical role in getting women's plays produced" (219). In addition to its importance within Toronto, Nightwood has played a national role by soliciting projects for its annual Groundswell festival of new works. Since Nightwood's inception in 1979, the company has produced collective creations and plays by single authors, mounted tours, collaborated with other companies, and sought out many ways to encourage new work by women; an on-line chronology, available in *Theatre Research in Canada*'s website publication of volume 18:2, provides dates and details for selected productions.[1]

Nightwood grew out of the alternative, collective theatre scene in Toronto and the international avant-garde and was initially committed to an experimental aesthetic. While not specifically intended as a feminist company by its four founders, Nightwood gradually became identified as feminist, largely because of external perceptions.[2] Over the years, the company presented itself as a producer of new works by Canadian women, as a provider of opportunities for women theatre artists, and, most recently, as an inclusive theatre company committed to producing work by women of colour; these variations have reflected the interests of artists and Board members at different stages.

For many years Nightwood also defined itself as a producer of collective work, although the creations were sometimes assigned to a main author. The company was also run, administratively, as a collective, although individuals always had separate titles and responsibilities. At different points, Nightwood's commitment to collectivity shifted emphasis between the works produced and the company's inclusive structure. Even as Nightwood moved steadily towards a more traditional structure throughout the 1980s, with a single Artistic Director and productions of plays by single authors becoming the norm, some of the collective spirit was retained in the existence of an Artistic Advisory group.[3] Perhaps for this reason, the collective way of working has continued to be identified with Nightwood's productions and administration, even though the company's mainstage productions have been scripted works by single authors and it has officially dissociated itself from the collective organizational model since the late 1980s. Just as Nightwood's feminist mandate has developed through a dialectic of external perceptions and internal process, so too has its relationship with collective creation; this dialectic has operated throughout its history in defining Nightwood as a company. It will be the purpose of this paper to chart Nightwood's movement from a collectively-run group that created theatre pieces collectively, to a more traditionally-structured company that produces scripted works by women. This movement has involved both ideological motivations and aesthetic aspirations, consistent with Nightwood's historical place within Canadian political theatre, and within the tradition of feminist theatre.

Theatre historian Denis Johnston refers to the late 1960s and early 1970s as the golden age of Canadian theatre, a time when a new and exciting wave of alternative theatres sprang up across Canada, especially in Toronto (3-4). These small, experimental companies, such as Theatre Passe Muraille, were reacting against the domination of the established regional theatre system by foreign productions. While the initial inspiration for the new companies came from the international avant-garde—companies like the Living Theatre in New York, for example—their motivation quickly came to include Canadian nationalism. Internationally and locally, alternative experimental theatre was co-existing with women's theatre: in 1968, Winnipeg's feminist Nellie McClung Theatre was formed; in 1969, new feminist theatres were founded in New York and Los Angeles; in 1972 the Women's Theatre Council was formed in New York; in 1977 Sistren was founded in Jamaica and, in England, Monstrous Regiment was collaborating with Caryl Churchill. Toronto got its first feminist theatre company in 1974, when Diane Grant and Marcella Lustig founded Redlight Theatre.[4]

Because Nightwood came into existence at the end of the seventies, it missed the period ten years earlier when the collective was most revolutionary in Canada, when the collective creation, the alternative theatre, the influence of an international avant-garde, and a passionate nationalism were all coming together in Canadian theatre. Nightwood also followed the initial period when many early women's theatre collectives were created as splinters from other groups, either experimental theatre companies or political associations, formed so that female members could work together on their own issues. In many ways, Nightwood reflected all that had gone on a short while before and yet developed in its own unique direction, learning from the theatre explosion of the late sixties and early seventies, and moving into the eighties. I would suggest that Nightwood's historical placement partly explains its longevity, in that its founders had a variety of successful models to emulate. For example, Cynthia Grant apprenticed in New York with Mabou Mines, an influential experimental company, just before Nightwood's first production, *The True Story of Ida Johnson*, was produced at the Annex Theatre in the fall of 1979; Kim Renders was a cast member in the Theatre Passe Muraille collective creation *Staller's Farm* in 1980. Their experiences with the international avant-garde and Canadian collective creation were reflected in Nightwood's early productions and in how the fledgling company positioned itself within the Toronto theatre community. On the other hand, the growing feminist movement meant that more and more women were feeling confident about finding their own voices in the theatre and creating new roles for themselves both on and off stage, and Nightwood became a focal point around which a number of projects could revolve; Nightwood's commitment to an inclusive, collective structure meant that many women could be accommodated. While the collective structure and the focus on producing collective work has altered considerably over the years, the need for a place where women's work is produced and women theatre artists can find jobs has (unfortunately) not disappeared; Nightwood has therefore remained relevant.

If we were to compare Nightwood to other Canadian feminist companies past and present, such as Nellie McClung, Redlight, Le Théâtre Expérimental des Femmes (founded in 1979), the Company of Sirens (founded in 1986), and Maenad Theatre (incorporated in 1989) for example, we would find similar struggles around obtaining funding, defining a mandate, developing an organizational structure and communicating with a desired audience.[5] The different kinds of feminist philosophy (cultural, materialist, postmodern, and so on) that individual theatre practitioners advocate will be reflected in the work they produce within these companies; at Nightwood, individuals have produced work that reflect a wide range of different types or approaches to feminism.[6] A commitment to any type of feminism will also influence how a piece of theatre is created, and each of the companies mentioned above have attempted to develop an appropriate, collaborative working model. As Nightwood founder Maureen White wrote in reference to the Anna Project, "it is not coincidence that a lot of feminists are choosing to work collectively: in exploring new material and breaking down old structures, a new process also should be explored" (Anna Project 173). Nightwood has always encouraged diverse perspectives and provided opportunities for women who might not find them elsewhere, and collective creation is in many ways an ideal model for empowerment; the process by which a project is organized can be as important as the finished product, and a collaborative model in which credit, creativity and responsibility are shared, as opposed to a strictly hierarchical structure, is a choice philosophically consistent with such goals.

Collective creation has come to connote a particular kind of theatre piece: episodic in structure, presentational, and made up of a number of stories that all contribute to some overarching theme or purpose. But collective creation is perhaps more accurately described as a process, a method of working in which authority is shared and each participant contributes in a significant way to the content of the work at hand. A collective might include one person who is designated as director or even playwright, but the other participants—actors, designers and so on—are understood to have more direct input than within a traditional, hierarchical situation, where everyone works towards realizing the playwright's vision. The end result of the collective creation process might be a play about a specific community or historical event (something like Nightwood's 1984 collective creation about pioneer women, *Love and Work Enough*, for example), and it might include an overt political motivation (such as the anti-nuclear weapons show *Peace Banquet* in 1983, or the work of companies inspired by Augusto Boal, for example). The collective process might also result in a piece like Nightwood's *Glazed Tempera* in 1980, which was intended to explore an interdisciplinary aesthetic rather than offer social commentary.

The work that is created through collective creation can be especially rich and powerful, benefitting from the combined efforts and gifts of a number of people, rather than the vision of a single individual. To quote Maureen White again:

> For me the greatest reward of working collectively is seeing a vision emerge that could *never* have come from just one person. A constant criticism of this method of working seems to be that it is a compromised vision. Yet I do not begin working collectively on a show with *my* vision in mind—that would certainly lead to compromise. Instead, ideas feed off one another to develop *into* a vision. (Anna Project 173)

On the other hand, working collectively can be difficult and time consuming, particularly if all the participants are not equally committed or comfortable with the process; as Mary Vingoe wrote, "the joys and frustrations of working collectively so often nearly cancel each other out" (Nightwood 48). Ann-Marie MacDonald acknowledged some of the hazards in her description of the Anna Project:

> the collective process has been fraught with more challenges and obstacles than any other I have known; struggles such as fund-raising and administration of one's own work, not to mention the constant striving for consensus in a process which is also a commitment to respect each artist's creative input. (Anna Project 170)

MacDonald concludes, however, that *This is For You, Anna* was "worth hanging in for" (170), and Vingoe writes that a collective creation is "distinct: it looks, tastes and feels different from script-based conventional theatre," and that each time a collectively created work challenges the audience's notions of a play, it has achieved a "tiny victory" (Nightwood 49). Because of this sympathy between feminism and collectivity, a collaborative, if not necessarily collective, method of working has continued to be associated with Nightwood and all other Canadian feminist theatre companies.

Theatre is naturally a collaborative art form, and in some cases the notion of "collectivity" is perhaps more accurately described as a kind of heightened and consciously implemented collaboration. Bañuta Rubess, a former Board member who has participated in a number of Nightwood productions as an actor, director and playwright, has done most of her directing in collectives and/or in situations where she is directing her own work. Rubess says that it is often painful and difficult for women to come into positions of power and that the collective process allows women to begin thinking of themselves in positions of authority.[7] Rubess outlines three different collective models in which she has worked: in the first model, there is no director, but there is a splitting up of responsibility in advance, with each person taking some authority in some area. In the second model, the collective has an outside director, but Rubess cautions that this can lead to conflict over who has final say and the collective members may end up experiencing a sense of aesthetic powerlessness. In the third model, the director is part of the collective and serves to translate the collective process by inspiring the actors to be concerned for each other onstage and to understand the larger context of what they are doing.

Rubess observes that two realizations are important for a collective to function effectively; first, it must be acknowledged that not everyone can do everything, so people should be encouraged to do what they are best at and also to discover other things they can do along the way. Second, each collective member must be committed to and understand why they are working as a collective. The first point explains why, even with the collective creations, the programs from Nightwood productions generally list certain people as being responsible for particular functions, while the show itself is credited to the group as a whole. The second point signals the greatest potential danger of working collectively, which is the question of "ownership." Part of the problem may be inherent in the process of collective creation itself, in that "job descriptions" may be largely self-defined and therefore easily subject to dispute. Individuals who put a lot of time and effort into a project are not always able to give up a sense of personal "ownership" of that work for the greater good of the company, and there are many who argue that they should not have to. But the issues can be further complicated when the collective members are assumed to share the same feminist principles; unspoken assumptions can be made that everyone is more in agreement than they really are, and individuals can be afraid of voicing dissenting views for fear of looking "not feminist enough." Apparently, collective creation may involve a discrepancy between process and product; in some cases a beneficial feminist workshopping process (as in the annual Groundswell festival, for example) may not necessarily result in a written script, while in the case of an example like *Smoke Damage*, an extremely troubled collective process still resulted in a valuable feminist play.[8] It is the combined efforts and enthusiasms (or lack thereof) which spark the creative process in a collective; individual moments of genius may not add up to an overall production, but the multifaceted result of collective effort may convey something about the process and the feminism of its participants which is valuable on its own terms.

In the beginning, collectivity, as a philosophy and working method, was ideal for the founders of Nightwood, who were searching for an opportunity for theatrical exploration. Kim Renders later explained: "I wanted to develop my own performance vocabulary with a group of people; I thought that would be more useful than roaming the streets as a freelance actor" (Renders "Interview"). Being part of a collective allowed Renders the opportunity, not only to act, but also to write, direct, and to exercise her artistic skills through design work, a range of input unavailable to an actor hired by a conventional company. Besides providing opportunities for personal growth, the collective experience fosters a sense of group identity. As Alan Filewod explains:

> in collective creation, the group mind must reconcile its differences to create a community statement. This can begin in one of two ways: either the cast is united by ideological consensus in the analysis of the subject

> … or the circumstances of making the play become a shared experience which becomes part of the substance of the play itself. (35)

In Nightwood's case, both elements were present simultaneously. The members of each collective creation were united through a common ideology (usually feminist, but in the case of a project like *Peace Banquet*, an anti-nuclear weapons stance), and a shared interest in a particular kind of experimental, multi-media aesthetic. Furthermore, financial constraints and a sense of being marginalized and avant-garde, gave them a feeling of group unity and common purpose.

Nightwood was very much associated with the artist-run Theatre Centre, its home for many years, and this status as a collective within a collective helped to define its place within the theatre community.[9] Nightwood was also associated with a number of feminist collectives, such as Women's Cultural Building which organized the first Five Minute Feminist Cabaret and the interdisciplinary Women's Perspectives series in 1983. As part of Nightwood's involvement in Women's Perspectives, the Anna Project formed to collectively create *This is For You, Anna*, a show that would identify Nightwood in the public eye for years to come.[10] Many of the women involved with Women's Cultural Building continued their involvement with Nightwood, such as Tori Smith, who became the stage manager for *This is For You, Anna*, and Kate Lushington, who became Nightwood's Artistic Coordinator in 1988. These examples illustrate how collectivity as a process serves to bring many women together who might otherwise never meet; the free flow of ideas, resources, and individuals is facilitated by the spirit of collaboration and a sense of common purpose. Also suggested is the important role of the audience to a feminist collective, as a spectator may well become a participant on future projects and the nurturing of a mutually supportive artist/audience relationship strengthens both the theatre company and the feminist community.

As the company continued to expand and include more artists, a structure was required to provide the necessary administrative and organizational support. By 1983, Cynthia Grant was consistently referred to as the Artistic Director in media coverage and on funding applications, and there was a Board of Directors in place. The definition of collectivity became a contentious issue over the years, as subsequent leaders struggled to balance their sense of individual responsibility with a desire to retain the company's collective spirit. There were adjustments to the title of Artistic Director; for example, during Mary Vingoe and Maureen White's terms of leadership (1985-1988), the position was re-named Artistic Coordinator. In a letter to the Canada Council dated March 17, 1986, Mary Vingoe described the reasons for the new title:

> For this season at least, we have created the position of artistic coordinator, as an alternative to artistic director, in order that the day to day artistic concerns of the company can be efficiently handled, while allowing more "collective" input on major decisions such as company programming.[11]

When Kate Lushington was hired in 1988, she was initially called Artistic Coordinator, but in 1990 the title changed to Artistic Director and remained so under the subsequent management team. The title adjustments reflect an on-going attempt to balance different agendas: the desire to be taken seriously within the theatre community, which demands artistic leadership; the desire to retain the support of the feminist community, which prefers alternative approaches to organization; and the desire for a clear working relationship between the Board and the staff, which is an issue for any theatre company.

Nightwood's Board of Directors has also changed its structure and purpose over the years. While initially an artist-run Board, emulating the Theatre Centre model, under Kate Lushington there was an emphasis on attracting women with certain skills, such as legal expertise and fundraising experience, to make the Board more "community-based."[12] The artistic decisions were taken over by the Play Group, a collective of artists working in conjunction with the Board and staff. At a meeting of an Ad Hoc Structure Committee in November of 1988, it was decided that the Board should be balanced between community and artist members. The Artistic Coordinator and General Manager were to be informed of all meetings and could attend with "a voice but no vote." The Play Group was to include the Artistic Coordinator and one or two Board members, plus four to six artists appointed by the Board. There is an amalgam of these approaches at present, with the Board of Directors taking on administrative tasks and a separate Artistic Advisory group in place, but with considerable overlap between the two (see endnote 3).

Throughout the changes in leadership and Board structure, Nightwood continued to identify itself as a collective, although it might be more accurate to say that it was a producing company that supported the creation of collective projects. Nightwood produced all their plays collectively in the early years, beginning with *The True Story of Ida Johnson* in 1979. The project began in 1976 with the Editing Group of the Women's Press, which included Cynthia Grant; she organized a dramatized reading of Sharon Riis's novel in March of 1977 with members of the Editing Group, and then a workshop production in 1978 which involved Maureen White, Kim Renders and Mary Vingoe. It played September 6 to 15 at the NDWT Side-Door Theatre (now the Annex Theatre) and later at the Adelaide Court Theatre (which no longer exists). The 1979 production listed Kim Renders, Mary Vingoe and Maureen White as actors and Cynthia Grant as the director; Renders also did the design. These four women, who came to be considered the founders of Nightwood, and six others, were listed on the program as the "Theatre Collective and Associate Members."

In terms of its formal qualities, the production was described as "a highly innovative and fascinating social document" by McKenzie Porter in the *Toronto Star*, and Kate Lushington wrote: "using slides and non-linear text to illuminate the relationship between two women and their worlds, a new style of feminist theatre was born" (Lushington, Letter). According to Cynthia Grant, "the work didn't abandon but rethought plot and character. The style wove a fabric of sense impressions through music, dance, mime, mask and visual images" (qtd. in Kaplan, "Cynthia Grant").

These two features—a collective structure with the four founders and others taking on different functions in each project, and a commitment to a multi-media, imagistic experimental aesthetic—continued to define Nightwood for several years, throughout their early productions. When Nightwood became involved with Buddies in Bad Times's Rhubarb! Festival in 1980, their mandate statement for the program read: "Nightwood Theatre operates as a collective to produce original or adapted material in a style which emphasizes the visual, musical and literary elements of the presentation." The earliest Nightwood shows demonstrated a consistent aesthetic vision: from *The True Story of Ida Johnson*, *Glazed Tempera*, *Flashbacks of Tomorrow* and *Mass/Age*, the reviewers always commented on the innovative use of multi-media techniques and the fragmented, nonlinear structure. By 1984, with other women like Bañuta Rubess having a strong presence at Nightwood, there was a corresponding diffusion of the "Nightwood show." In fact, one reviewer of Rubess's *Pope Joan* (1984) commented that the plot is unusually linear for a Nightwood production, indicating that there had been a certain loosening of the established model for the company's work (Lazier);[13] the obvious difference, of course, is that *Pope Joan* is not a collective creation.

In 1986 Cynthia Grant left Nightwood to form the Company of Sirens, a feminist collective which works at a much more grass-roots level than Nightwood, most often outside the framework of traditional theatre. In *Theatre Audiences*, Susan Bennett uses Cynthia Grant and the Company of Sirens as an example of theatre-makers who want to work directly with the audience:

> Cynthia Grant made it clear that her decision to leave her post as artistic director of the successful Nightwood Theatre in Toronto was the result of a growing dissatisfaction in working within an established institution. Her present participation in a co-operative venture, the Company of Sirens, permits a more direct and important contact between actors and audience without the constraints of the conventional theatre system. (62)

In a 1990 article in *FUSE* magazine, Susan G. Cole suggested that the creation of the collectively-based Sirens freed Nightwood to concentrate less on collective work and more on developing individual writing talents. Nightwood was moving more towards the mainstream at this point, in what could be seen as the second phase of its development. In their February 13, 1986 funding application to the Municipality of Metro Toronto, Mary Vingoe introduced herself as the new Artistic Coordinator of Nightwood and Linda Brown as the first full-time office person. Their application emphasized events that traditionally define success: a fundraising production by the American company Plutonium Players made $8,000 in one week; Nightwood's collective creation *Love and Work Enough* won a Dora award; the tour of *This is For You, Anna* sold out in England, was voted one of the top fifteen shows in London, and was also invited to the DuMaurier World Theatre Festival in Toronto. Upcoming projects included the English-language premiere of *The Edge of the Earth is too Near, Violette Leduc* by Jovette Marchessault and a 1987 production of *War Babies* by

Margaret Hollingsworth, two very literary scripts by individual authors with little previous contact with Nightwood. However, Nightwood was not ready to give up its more community-based objectives completely; in the application letter, Mary Vingoe explained:

> While we have begun seriously to work with writers and scripts, we have not abandoned our commitment to the more innovative, collaborative way of play-making which has been our strength in the past. Both *This is For You, Anna* and *Love and Work Enough* were created through painstaking collective work, refined over a number of workshops and productions.

Their commitment was centred in plans for "a collective, comic collaboration on the theme of female eroticism, inspired by photography by Marcia Resnick." The creative team working on the project included Bañuta Rubess, Maureen White, Louise Garfield (a member of the lip synch trio the Clichettes) and playwright Peggy Thompson; collectively named the Humbert Humbert Project, their collaborative effort became *The Last Will and Testament of Lolita* (1987), Nightwood's last mainstage collective creation.[14]

The founding members were well aware that the introduction of single-author texts was a new direction for the company. In an article published in 1987, Kim Renders acknowledged that the production of scripted works was a new development for Nightwood:

> The promotion of female talent is still one of the company's strongest features. But in the past two and a half years, Nightwood has been putting on fewer collectives and become more script-oriented. This is a broadening of the group's method, since previously it had been adamantly opposed to scripted material. (qtd. in Kaplan, "Renders")

And in a later article, Maureen White and Mary Vingoe commented on their working relationship as director and playwright for the production of Vingoe's play *The Herring Gull's Egg*: "'This is the first time we've worked together in this configuration,' says White. 'In our earlier days at Nightwood, collective creations were more common. It's exciting to see Nightwood now, at a time when more input is coming from outside people, those who weren't founders. It's good,' she smiles, 'that the company can exist without its mothers'" (qtd. in Kaplan, "Bearing"). We can see the dialectic of accident and intention at work here: when the founders and their colleagues were interested in creating collectively, this was defined as part of Nightwood's mandate, but as company members became more interested in writing and directing conventionally scripted plays, the mandate changed to emphasize the production of Canadian work and the creation of opportunities for women, while shifting the collective ideal to the company's administration. In an October 22, 1986 application to the Ministry of Citizenship and Culture, Internship Training Program, Vingoe explained that: "Major decisions such as programming, are made in conjunction with a programme committee from the Board. The new structure has allowed Nightwood to retain a functioning collective sensibility while evolving an efficient management structure."

In 1988, however, Nightwood moved into its third phase as a company with the hiring of Kate Lushington as Artistic Coordinator. In a July 1989 application to the Ministry of Culture and Communications for money to hold a Board retreat, Lushington wrote:

> Since I joined Nightwood last September as the first Artistic Coordinator from outside the group of founding members, the Board has been undergoing a year of structural transition, from an open ended collective approach to a more traditional structure, with the establishment of standing committees to handle tasks, intensive Board recruitment, and the setting up of terms for Board Members.

The Mission Statement had also been re-written to read:

> To provide opportunities for all women to create and explore new visions of the world, stretching the concept of what is theatrical, and to hone their skills as artists, so that more of us may see our reality reflected on this country's stages, thus offering theatre goers the full diversity of the Canadian experience.

By the fall of 1989, in the first issue of the Nightwood newsletter *Nightwords* (vol.1 no.1), Lushington explicitly charted what she saw as the company's new identity in a column entitled "A Word, or two, from the Artistic Coordinator." The 1989/90 season was celebrated as Nightwood's tenth anniversary, and in her column Lushington recounted Nightwood's origins with *The True Story of Ida Johnson* and expressed the opinion that Nightwood had grown beyond the wildest dreams of its founders: "No longer a collective, the collaborative spirit lives on in the artistic heart of the company, The Play Group...." With this statement, Lushington redefined the way Nightwood would present itself. There would be a stronger focus on administration, on having adequate office staff and large enough budgets to mount higher profile shows (although these intentions were undermined by government funding cuts to the arts). The Board was increasingly made up of professional women, lawyers, accountants and executives, and there were more fundraising events. The "collaborative spirit" shifted to the Play Group, a collective of women who formed the selection committee for Groundswell and planned each season. Instead of sponsoring co-productions with collectives, Nightwood supported its own playwrights-in-residence; for the 1989/90 season, Sally Clark worked on *Life Without Instruction.*

A further development in Nightwood's structure was announced in the Winter 1991 newsletter (vol. 2 no. 2, re-named *Night Talk*). In a report on board news, Phyllis Berck explained that there had been another Board retreat in October of 1990: "During a special meeting about the artistic vision of Nightwood, it was agreed that the title Artistic Coordinator should be changed to Artistic Director, to better reflect the duties of the position." Accordingly, Lushington's regular column is re-titled in this issue to read "A Word, or two, from the Artistic Director." In her *FUSE* article about

Nightwood the previous year, Susan Cole had suggested that the absence of a traditional Artistic Director may have lost Nightwood some support in the theatre community and may also have confused potential funders. While these issues may have been part of the reason for the change, the predominant consideration seems to have been a desire to reflect Nightwood's new identity as a traditionally structured theatre company, no longer a collective.

However, another very telling document from this period is an article in *eye Magazine*, reporting on *Charming and Rose: True Love* (1993), Lushington's final directing project at Nightwood before she left the position of Artistic Director. The reviewer described Lushington as directing a farewell show for "the feminist theatre collective she helped start five years ago" (Zeitoun 24). Of course, on one level this is merely bad reporting, mistaking the date when Lushington began working for the company with the date when the company was founded. But it also points to the fact that, even though Lushington had been consistently disassociating Nightwood from the collective label in those five years, it was still being considered as such by that theatre reviewer.

Nightwood continues to be thought of as a collectively-run organization, perhaps because of the existence of the Artistic Advisory and the presence of artists on its Board, and perhaps because it is perceived by some as a "community theatre." This was reinforced when a leadership team of three women took over from Lushington in 1994, even though each had a title and separate responsibilities. Since Diane Roberts left her position with Nightwood in the spring of 1996, Alisa Palmer is the sole Artistic Director, Leslie Lester has continued as Producer, and two other women, Soraya Peerbaye and Jay Pitter, have worked as their associates. Palmer may succeed in shaking the collective label because of her strong profile within the theatre community as an award-winning playwright, director and actor; she has been associated with other companies, and this may actually help her to establish Nightwood's identity, as will the critical success of their most recent production, Djanet Sears's *Harlem Duet*. Nightwood does retain its collective spirit, however, in the sense that it strives to be inclusive and accessible, and continues to be part of a long tradition of political theatre in Canada, the legacy of socially-conscious collective creation of the 1960s and 1970s, and also the on-going development of models for feminist theatre. Particularly for feminist groups, the value of collective creation lies in both the process and the product. How this balance is achieved, however, can take different turns, and the element of risk involved seems appropriate to theatre-makers defining themselves as alternative and socially-conscious. In Nightwood's case, however, the external perception of the company's commitment to collectivity has been greater than the internal development, in which collective creation has been only one means to evolve a feminist mandate.

(1997)

Notes

1 A complete chronology of Nightwood's activities (1979-1998) is available in searchable format and appended to the electronic version of this article at this journal's website <http://www.lib.unb.ca/Texts/TRIC>. This chronology also appears in the author's unpublished dissertation "Feminist Theory and Nightwood Theatre." See also Glen, Hunt, Ives, Keeney Smith, Levine, Lushington "Fear" and "Possibility," Peerbaye, Roberts, and Wilson for further information on Nightwood Theatre.

2 For example, Mary Vingoe writes: "Feminism was not the primary reason for starting the company. Only later did it become a significant factor when we began to be identified as a group of four women running a theatre company" (Nightwood 48).

3 The Board of Directors takes on administrative tasks while a separate collective called the Artistic Advisory assists the Artistic Director with programming the season and reading scripts for Groundswell (during Kate Lushington's tenure they were referred to as the Play Group). For 1997/98, the Nightwood Board of Directors is Sierra Bacquie (Co-Chair), Shirley Barrie, Diane Flacks, Jennifer Kawaja, Danielle LiChong, Ann-Marie MacDonald (Co-Chair), Dawn Obakata, Angela Robertson and Eiko Shaul, and the Artistic Advisory is Alex Bulmer, Karen Glave, ahdri zhina mandiela, Erin McMurtry, Sonja Mills, Melanie Nicholls-King, Dawn Obakata, and Sheyfali Saujani. Jacquie Carpenter is apprentice producer and M.J. Kang is playwright in residence.

4 Redlight's first production was *What Glorious Times They Had*, written by Diane Grant. A humorous and episodic portrait of Canadian suffragette Nellie McClung, it was originally produced at Bathurst Street United Church on May 8, 1974, directed by and starring Diane Grant as Nellie and also featuring Francine Volker, who would later go on to develop her play *The Paraskeva Principle* with Nightwood.

5 For example, in "Bad Girls Looking for Money" Bennett and Patience write: "What Maenad is exploring is an administrative and artistic structure that makes possible a wide range of work by a diversity of women who do not or cannot, for a number of reasons, produce their theatre in more traditional structures" (12).

6 For an early categorization of different schools of feminist thought as they relate to theatre, see Case.

7 Rubess, speaking to Canadian Theatre and Drama class. Graduate Centre for Study of Drama, University of Toronto. 11 March 1993.

8 *Smoke Damage*, which was produced by Nightwood in 1983, was created collectively but assigned to Bañuta Rubess as the principal author and grew out of an earlier collective piece called *Burning Times*. It was the subject of a legal dispute that revolved around the question of who had copyright over the play.

[9] In Sheehan, the Theatre Centre is depicted as the product of a younger generation, set up in opposition to the "establishment alternative theatre" of the 1960s, represented by Passe Muraille. Grant is quoted as saying: "Yes, the 60's have passed, but that spirit of collective effort in which new work can develop still exists … there is a whole generation below us anxious to get space to work in, to develop even newer ways of communicating. I really feel we should do something to make sure that opportunity is there." The model of collectivity being espoused here is mainly about access, with less focus on an aesthetic type than on a policy of inclusiveness; the discussion is situated in a discourse of youth versus age, new versus established theatre artists.

[10] Of the Anna Project members, only Maureen White was also a Nightwood member, but two others, Bañuta Rubess and Ann-Marie MacDonald, went on to extensive involvement, including sitting on the Board of Directors.

[11] The author wishes to thank Nightwood Theatre for granting her access to their private archives. All Nightwood correspondence (including grant applications) and theatre programs cited in this article can be found in these archives.

[12] In Green and Buck, a community-based board of directors is defined as one made up of non-artists, people in the patron and business communities. They have final legal responsibility and the authority to approve or disapprove anything. Funding agencies require that publicly funded institutions have a board.

[13] Kate Lazier, the reviewer in questions, writes: "Rubess's linear plot is a departure for Nightwood, whose work is usually more associative. But in typical Nightwood fashion, the transitions between scenes are smooth…."

[14] Some presentations at subsequent Groundswell Festivals have been by collectives. For example, the 8th annual Groundswell, "Making Waves," held at the Tarragon Theatre Extraspace, in October and November of 1992, featured three collective creations: *A Savage Equilibrium* by Monique Mojica, Fernando Hernandez Perez, Jani Lauzon and Floyd Favel; *Coming from the Womb* by the Red Sister/Black Sister Collective; and *Girls in the 'Hood* by Catherine Glen with young women from Metro Housing.

Works Cited

Anna Project, The. "Fragments." *Canadian Theatre Review* 43 (Fall 1985): 167-73.

———. "This is For You, Anna: A spectacle of revenge." *Canadian Theatre Review* 43 (Fall 1985): 127-66.

Bennett, Susan. *Theatre Audiences.* London: Routledge, 1990.

Bennett, Susan and Alexandria Patience. "Bad Girls Looking for Money—Maenad Making Feminist Theatre in Alberta." *Canadian Theatre Review* 82 (Spring 1995): 10-13.

Berck, Phyllis. Report on Board News. *Night Talk* 2.2.

Burke, Kelley Jo. "*Charming and Rose: True Love.*" *Amazing Plays: 3 from the '92 Winnipeg Fringe.* Winnipeg: Blizzard, 1992. 31-62.

Case, Sue-Ellen. *Feminism and Theatre.* London: MacMillan, 1988.

Cole, Susan G. "Ten Years and Five Minutes: Nightwood Celebrates a Decade of Feminist Theatre." *FUSE* (Spring 1990): 12-15.

DiCenzo, Maria. Rev. of *Fair Play* by Much and Rudakoff, *Theatre History in Canada/Histoire du théâtre au Canada* 12.2 (Fall 1991): 219.

Filewod, Alan. *Collective Encounters: Documentary Theatre in English Canada.* Toronto: U of Toronto P, 1987.

Forsyth, Louise H. "Feminist Theatre." *Oxford Companion to Canadian Theatre.* Ed. Eugene Benson and L.W. Conolly. Toronto: Oxford UP, 1989. 206.

Glen, Catherine. "On the Edge: Revisioning Nightwood." *Canadian Theatre Review* 82 (Spring 1995): 36-39.

Grant, Diane. *What Glorious Times They Had: a satire.* Toronto: Simon and Pierre, 1974.

Green, Joseph and Douglas Buck. "Responsibility and Leadership in Canadian Theatre." *Canadian Theatre Review* 40 (Fall 1984): 4-8.

Hunt, Nigel. "Bringing the Heroine Back to Life." *Performing Arts* (March/Spring 1990): 27.

Ives, L. Patricia. "The Very Best Bad Girls Create…" *Canadian Theatre Review* 50 (Spring 1987): 30-33.

Johnston, Denis W. *Up the Mainstream: The Rise of Toronto's Alternative Theatres.* Toronto: U of Toronto P, 1991.

Kaplan, Jon. "Cynthia Grant Builds Images," *NOW* August 1982: 13.

———. "Bearing the fruit of a polluted world," *NOW* 4-10 May 1989: 47.

———. "Renders goes solo in noisy kids' show," *NOW* 17-23 December 1987: 19.

Keeney Smith, Patricia. "Living with Risk." *Canadian Theatre Review* 38 (Fall 1983): 34-43.

Lazier, Kate. "Pope Joan's Infallible Wit." *The Varsity* 10 September 1984: 16.

Levine, Meredith. "Feminist Theatre—Toronto 87." *Theatrum: A Theatre Journal* (Spring 1987): 5-10.

Lushington, Kate. "The Changing Body of Women's Work," *Broadside* August/September 1989: 20-21.

———. "Fear of Feminism." *Canadian Theatre Review* 43 (Summer 1985): 5-11.

———. Letter to Ministry of Culture and Communications. July 1989.

———. "The Possibility and the Habit." *FUSE* (Summer 1983): 62-63.

———. "A Word, or two, from the Artistic Coordinator." *Nightwords* 1.1.

Much, Rita and Judith Rudakoff, ed. *Fair Play: Twelve Women Speak: Conversations with Canadian Playwrights.* Toronto: Simon and Pierre, 1990.

Nightwood Theatre. "Notes from the Front Lines." *Canadian Theatre Review* 43 (Summer 1985): 44-51.

Peerbaye, Soraya. "Look to the Lady: Re-examining Women's Theatre." *Canadian Theatre Review* 84 (Fall 1995): 22-25.

Porter, McKenzie. "Ida: postgraduate study in wasted intelligence." *Toronto Star* 26 October 1979: 101.

Renders, Kim. Personal Interview. 11 May 1996.

Riis, Sharon. *The True Story of Ida Johnson.* Toronto: The Women's Press, 1976.

Roberts, Diane. "Dramaturgy: A Nightwood Conversation." *Canadian Theatre Review* 87 (Summer 1996): 22-24.

Rubess, Bañuta. Address. Canadian Theatre and Drama class. Graduate Centre for Study of Drama, University of Toronto, 11 March 1993.

———. *Pope Joan: a non-historical comedy.* Toronto: Playwrights Union, 1984.

Rubess, Bañuta with Peggy Christopherson, Ann-Marie MacDonald, Mary Marzo, Kim Renders, and Maureen White. *Smoke Damage: A story of the witch hunts.* Toronto: Playwrights Canada, 1985.

Scott, Shelley. "Feminist Theory and Nightwood Theatre." Diss. U of Toronto, 1997.

Sheehan, Nick. "Theatre Centre's collective core." *NOW* 15-21 March, 1984: 7.

Vingoe, Mary. "Internship Training Program Application." Ministry of Culture and Communication. 22 October 1986.

———. Letter to Jeremy Long, Theatre Officer, Canada Council. 17 March 1986.

Wilson, Ann. "The Politics of the Script." *Canadian Theatre Review* 43 (Summer 1985): 174-79.

Zeitoun, Mary Lou. "Sex and the working theatre girls." *eye Magazine* 14 October 1993: 24.

A Feminist Absurd: Margaret Hollingsworth's *The House That Jack Built*

by Celeste Derksen

Theatre scholars with an interest in absurdism are likely to find the name Margaret Hollingsworth oddly out of place on a list including such canonical representatives as Samuel Beckett, Eugene Ionesco, Harold Pinter, and Vaclav Havel. This is particularly the case given that the playwright is a contemporary Canadian woman and a feminist. The profits of this inclusion are found in its very disjunction: to consider Hollingsworth as absurdist is at once a challenge to the male exclusivity that is a defining feature of absurdism and an argument for revitalizing absurdism as a contemporary critical term.[1] Indeed, I contend that much of Hollingsworth's drama draws from, and is illuminated by, consideration of absurdist technique, philosophy, and subject positions. Further, she deploys absurdism in a manner that foregrounds gender concerns and so points to the exclusion—or incomprehension—of gender as a controlling framework of meaning in the established tradition. As such, Hollingsworth's dramatic vision presents the potential for an enlivening new critical conception: the "feminist absurd."

Hollingsworth's plays have a tendency towards experimentalism and variety; thus, any alignment of her work with a single writerly position/style or philosophical stance should be provisional and experimental. Caveat in hand, I argue that many of her plays—particularly her early work[2]—are clearly layered with seams of absurdism. This essay focuses specifically on *The House That Jack Built*, one of four short plays in Hollingsworth's 1988 collection *Endangered Species*, in which the effects of gender become ludicrous and ominous, to the point of comic absurdity. *The House That Jack Built* features Jack and Jenny, a married couple who sit onstage in rocking chairs through virtually the entire play. While the character notes state that they are only twenty-four years old, the rocking chairs ominously suggest that the couple has prematurely aged for some reason. The rocking chairs also create an effect of repetitive motion with no progress—visibly and acoustically—onstage.[3] Hollingsworth's settings allude to George Toles's description of "Beckett's eternal waiting room, where one is condemned to speech and repetitive activity simply because one *cannot* leave" (162, emphasis in original). In this play, Jack and Jenny are entrapped in preconceived gender and marital structures. Throughout the play they rock, moving backwards and forwards in time, each relating their separate version of how they reached their current condition. Jack's story tells of his Herculean effort to make his wife happy by building her a home in the country; Jenny's narrative exposes her attempts to gain autonomy within the confines of marriage, her resistance to the house, and her eventual containment in that structure and what it represents.

The House That Jack Built takes its name from a traditional nursery rhyme that employs a repetitive type of word play known as accumulation:

> This is the house that Jack built.
> 2. This is the malt
> That lay in the house that Jack built.
> 3. This is the rat,
> That ate the malt,
> That lay in the house that Jack built.
> 4. This is the cat,
> That killed the rat,
> That ate the malt,
> That lay in the house that Jack built.

The rhyme continues, accumulating a dog, a cow with a crumpled horn, a maiden all forlorn, a man, a priest (who marries maiden and man), a cock, and a farmer. Like other nursery rhymes of this type, the accumulative pattern conforms to recognizable social patterns and hierarchies. These include the ascendancy of larger mammals (which culminates in the human male), the desirability of material accumulation and consumption, and the inevitability of heterosexual marriage. Still, there is a trouble-spot in the rhyme's comfortable wor(l)d order. Jack appears to represent its apex, since his name is repeated as the agent of the cumulative action. But Jack's action is silly, even ignorant: he leaves malt in the house for the "lesser" animals to find. In other words, while Jack appears to be the pivotal character, he is less than dependable and certainly less than heroic. He is, in short, fallibly comic. Thus, the title itself draws attention to several thematic effects that operate within Hollingsworth's play: the persistent reiteration of hierarchies through verbal and social patterns; the importance of unearthing those fallible and comic elements that may trouble such patterns; and, on a simpler note, the dubious reliability of even well-intentioned "Jacks."

The Jack of Hollingsworth's play does not question the social blueprint that provides his primary motivation, which is to build a house for his wife:

> **JACK.** [...] So I built her a house. I mean, what more can a man do for his wife? You meet a girl. It's too soon. High school, but what can you do when she's the right one. Chew on your nails? Jerk yourself off? No. You buy her a ring, right? You buy her a ring, and then you marry her. You do it right. You work for her, and you just have to hope she doesn't get herself pregnant before you've got her a house. That's the way it is. I mean you tell me different, don't matter who you are. There's no other way when you come right down to it.
> **JENNY.** There's no other way. (11-12)

This quotation, like the title rhyme, adheres to an accumulative structure and logic. Jack follows the socially prescribed direction for a middle-class performance of his gender: first you find a girl, then you get married, then you get her a house, then you have kids. The play takes this accumulative pattern, which poses as the key to personal success in North American middle-class society and which Jack supposes is his rightful duty, and then exposes its dangers, weaknesses, and futility. It does so in part by foregrounding the fallibility of Jack's assumptions. In this passage, his use of bravado, rhetorical question, and repetition comically exaggerates the uncertainty that lurks behind the certainty. Jenny's affirmation of Jack's speech suggests her complicity with this framework, although her robotic repetition has both a comic and a menacing undertone.

Such depiction of characters caught in patterns of thought and language, endlessly and menacingly reiterating those structures, characterizes Hollingsworth's vision as absurdist. Conversely, her focus on gender and marriage as primary, confining structures of meaning differentiates her work from the absurdist canon and calls for a more expansive conception of absurdism.

The House That Jack Built constructs what I call a feminist absurd subject position for its readers, spectators, directors. This should appear an odd bifurcation/combination of positionalities, given that usual conceptions of the subjects of absurdism and feminism are quite unlike, the former being a kind of politically neuter non-subject and the latter implying an inherently political quest for subjecthood. However, the subject positions associated with absurdism and feminism are neither monolithic nor stable; this acknowledgement offers the potential to extend both strands of dramatic criticism. Precedent is even found in the differences between the 1961 and 1969 editions of *The Theatre of the Absurd*, through which Martin Esslin revises and expands the notions of subjectivity that underpin the plays he describes as absurdist. The 1961 edition constructs the following (distilled) portrait of an absurdist subject. Western absurdist plays dramatize the modernist challenge to the notion of a centred subject who is in control of his universe and understands its meanings. The subject of absurdism is characterized by metaphysical anguish and a profound mistrust of those structures of meaning that society employs to buttress his sense of subjecthood. Through a variety of techniques (repetition of language and movement, plotted inactivity, theatrical images of enclosure, and so forth) absurdist drama presents a vision of people caught in arbitrary patterns of behaviour which affect but do not appear to have meaning. Such patterns of domination or submission seem random. These characters are virtually non-subjects, given that their ability to act or speak meaningfully or autonomously is doubtful at best. Such plays construct for readers/spectators a subject position (a psychic/philosophical position from which they are most readily intelligible) characterized by co(s)mic angst at this lack of meaning and agency. In keeping with male-modernist-humanist notions, absurdist characters represent an abstract conception of "all man," and their dilemmas represent the essence of the general human condition. As such, the subject of absurdism, as conceived by Esslin—at least in 1961—is supposedly apolitical and universal (293-94; 311-13).[4]

Yet in Esslin's second edition of *The Theatre of the Absurd* (1969) a more malleable and expansive notion of subjectivity emerges with his added consideration of Eastern European playwrights. Here he acknowledges that absurdist theatre may comprise subversive political critique: "a theatre of such concretized images of psychological dilemmas and frustrations which transmuted moods into myths was extremely well suited to deal with the realities of life in Eastern Europe, with the added advantage that, concentrating on the psychological essentials of the situation in a setting of myth and allegory, it had no need to be openly political or topical by referring to politics or social conditions as such" (272). In other words, absurdist plays may be read as political allegories and are effective precisely because their particular oppositional messages are "hidden" in notions of universality and thus protected from censorship. The political subject of Eastern European absurdism is still male-defined and focused (all the plays Esslin cites are written by men).[5] His potential for subjecthood is foreclosed by political and social structures, and he gives voice to the angst of many Eastern Europeans regarding their lack of agency and individuality under Soviet-dominated governments. The random effects of domination and submission to which he is subjected have, in this context, definite political implications. Political resonance exists also in those surreal elements that appear in the plays of Adamov, Mrozek, Rozewicz, and other Eastern European absurdists. Lyrical, surreal, and darkly comical passages and theatrical effects give voice to a kind of subterranean protest that will not be repressed.[6]

In Hollingsworth's feminist absurd, the subject of absurdism can be constructed and read from a more overtly political, socially engaged standpoint. This develops from and expands upon earlier conceptions of the metaphysical/apolitical and surreal/political subjects of absurdism, draws attention to those theatrical conventions and ideas that align Hollingsworth's play with absurdist traditions, but notes particularly how her treatment of gender shifts their focus. For instance, in *The House That Jack Built*, both male and female characters could be called absurd (non)subjects, since both are caught in the controlling structures of gender, heterosexual, and capitalist imperatives. The play's *mise en scène* constructs a sense of their enclosure in systems of language and in personal and economic relationships that, while they might provide the illusion of meaning and agency, in fact control their potential meanings and actions. Both characters are caught in stultifying social scripts; however, the male character, Jack, adheres hopefully to them, while the female character, Jenny, reveals more angst and oppositionality towards them—at least initially.

Jenny's acquiescence in Jack's assumption that "[t]here's no other way" (but to follow their middle-class gender script) reflects the couple's current condition. As they recount the story of their marriage, Jenny alternately reiterates and thwarts his assumptions, to the point where Jack himself becomes less than certain of their inevitable success. Indeed, the more Jack tries to follow the "rules" for a happy marriage, the more he exposes the flaws in his social blueprint—the "cracks" in his patriarchal foundation. One such flaw is the fact that Jenny does not want a house in the country. Jack, however, refuses to see that his wife does not correspond neatly to his gender expectations. The play continually highlights the characters' inflexibility and inability to understand or to communicate with one another and shows that much of this difficulty is due to rigid gender prescription that sets them at odds. In this passage, the couple moves back in time, to survey the lot Jack has purchased for their home:

> **JENNY.** This is it?
> **JACK.** What's wrong with it?
> **JENNY.** It's wet.
> **JACK.** Of course it's friggin wet what do you expect!
> **JENNY.** It's a swamp.
> [...]
> **JENNY.** What about a basement?
> **JACK.** You want a basement?
> **JENNY.** It's too wet for a basement.
> **JACK.** You want a basement you'll get a basement
> **JENNY.** Don't all houses have basements?
> **JACK.** If that's what you want, you'll have one. All you gotta do is just say what you want.
> **JENNY.** I wanna stay on Queen.
> **JACK.** You just gotta say the word. Basement. (12-13)

In this dialogue, Jenny articulates her desire to remain in their Toronto apartment; Jack's fixation on the word basement evades that desire and allows him to reconfirm his preconceived pattern of action. Cynthia Schnebly notes that absurdist drama often employs repetitive patterns to signify failed conversation; instead of denoting interpersonal involvement, such repetitions may be manipulated so that "characters often seem only marginally aware of what is being said, and they repeat to clear away the obligation to reply or to evade substantive response" (99). In typical absurdist fashion, Jack and Jenny's bickering indicates language as a fallible system that is just as likely to refuse as to allow communication. But here, Hollingsworth particularly foregrounds the dynamics of intergender communication and how dialogue involves patterns of domination. While the audience may find Jack's gullibility (as the proverbial dupe who buys swampland) and miscomprehension amusing, his fixation on the basement (dark, damp, dungeon-like) provides an image of ominous foreboding. This dialogue provides both a discursive and a figurative impression of Jenny's impending imprisonment in Jack's design.

The house that Jack builds clearly represents a threat to Jenny. Through pieces of information interspersed throughout the play, we learn that Jenny enjoys the city, its distractions, her work and friends. The urban environment provides her with a sense of adult autonomy, whereas the country house surrounded by trees reminds Jenny of her insular childhood home in Kapuskasing. Very simply, then, the house appears to represent a way of life that she rejects in favour of one of her own making. Jenny's personal dislike of the house has wider gender significance. Hanna Scolnicov, following other feminist critics, argues that "[g]ender roles are spatially defined in relation to the inside and the outside of the house. Traditionally, it is the woman who makes the house into a home, her home, while the world of commerce, war, travel, the world outside, is a man's world" (6). She further notes that the "house" can have either positive or negative gender associations. On the one hand, the house may be viewed as a space in which women can exercise their creativity and control; on the other hand, "especially in modern times, the problem is how to escape the restrictive space of her house" (8). In Hollingsworth's play, Jenny's relationship to the house corresponds clearly to the latter attitude.

The female/passive/inside versus male/active/outside binary opposition operates throughout the play, and it is this binary type of thinking that contributes to the characters' estrangement. Initially, Jack, who drains the swamp, cuts down the trees, and builds the house, is associated with the active outdoors. Ironically, his relationship to that environment is primarily destructive, as he obliterates the trees and animals that populate the building site.[7] While he associates himself with the building and the outside of the house, he expects Jenny to take care of the inside decor and to consume domestic goods. He brings her decorating catalogues to look at and becomes violently frustrated that she hasn't "as much as picked out a shower curtain" (18). For Jack, the indoors/female and outdoor/male binary is assumed and accepted. For Jenny, it is a site of gender and power struggle.

Importantly, while Hollingsworth's play draws attention to the "house" as a gender- and power-charged environment, she does so primarily through words. While the rocking chairs connote the inside of the house, the stage directions call for no doors, no windows, no other realistic details of the house. Many absurdist plays tend towards such emptiness (bare stage, scarce props, plain costumes), which signifies a world emptied of meaning and fixed points of reference. Similarly, the stage of *The House That Jack Built* is delimited in order to foreground conceptual spaces. But here it draws attention to the power of the "house" and its gender restrictions as a structure/product of language and thought as opposed to a realistic physical space. In this exchange, Jack heroically describes his struggle to build Jenny's house and Jenny makes an attempt to articulate her sense of resistance—not to the house itself—but to what it represents:

> **JACK.** [...] Billy bet me I couldn't get the roof on by mid-July.
> **JENNY.** See I wanted—
> **JACK.** I won, then I got the dry-wallin started.
> **JENNY.** I wanted.
> **JACK.** Plaster dust everywhere—I guess I shoulda had that under control right?
> **JENNY.** I wanted— (*Drinks.*) I love him. It's not that but I wanted... I wanted a house, it's not that.
> **JACK.** I shoulda friggin had it under control right? (18)

Jenny can articulate neither her desire nor her fear, yet her apprehension is all the more evident through the pattern of her silences. It appears that it is not the physical house itself that threatens but what it represents—seclusion, possession, and passivity. In addition, the passage demonstrates Jack's proprietary belief that he must maintain power and control not just over the plaster dust, but also over his wife. While Jenny's desires appear to be in formation Jack's belief that he must follow his gender program and assert control (and thwart Jenny's desires when they deviate from that program) is palpable. His ability to fulfill the agenda for masterful manhood is, however, frustrated throughout the play.

In a world of uncertainties and missing points of reference, gender hierarchies remain largely unquestioned in both Western and Eastern European absurdist traditions. Hollingsworth's play takes as its subject those gendered patterns of domination and submission; it acknowledges the power of such hierarchies in language and in personal and economic relationships, but it also calls into question their necessity and desirability. So, while in dialogue with "classic" absurdism, *The House That Jack Built* deviates from its presumptions in a significant fashion. Certainly, the play challenges the assumed primacy of the male hero in the comedy-of-despair. The male character—our quintessential Jack—thinks himself the hero of the play's action, but it is Jenny, the female character, who is the more provocative source of action, albeit a seemingly futile resistance. Correspondingly, the play considers gender not as a fixed state-of-being, but as a structure that, like language, has dangerous—if dubious—power. Hollingsworth combines an interest in the social with an interest in the psychological, an interest in the philosophical with an interest in everyday practice and, in so doing, interrelates feminist and absurdist practices and concerns. The female protagonist in this comedy-of-despair is herself, however, anything but consciously feminist. Jenny is at once submissive, complicit, and resistant to those patriarchal power structures determining her life. At no point in the play does she envision leaving her marriage, although she describes her increasing dissatisfaction and yearning for independence. Marriage is like Beckett's waiting room: she cannot see an exit and can barely imagine an outside, independent female life. When she does begin to find an interest in a new job and female community of co-workers, Jack is immediately threatened:

> **JACK.** [...] She went to work for Canadian Tire.
> **JENNY.** I went to work at Canadian Tire. They give thirty percent discount to employees but you have to work Saturdays.
> **JACK.** It paid good. Thing is it paid in Canadian Tire money!
> (*Laughs.*)
> **JENNY.** I liked it—see me and the other girls—
> **JACK.** She knew she'd have to give it up once we moved.
> **JENNY.** We were always horsin around on our lunch break. Me and the other girls.
> **JACK.** I went there once and watched her. She didn't see me. She was on the cash register and this other girl. It was like watchin a stranger or somethin. I never let it bother me. (17)

Jenny transgresses Jack's formula by finding companionship outside their marriage and purpose in work—and at none other than the iconic bastion of Canadian maleness, the Canadian Tire store.[8] By now, the reader is familiar with Jack's characteristic self-delusion and can read his bravado with comic irony. His assertion "I never let it bother me" betrays his jealousy and need for domination. Jack's denial confirms that he is threatened by Jenny's economic independence (note, for instance, how his Canadian Tire money joke belittles her status as a wage earner) and female community and that he fears losing Jenny as that possession that ultimately defines his masculinity. And so, he escalates the house-building project.

The House That Jack Built brings to the foreground the collusion of capitalist consumerism with gender and marital structures by having Jenny trouble this equation, first through her desire to step outside her traditional role as wife (who supports her labourer husband, who consumes domestic goods, and whose own labour is unpaid) and second through her attention to the environmental destruction caused by Jack's need to build, or accumulate, in service of his marriage. The play's absurdist portrayal of gender and marriage is thus connected integrally to its portrayal of consumerism: they are structures of meaning that allow people to construct themselves as subjects (that seem to offer purpose, value, and the promise of autonomy in their lives) but that also subjugate them (that foreclose other purposes and values and other configurations of gender, human, and environmental relations). From this standpoint, Jack is as much a hapless victim of capitalist/gender ideologies as Jenny. The difference between their standpoints is, in Hollingsworth's words, that the men in her plays "are [...] much more secure in their worlds, and in order to keep that security they use words as weapons, they intimidate by silence" ("Introduction" 7).[9] Jack belittles Jenny's tentative attempts to construct a different role for herself through his jokes and his dogged reiterations of the rightness of his motives and plan. He uses language as a means of control, although, ironically, language also controls him (it determines what he thinks, how he behaves) and betrays him (it exposes his self-delusions and presumptions). Because Jack follows so closely the script for a middle-class performance of his gender, words come easily—indeed too easily—from that script to assert the value and necessity of his actions and beliefs. Whereas, when Jenny attempts to conceive a role outside that script for herself, words do not come so easily or coherently at all.

Jenny's voice of resistance and protest against repression becomes increasingly nonsensical and surreal, both verbally and non-verbally, once she describes the period after they move to the new house. She becomes obsessed with the "outside," particularly with those elements of the environment that Jack's enterprise threatens to destroy. At one point, as Jenny tries to articulate her unhappiness with their change of home, she reaches into her knitting bag and empties out an array of sponges. During the dialogue that follows, she squeezes, rocks, and strokes the sponges (18). Initially, this action seems incongruous. The "surreal" logic[10] of Jenny's attachment to the sponges becomes clearer when she describes how she came to have them:

> I was arrested for shoplifting from Shoppers Drug Mart. They asked me why I did it. I said I didn't know. We don't need that many sponges. They didn't charge me so I didn't have to tell him. I paid for them so now

> they're mine. This was alive once. (*Tears the plastic wrap off one of the sponges with her teeth*) (19)

Jenny treats the sponges as if she were trying to set them free (by tearing off the plastic wrap) and as if they were still alive (stroking and rocking them like a child). The sponges are a fitting symbol of Jenny's repressed self that, while inarticulate and imperilled, is nonetheless alive. Her maternal actions suggest that this part of herself is newly born and thus all the more fragile and cherished. It is also significant that Jenny says, in her now halting, disjunctive voice, that she tried to shoplift the sponges. This could be seen as her attempt to circumvent the necessity of ownership, so pivotal to Jack's middle-class, accumulative logic—a logic that extends to his proprietary attitude towards Jenny and her happiness. The line "I paid for them so now they're mine" draws attention to this and ominously signals Jenny's acquiescence in that equation she first intuitively tried to avoid.

The sponge episode introduces Jenny's increasing obsession with endangered species (which is also the name of the collection in which this play appears). To Jack's dismay, instead of focusing on the new house, Jenny becomes fixated on those elements of the environment destroyed in order to build it:

> They drained the swamp. Endangered species include two varieties of orchid under our driveway. Mud puppies right where the double sink is—they're dying out—they use them for research. A Canada Goose nest under the garage. Geese mate for life. Treefrogs, Fowler's toads, lungless salamanders. Bullfrogs. We eat their legs. A frog. Does not. Drink up. The pond. In which he lives. (20)

This rich moment has several potential layers of meaning and effect. On the most basic level, Jenny questions the wisdom of destroying the environment one plans to live in. Moreover, this passage establishes her obsession with those species that, like her own sense of self, are threatened by the destruction that accompanies Jack's act of construction. Those creatures she names are mostly reptilian and, like the deep-sea sponges, symbolize the "underbelly" of her consciousness. In this passage, it is as if that subterranean consciousness (so long and increasingly repressed) finds its correlative in the environment and is able to touch the surface and find a language. That language is different from the everyday, repetitive, and "realistic" dialogue of most of the play. Its tone is urgent; its syntax fragmented; its pacing and sound patterns, poetic. Jenny's final line also provides an ironic echo of the rhyme that gives the play its title, given that her halting speech undercuts the smooth unravelling of its (and Jack's) accumulative logic.

Jenny's rich, disjunctive speech suggests that her interest in those endangered species is more symbolic of her psychological state than literal. She speaks in short sentences, in short breaths, as if she were having difficulty getting the words out of her body. Like the sponges, those endangered species represent an inner self that begins to come to the surface, and her struggle to save them is thus also a struggle for self-projection and self-protection. Her speech and actions signify attempts to express herself outside of, or in resistance to, the patriarchal frame Jack erects and, as such, they constitute a form of gentler protest. Thus, Hollingsworth's drama draws attention to the pivotal relations among psychological unease, isolation, submission, and the power dynamics of gender in language and in economic and marital frameworks.

This turn to a surrealistic depiction of Jenny's psychological repression deviates from what I earlier called the Western "metaphysical" absurdist tradition, which arose in part as a critique of the psychological focus of post-war drama. However, its surrealistic depiction of a character's psychological state, which has distinct political resonance, is not unlike that ascribed by Esslin to Eastern European absurdist practice. The difference, again, is that Hollingsworth is interested in foregrounding the psychological effects of gender politics. Her characters are at once almost clown-like, emblematic representations of social conditioning taken to an absurd degree and semi-realistic characters whose psychological processes are available to interpretation. The metaphysical abstraction that characterizes early Western absurdist practice is inadequate to Hollingsworth's contemporary vision: she insists that we see the operation of those abstract structures that control human behaviour as having very real costs. Thus, Hollingsworth employs absurdism in a manner that probes its limitations and expands its concerns.

Initially, Jenny attempts to resist enclosure and instead embraces the outside and what it represents through her environmental activism. She joins a group of women concerned with saving the frogs in the disappearing swamps.

> **JENNY.** Save the swamps!
> **JACK.** It gave her somethin to do. Didn't bring no money in, but I didn't say nothin. She was on the phone for hours to this one and that one. Then I'd come home and there'd be all these women in rubber boots in our kitchen. I didn't say nothin. (20)

Jack's comical reference to "all these women in rubber boots" suggests that his anxiety stems, at least in part, from the blurring of the boundaries between indoors and out, between female and male realms of activity. More simply he is threatened by Jenny's preoccupation with a world beyond him and, once again, by her association with other women. While Jack feels his hold on their world weaken, Jenny draws strength from her activity, her female community, and her commitment to issues of survival. On a personal-symbolic level, Jenny engages in a kind of (un)consciousness-raising activity. With the help of other women, she begins to identify a world outside her role in marriage and so begins to articulate (albeit indirectly) issues of repression and endurance that apply not only to the endangered amphibians but also to herself. Still, while the audience/reader may perceive the significance of Jenny's activities, she herself does not appear fully aware of it. Ironically, Jack perceives this connection on a somewhat more conscious level.

Her work to save the frogs at first appears to be a success, as they begin to return to the drained swamp that now supports their home.

JACK. [...] It was the next spring. The next spring that they came back.
(*JENNY suddenly becomes alert.*)
They were in the basement. Just a few of them at first. Cute little green ones.
JENNY. Oh look Jack!
JACK. Then they moved into the kitchen.
JENNY. I told you they'd keep coming back! (22)

Ironically, Jenny's victory falters when she—and Jack—realize that she is afraid of frogs. For Jenny, the frogs represent an abstract cause and hope. But when the outside actually begins to come in and invade the garrison of what is safe and expected, she reacts with fear. Jack seizes his opportunity to re-establish conventional boundaries by capitalizing on her trepidation:

JENNY. I told you they'd keep coming back!
JACK. The living room. They sat down to meals with us.
(JENNY *draws her feet up, scared.*)
(Opening his eyes, and getting into it.) She went up to Kap for a visit and when she came back I told her they were in all the cupboards, in the sink...when you sat on the toilet...
JENNY. Where? Where?
JACK. I told her they were in the bedroom. They were jumpin and crawlin all over Meryl Streep's face. They were in the friggin bed. (*Jumps to his feet.*) The whole friggin house is overrun! The whole street! (JENNY *screams.*) Like a slimy green rug, heavin under your feet—and when you walk on it you feel it squelch...you feel it under your feet, and then you're up to your knees in it and then it's up to your chin. They're on your shoulders, in your ears...they're takin over! It's frogs. Your friggin frogs! (22)

At this point, the characters finally leave their rocking chairs to enact the scene in its immediacy. Hollingsworth leaves us wondering whether the frog invasion is real or a calculated embellishment manufactured by Jack to reassert his control.[11] Jenny calls to Jack to "Kill them! Kill them! Kill them! Kill them! Kill them!" and both characters, transfixed by the repressed violence they have unleashed, "*shrink back to either side of the stage*" (22). The lights go down and when they come back up, Jenny and Jack are back in their chairs, rocking almost catatonically.

The end of the play finds both characters safely re-ensconced inside the house and their gender roles:

([...] Lights come up to reveal JACK *and* JENNY *back in their chairs.* JENNY *is very pregnant.)*
JACK. I decided against a lawn. I put down gravel and cedar chips. The weeds got through so I kept a bunch of weedkiller in the garage. It's not hard to control them if you get the right stuff. *(Picks up the*

> *binoculars.*) You can't go on livin in the past. You gotta look forward. Right? (*Hands binoculars to* JENNY.) You ever look at the sky Jenny? You ever look at the stars? Really look I mean. Really look. (23)

This final scene is at once ominous and ambiguous. Certainly, the final, static image of Jenny suggests her recontainment in the oppressive gender system represented by their middle-class marriage. Jack's accumulative project—marriage, house, now kids—is right on track at the play's end. After all, "You gotta look forward. Right?" Once again, Hollingsworth employs repetition to make readers doubt the necessity and desirability of Jack's forward-looking vision. Further, Jenny's pregnant silence, like the doubts lurking behind Jack's certainty, leaves the potential for further disruption ominously present.

Jenny's pregnancy presents both a troubling and a hopeful image to end the play. As Jack updates his house-building project, we learn that he has put down a non-organic lawn (gravel and cedar chips), but the weeds have begun to come through, so he is using poison to control them. Jack gives no thought to the potential side effects of herbicides on his pregnant wife and so, with very dark comedy indeed, Hollingsworth leaves the reader/spectator with an image of the potential deformity (at once symbolic and actual) that haunts their marriage. Neither have Jack's fears dissipated entirely. Weeds are nuisances that threaten his image of the perfect home, just as Jenny's troubling thoughts are blights that once threatened Jack's progress. Like weeds, these must be stopped from growing through again.

Despite these ominous undertones, Jenny's pregnancy can also be viewed more hopefully. She holds a new life within her body, which Jack cannot entirely control (although he may poison it). Further, this scene recalls an earlier vision of Jenny rocking the sponges as if they were children, thereby suggesting that something precious, if unformed, remains inside her waiting to be born. Thus, Jenny's pregnancy can be viewed as a tentative expression of hopefulness for future evolution. Something similar may be said of Jack. On the one hand, both characters are recontained in solid, conventional gender roles. Jenny is silent, passive, and dominated by her female body. Jack is vocal, active, and looks out to the abstract world—the stars. While they remain together in the agreed upon social unit of marriage, clearly Jack and Jenny are more estranged than ever. On the other hand, if we can view Jenny's pregnancy as offering a glimmer of hope, we can view Jack's star-gazing that way also. Certainly Jack continues to ignore his wife's own desires and realities, but his desire to communicate something to her about the stars suggests a yearning on his part for some form of shared understanding. The problem is that Jack is still trying to control where and how Jenny looks. He is unwilling to share her view. Tellingly, Jack does not comment on his wife's pregnancy. Instead, he looks to the stars. Because of those gender-divided roles they follow, Jack and Jenny each look and reach out in different directions. In this way, the ending of *The House That Jack Built* remains fraught.

This difference in vision is also emblematic of what I hope is a productively fraught alliance between feminism and absurdism running through this analysis.

Jack's subject position and his abstract vision recall the metaphysical focus of the Western absurdist tradition, whereas Jenny's subject position, and her pregnancy, suggest the importance of the social and physical realities that feminism seeks to redress. Thus, through attention to gender, Hollingsworth's play can be read as at once criticizing and expanding earlier forms of absurdism.

Hollingsworth is not the only playwright to reassess the relation between absurdism and feminism. In a panel at the 1988 Women Playwrights Conference (at which Hollingsworth was also present), Nataša Tanská made the comment:

> We are regulated by external mechanisms [...] to the degree of absurdity. It's not surprising that absurd comedy has emerged as the adequate mirror of our times. Yet, it is still more the domain of men. Is this because it requires generalizations, whereas women tend to realistic detail? (98)

Tanská wonders further whether the realistic focus of much women's comedy is "the adequate response to contemporary reality" (98) and argues that absurdist humour best offers the modern woman "an ability of self-assessment from a distance" and the occasion "to see herself critically" (97):

> It is here we have an opportunity to widen the range of seeing and understanding the world and its mechanisms, an opportunity for a more philosophical approach to the subject, for demonstrating a global view of life as it surrounds us. (98)

As Tanská suggests, the absurdist theatre tradition has long been conceived of as a male domain characterized by an abstract, apolitical vision. And yet she proposes that women can benefit from the kind of self-critical, philosophical humour that mode allows.

I see these benefits and others in the feminist-absurd subject position that emerges from Hollingsworth's work. As I have argued, envisioning such a position necessitates the acknowledgement that notions of subjectivity constructed by absurdist theatre shift according to context and practice. The same is true when it comes to discussion of subject positions that can be termed feminist. In her study of Maria Irene Fornes (which is, I believe, the only extended critical discussion of absurdism and women playwrights), Toby Silverman Zinman contends that feminism and absurdism cannot coexist because feminism necessarily exhibits a commitment to promoting social change, which assumes a degree of agency that is anathema to absurdist philosophy. Contrary to the Beckettian "[n]othing to be done" premise, she argues, "[t]he new feminist theatre [...] obviously believes that there is much to be done" (205). While feminist comedies may employ absurdist techniques and address issues of miscommunication, mistrust of language, and other structures of meaning, she argues that they refuse the pessimistic, abstract philosophies that define absurdism. By and large, she argues, women playwrights are interested in finding the means of asserting themselves as subjects, rather than dismantling the very notion of an assertive subject who can act and create her own meanings. Certainly, some critics, such as Susan Carlson, do suggest that optimism characterizes not only feminist comedies, but female-authored comedies generally. Other critics, like Gloria Kaufman, argue that feminist comedy contains an explicit, and sometimes implicit, didactic and revolutionary purpose: "The persistent attitude that underlies feminist humor is the attitude of social revolution—that is, we are ridiculing a social system that can be, that must be changed" (13). Because of a distrust in the promises of rationalism and rational discourse, absurdism—as Zinman conceives it—refuses such didactic messages and methods.

Zinman's description of absurdism follows, rather than challenges, its critical ancestry, which is that of Western male modernism. As a result, it is not surprising that virtually no female-authored works fit her definition. Her conceptions of feminist and absurdist practices both appear to my mind unnecessarily monolithic. In order to reanimate the concept of absurdism—whether for feminist or other critical intents—it is useful to look at the ideological underpinnings of the modernist-absurdist tradition and to consider how they intersect with, and may be enriched by, contemporary ideologies and practices. This can be done only by paying close attention to particular manifestations of absurdist practice.

Indeed, *The House That Jack Built* can be read as a critique of the modernist notions that underpin the absurdist tradition. As I have argued, the play's techniques and vision clearly situate it within the realm of absurdist practice, but, immediately, its focus on gender and on characters/situations at once abstract and specific complicates that position. In particular, the play calls into question the primacy of the male hero in this comedy of despair. While it portrays Jack as having a "stronger" sense of selfhood and agency (he is sure that he knows what's right for himself and for Jenny), it also suggests that his assumptions are not autonomous or inevitable but are rather the effects of capitalist and heterosexual ideologies that he unthinkingly endorses (and that endorse him). Whereas both Western and Eastern European modes of absurdism seem to mourn the "universal" loss of agency and meaning, Hollingsworth questions the power and presumptions that underlie different assumptions of agency. It indicates, for example, that both male and female characters are subjected by and subjected to gender (through the construction of themselves as subjects in linguistic, economic, social, and sexual relations). It also indicates that, while Jack's maleness may be a construct, it is a powerful one, with detrimental effects. *The House That Jack Built* performs what could be called both a feminist and a postmodernist critique of the modernist conceptions that underpin absurdism. That is, it places the "*modernist* search for order in the face of moral and social chaos" in dialogue with the "*postmodern* urge to trouble, to question, to make both problematic and provisional any such desire for order or truth through the powers of the human imagination" (Hutcheon, *Canadian Postmodern* 2, original emphasis). *The House That Jack Built* engages in the "paradoxes of postmodernism [...] those contradictory acts of establishing and then undercutting prevailing values and conventions in order to provoke a questioning, a challenging of 'what goes without saying' in our culture" (3). This kind of interrogative literature is political because it invites readers/spectators to consider assumptions and vectors of power that seem to "go without saying" in literature and in life.

From this perspective, the play's use of repetition needs to be read not only in traditional modernist fashion as an indication of the emptiness of words or lack of direction, but also as an indication of the power of words to shape the subject and also as an indication that this power is not total. Judith Butler has argued that the necessity of repeating gender, of performing it over and over again, indicates first that gender is an effect of reiterated ideological norms (and so not "natural") and second that gender is not totalizing (because the potential for difference haunts each repetition) (271). *The House That Jack Built*, which repeats the story of how Jack and Jill ended up rocking endlessly in their chairs, employs repetition both to show how the characters are enclosed in external structures of meaning and also how they indicate or enact moments of subversive resistance. For instance, Jack's need to reiterate and justify his plans makes the reader doubt the necessity and rightness of his goals. Jenny's surreal comic expressions trouble the expected patterns of word and thought and so suggest that resistance to control is as inevitable as it is perhaps futile. Indeed, Hollingsworth invests this play with a sense of the importance of language. Words can be used as weapons that wound women particularly (Jack's frog fantasy). Words can be used by women to wound phallocentric logic and power (Jenny's surreal environmentalist speech). Words can also denote the attempt, as well as the refusal, to forge communication and change (Jack's final plea to Jenny to look at the stars).

Each repetition of absurdist practice can be read with an eye to difference rather than coherence, which means that those practices, and the subject positions they construct, are always available to redefinition. But why redefine? What is to be gained by reading *The House That Jack Built* from a feminist-absurdist (now postmodernist) subject position? This term is provocative first, as I have argued, because it challenges the usual exclusion of gender from absurdist conceptions. Second, the designation "feminist absurd" suggests that feminism itself can be portrayed or read as an absurdist proposition. In other words, a playwright or critic may be disillusioned with, or mistrustful of, aspects of feminist ideology and still wish to write about the effects of gender, with a view to both understanding and change. So, while this analysis of *The House That Jack Built* offers the potential for re-considering conceptions of absurdism, it also offers the opportunity to reconsider what might constitute feminist comedy.

Toby Silverman Zinman and others view feminist ideology as pre- or over-determined by revolutionary optimism and agency. Yet this assumption does not mirror the multiplicity and self-questioning characteristic of much contemporary feminist discourse and practice. For example, Deborah Silverton Rosenfelt refers to a tendency in recent fiction that she terms "post-feminist." She employs this term "to connote not the death of feminism but its uneven incorporation and revision inside the social and cultural texts of a more conservative era. The term, read analogously to terms like *postmodernist* or *post-revolutionary*, acknowledges the existence of a world and a discourse that have been fundamentally altered by feminism" (269, emphasis in original). In comparison to feminist texts, she argues, post-feminist texts "retain an awareness of male domination in gendered relationships"; however, they are "less clear about what can be done" (270). Those texts mark a return to the theme of heterosexual love and are "more aware of limits than transgressive of traditional boundaries" (270). Another quality she identifies, which relates to the ending of Hollingsworth's play, is a predilection for ambiguity. And while such ambiguity might indicate a retreat from the visionary politics of some early feminist texts, Rosenfelt argues that these works "may nevertheless through their very contradictions help in reformulating a more honest and inclusive feminism" (270). She allies this more "honest" vision with the post-modernist attack on any "unifying, totalizing" system, including the "feminist myth" of "a progress toward liberation surely attainable within the immediate future" (287). Post-feminist texts represent "multiple stories, multiple narrations" which account for "the complexity of women's experience, gendered relations, and relations of dominance in general in the modern world" (287). Whether one employs the terms common to fiction (post-feminist) or, as I have done, "feminist absurd," Hollingsworth's *The House That Jack Built* engages in precisely this form of feminist (self)interrogation.

Hollingsworth's unwillingness to support a unifying or totalizing vision of feminism is apparent in her introduction to *Endangered Species*, where she addresses the imagined feminist reader who is critical of her presentation of women:

> Many of the women in these plays may well be viewed as victims, and I am sure that this will not sit well with those who feel we should be presenting positive images of women on stage. I can only answer by saying, as many other writers have said, I call it as I see it, change cannot come without understanding and understanding can't happen without elucidation. (8)

The subject position from which Hollingsworth writes, and hopes her plays will be read, is feminist, in that it hopes for change through understanding and elucidation. Although Hollingsworth recognizes that her vision is bleak, she asserts that there is a degree of faith in the process of stimulating consciousness and in addressing the complexities and complicities that make change difficult. While Hollingsworth appears to share a "feminist" agenda for social and personal change, her work deviates from the assumption that an optimistic representation of female subjects is a necessary or even "realistic" tactic. Deborah Silverton Rosenfelt is only one of many feminist critics who challenge potentially totalizing definitions of feminism. Other critics, such as Teresa de Lauretis, acknowledge openly that feminism is a volatile ideology, riddled with contradictions (10). Hollingsworth makes no effort to smooth those trouble spots over but allows the cracks in feminist systems of meaning to open up and reveal themselves. For instance, *The House That Jack Built* situates the female body, or femaleness, as at once a site of resistance and a site of women's containment. The moment when Jenny's femaleness is most manifest, when she is pregnant, is also the moment when she is most silent and socially scripted according to Jack's plan. Further, the entire *Endangered Species* collection recognizes that many women continue to choose to remain in heterosexual relationships, despite the economic and power imbalances that, as feminism has taught, almost inevitably arise from that social/personal framework. And the collection refuses to focus exclusively on the negative dimensions of just one part of that gender/power equation. Hollingsworth does not shy away from the complexity of gender relationships, the negative aspects of both female and male power matrixes, or from the notion that women are often complicit in their victimization. She does not present a vision of either social relations or individual self-determination as easily remediable, yet she clearly sees herself and her work as "feminist."[12]

As *The House That Jack Built* ends, Hollingsworth leaves her audience with a vision of Jack's abstract star-gazing and Jenny's physical state of expectancy, communicating both dreams and fears, the desire for something beyond and the reality of enclosure. Although there is a glimmer of hope in this final vision, even that reveals divergent gender experiences and even philosophies. In absurdist fashion, the play presents these characters as isolated and confused pawns who fruitlessly resist and reiterate those structures of meaning to which they willingly or unwillingly, knowingly or unknowingly, submit. Over the course of the play, Jenny and Jack repeat the story of their attempts at communication and inevitable miscommunications, attempts at autonomy and inevitable power skirmishes (which act as correctives to autonomous acts), attempts to find meaning and ultimate refusals of meaning, attempts at action and final lapses into inaction. The play's feminist absurd subject position does not present a positive, optimistic vision of the possibility of gender equality, or of self-knowledge and self-determination within heterosexual and patriarchal structures, but it does create consciousness of those structures and elicits an appreciation of oppositional possibilities. While it suggests that power relations between men and women continue to be unequal, with men invested in maintaining the status quo, the potential for women's resistance and resilience (like Jenny's) continues to exist in subversive expressions. In *The House That Jack Built* the absurd joins feminism in a fraught marriage, in which the potential for change threatens to be born.

(2002)

Notes

1 In recent decades, discussions of theatre employing "absurdism" as a critical/theoretical category have largely been replaced by discussions employing a variety of poststructuralist theories. A notable exception, which itself reflects this shifting critical terrain, is the collection of essays *Around the Absurd: Essays on Modern and Postmodern Drama*, edited by Enoch Brater and Ruby Cohn.

2 Some of Hollingsworth's early plays incorporating both surreal and absurdist elements include *Alli Alli Oh* (1979), *Mother Country* (1980), *Operators*, and *Bushed* (1981), *Islands* (1983), *War Babies* (1985), and *It's Only Hot for Two Months in Kapuskasing* (1988).

3 A rocking chair is used similarly in Samuel Beckett's *Rockabye.*

4 From a feminist subject position, it is anything but. Critical discourse on absurdism and the plays that make up its canon are marked by a lack of awareness of gender as a structure of meaning and, ironically, are further marked by male focus. As Regina Barreca (following Judy Little) notes, the male modernist comedy-of-despair presumes the fixity and centrality of the male hero (9). For the most part, canonical absurdist dramas treat the frustration of the male's quest for identity and mourn his loss of agency. They employ a language and set of images of domination and submission that follow conventional male and female gender patterns. For instance, the loss of agency appears simultaneously as a loss of virility. While Gay Gibson Cima allows that some plays conceived of as belonging to the absurdist canon, particularly those of Beckett, can be performed and read in such a manner as to foreground, rather than endorse, stereotypical views of gender roles and power relations, she concludes that gender is still inscribed as a kind of "mystical" and "*universal*" force (216, emphasis in original). Critics who have constructed the critical discourse on absurdism have either echoed this attitude as unquestionable or ignored the implications of gender representation entirely. Absurdism, then, would seem to be an uninviting theatrical tradition for feminist practitioners to engage in, not only because of its universalist male focus and its lack of awareness of gender as a controlling structure in language and meaning, but also because it laments the loss of subjecthood at a time when women are striving to represent themselves as subjects. Nancy K. Miller, for instance, takes issue with the dispersal of identity associated with both modernist and post-modernist treatments of subjectivity: "Because women have not had the same historical relation of identity to origin, institution, production, that men have had, women have not, I think, (collectively) felt burdened by too much Self, Ego, Cogito, etc." (qtd. in Hutcheon, *Politics* 39). Despite these problems, I argue in this essay that the production of a feminist subject position is enabled by Hollingsworth's treatment of absurdism.

5 A specific example of what I mean by a male-defined subject position may be useful here. Consider these stage directions from Rozewicz's *The Witnesses* (which features two characters named Man and Woman): "*WOMAN turns to face the*

window and even leans over as if she has just seen something. Her back is turned towards us. It is not just a specific shape, but a stylistic one as well. This turning back not only affects the spectator's perception, it is also a kind of archetype, an embodiment of an idea slumbering in men's subconscious" (22). I would argue that the spectator's subject position is clearly male: WOMAN is eroticized by the stage directions; her stance is an archetype of *men's* subconscious.

6 Another precedent is Harold Pinter, an author initially associated with the metaphysical, apolitical tradition of absurdist theatre, who has in recent years re-read his own plays from a consciously political standpoint and in so doing has redefined the subject position from which they were written and are now read. See Benedict Nightingale's article "Harold Pinter/Politics."

7 Hollingsworth's stage directions draw particular attention to this strand of critique. They call for a series of backdrop slide projections that are interspersed, sometimes disruptively, throughout the narrative. The initial projection shows a fecund forest. As the story of Jack and Jenny's relationship progresses (or rather deteriorates), the slides focus more closely on the forest to show a few trees, then one, then a trunk, then a cross-section of the stump's rings. The movement of slides parallels the way that their relationship comes closer into our view, as if it were being presented for our dissection. This creates a kind of scenic irony, since the slides depict a process of deforestation that contrasts with the accumulative motion of Jack's plan. The slides also emphasize the environmental destruction that accompanies the middle-class accumulative logic.

8 Canadian Tire is the name of a popular, Canada-wide chain of stores that specialize in automotive goods and hardware. They give their customers "Canadian Tire money," which is a form of coupon.

9 The notes to *The House That Jack Built* state that the play "is designed to be presented with *It's Only Hot for Two Months in Kapuskasing*" (10), another short play in the collection. In that play, the violence that results from gender friction is verbal, psychological, and physical. In contrast to Jack in *The House That Jack Built*, the male character in *Kapuskasing* dominates through silence. As a point of similarity, in both plays it is the female characters who ultimately enact the violence submerged in their heterosexual relationships.

10 I employ the term "surreal" to describe a theatrical effect that provides a visible and/or acoustic image of, and appeals to, what surrealists call the "deep mind" (the realm of dreams and hallucinations). The association between surrealism and absurdism (in tactics and in historical development) has been widely noted; see Esslin and Ruby Cohn's introduction to *Around the Absurd*.

11 Critics are understandably confused by the truthfulness of his account of events. Jerry Wasserman calls this scene "surreal" (69) but goes on to take Jack's speech quite literally, when he states that "a plague of frogs wreaks nature's revenge" (69). Oddly, he does not wonder why Jenny—not Jack—should be the victim of this reprisal. Rita Much's interpretation is more subtle, but it also takes Jack's narrative

at face value: "the dream home is invaded by hordes of slimy, croaking frogs: Hollingsworth's hilarious inversion of fairy tales about princesses and amphibians" (xvi). Neither critic questions the credibility Jack's narrative. Certainly the play gives ample precedent for Jack's dubious reliability and his capacity to manipulate reality to suit preconceived needs. When he sees Jenny bridle at his description of frogs sitting down to dinner, the stage directions state that he opens his eyes "*getting into*" his story, which becomes increasingly exaggerated and suspect. The play also states that after Jenny returns from her trip, Jack "told" her that the frogs were in the toilet, the cupboards, the sink. To which Jenny responds. "Where? Where?" (22). Jack takes a portion of reality and exaggerates it so that it becomes a surreal nightmare that has the desired effect on his wife his description of slimy frogs up to the chin is a fantasy that perfectly articulates the fears within Jenny of allowing her repressed anger into their safely gendered world. Contrary to Wasserman's analysis, it is Jack, not the frogs, who wreaks revenge. To expand upon Much's analysis, Jack's inversion of the fairy tale turns Jenny against her saving frogs so that he can be, once again, her "prince." Jack's discourse, as he wrests power from Jenny, conveys a release of his anger, ugliness, and even repressed violence. And while his psychological assault may appear spontaneous it is also calculatedly cruel.

12 When asked by a journalist if she considered herself feminist Hollingsworth answered, "I think that any thinking woman has to call herself a feminist. I think any thinking man, any thinking *person* has to. What worries me is the connotations of the word" (Dykk, emphasis in original). This comment again points to her desire to trouble totalizing and exclusive notions of feminism. Her feminist commitment is further described by Hollingsworth in the article "Collaborators."

Works Cited

Barreca, Regina. "Making Trouble: An Introduction." *New Perspectives on Women and Comedy.* Ed. Regina Barreca. Philadelphia: Gordon and Breach, 1992. 1-11.

Brater, Enoch and Ruby Cohn, ed. *Around the Absurd: Essays on Modern and Post-modern Drama.* Ann Arbor: U of Michigan P, 1990.

Butler, Judith. *Bodies That Matter: On the Discursive Limits of Sex.* New York: Routledge, 1993.

Carlson, Susan. *Women and Comedy: Rewriting the British Theatrical Tradition.* Ann Arbor: U of Michigan P, 1991.

Cima, Gay Gibson. *Performing Women: Female Characters, Male Playwrights, and the Modern Stage.* Ithaca: Cornell UP. 1993.

Cohn Ruby. "Introduction: Around the Absurd." Brater and Cohn 1-9.

De Lauretis, Teresa. *Technologies of Gender: Essays on Theory, Film, and Fiction.* Bloomington: Indiana UP, 1987.

Dykk, Lloyd. "Drama with the Feminine Touch." *Vancouver Sun* 25 January 1984: D1.

Esslin, Martin. *The Theatre of the Absurd.* New York: Doubleday, 1961.

———. *The Theatre of the Absurd.* Rev. ed. New York: Doubleday, 1969.

Hollingsworth, Margaret. *Alli Alli Oh: A Play in One Act.* Toronto: Playwrights Co-op, 1979.

———. "Collaborators." *Canadian Theatre Review* 69 (1991): 15-19.

———. *Endangered Species. Four Plays by Margaret Hollingsworth.* Toronto: Act One, 1988.

———. "Introduction: Margins." *Endangered Species* 7-8.

———. *Islands: A One-Act Play.* Toronto: Playwrights Canada, 1983.

———. *It's Only Hot for Two Months in Kapuskasing. Endangered Species* 33-45.

———. *Mother Country.* Toronto: Playwrights Canada, 1980.

———. *Operators; Bushed: Two Plays.* Toronto: Playwrights Canada, 1981.

———. *The House That Jack Built. Endangered Species.* 9-32.

———. *Willful Acts.* Toronto: Coach House Press, 1985.

Hutcheon, Linda. *The Canadian Postmodern: A Study of Contemporary English Canadian Fiction.* Toronto: Oxford UP, 1988.

———. *The Politics of Postmodernism.* London: Routledge, 1989.

Kaufman, Gloria. "Introduction." *Pulling Our Own Strings: Feminist Humor and Satire.* Ed. Gloria Kaufman and Mary Kay Blakely. Bloomington: Indiana UP, 1980. 13-16.

Much, Rita. "Introduction." *Women on the Canadian Stage: The Legacy of Hrotsvit.* Ed. Rita Much. Winnipeg: Blizzard, 1992. ix-xxiv.

Nightingale, Benedict. "Harold Pinter/Politics." Brater and Cohn 129-54.

Rosenfelt, Deborah Silverton "Feminism, 'Postfeminism,' and Contemporary Women's Fiction." *Tradition and the Talents of Women.* Ed. Florence Howe. Urbana: U of Illinois P, 1991. 268-91.

Rozewicz, Tadeusz. *"The Witnesses" and Other Plays.* Trans. Adam Czerniawski. London: Calder and Boyars, 1970.

Schnebhy, Cynthia. "Repetition and Failed Conversation in the Theater of the Absurd." *Repetition in Discourse: Interdisciplinary Perspectives.* Vol. I. Ed. Barbara Johnstone. Norwood, NJ: Ablex, 1994. 98-112.

Scolnicov, Hanna. *Woman's Theatrical Space.* Cambridge: Cambridge UP, 1994.

Tanská, Nataša, et al. "What's So Funny: The Use of Humor, Comedy, Satire." *International Women Playwrights: Voices of Identity and Transformation—Proceedings of the First International Women Playwrights Conference, October 18-23, 1988.* Ed. Anna Kay France and P.J. Corso. Buffalo: Scarecrow, 1993. 96-104.

Toles, George. "Enclosures." Rev. of *Endangered Species*, by Margaret Hollingsworth. *Canadian Literature* 127 (1990): 162-64.

Wasserman, Jerry. "Drama." *University of Toronto Quarterly* 59 (1989): 61-78.

Zinman, Toby Silverman. Brater and Cohn 203-20.

Still "Activist" after All These Years? Reflections on Feminism and Activist Theatre, Then and Now

by Cynthia Grant

"Feminist activist theatre worker" was an identity that I was more comfortable with as a moniker in the eighties and nineties. Yet, I still attempt to live as a person who seeks justice, who is engaged in transformative learning as an educator, who still will challenge the power structures. During my many years running theatre companies, first Nightwood Theatre (1979-1985) and then Company of Sirens (1985 until recently), and as a working Board member of the Theatre Centre (1979-1994), my interest was in "creating spaces"—both in the literal sense and in the sense of context—where meaningful theatre would flourish, where social change was possible.

Brecht, as we know, argued that "all art is political." So, whoever reads this might consider how her or his actions might define his or her identity, particularly as an artist. As for me, we might begin with the highlights.

The Activist Move ... Creating a Space for Women in Theatre

It's twenty-five years since I founded Nightwood Theatre. Nightwood was a baby and child for me, absorbing my entire being. Although it is often referred to as an early collective, that is not really the case.[1] In the early years of Nightwood, I nurtured the projects, demanding funding and pushing hard for the support of audience and significant theatre folks. Paul Thompson, who at the time, was chief animateur of a growing set of theatres right across the country, was an valuable ally ... at least until I declined to create a show about strippers.

I did battle in defence of the right of audiences to see new work by women. We, at Nightwood (close colleagues Maureen White, Kim Renders, and Mary Vingoe), created new work ourselves and, over time, brought on talented actors who subsequently became much more. Ann-Marie MacDonald, Bañuta Rubess, Amanda Hale, Lina Chartrand, Aida Jordao were women who found support there in the early eighties.

Sometimes, when I stand before an audience of young people and have to tell them that women were not playwrights or directors in any significant numbers, I feel that I must be a holdover from some bygone era. They must know the struggle. When, in 1982, the Status of Women, a federally funded agency now defunct, commissioned a study authored by Rina Fraticelli on the participation rates of women in the theatre, the statistics presented an unarguable picture of minimal access for women to the positions of playwright, director, or artistic director. Sometimes, when I see seasons' listings that disproportionately feature men as playwrights and directors, I think that the problem remains.

In contemplating these questions, I felt the need not only to reflect on my own experience but also to discuss with other women what motivated them to form theatre companies in circumstances much more dangerous than those I had faced.

What Was the Impetus to Form Nightwood Theatre?

In retrospect, it's plain to see some of the influences on me at the time Nightwood came into being. I was living through a time when feminists were speaking up. I had read Germaine Greer's *The Female Eunuch* in high school, seeking to understand women's place in society. This coincided with the year when I was president of the Student Council and tried to revolutionize the educational practices at a small town rural high school in Aylmer. The student radicalism of the SDS in the United States had reached conservative farmlands. I had studied with a young Professor Kay Armitage, who was offering the Women in Film and Literature course in 1973/74, which was a precursor to the Women's Studies program at University of Toronto. In that course, I would be utterly chilled and intrigued by the underground classic novel *Nightwood*, by Djuna Barnes—the history and the lyricism of *Nightwood*, an enigmatic title by a brilliant, under-recognized female author whose own story was at once both stellar and tragic. Years later, I would be drawn to the title to name a new theatre company. While in university, I had hooked up with women who had formed the Women's Press, a publishing venture of the growing feminist community, joining their fiction collective.

The inaugural production of Nightwood Theatre came about because of my involvement with the Women's Press, whose mandate was to publish works by women about women's social realities. *The True Story of Ida Johnson* was the first novel published by the Women's Press. The book captures the voices of two compelling female characters within a lyrical narrative … a highly dramatic piece. With the fiction collective (including Liz Martyn, Christa Van Daele, Lois Pike), we would launch the book with a haunting dramatic reading in 1976.

The seventies were intoxicating times, as many women's groups came into being, from the grassroots to the corporate women's networks. Plus, there was a growing cultural funding base for the arts generally, with the inception of the Toronto Arts Council and the bolstering of the Ontario Arts Council and Canada Council. My passion for theatre, nurtured at University of Toronto, combined with my feminist activism. These coalesced around this project, *The True Story of Ida Johnson*, as I determined to fully develop a play based on the novel by Sharon Riis. Like many of my generation, I pursued an Explorations grant to fund this first wonderful production based on the novel. By then, I had met actors Maureen White and Kim

Renders on a project with Open Circle Theatre. Because we received this funding, I returned from New York where I was on a Professional Theatre Training grant from Theatre Ontario, to learn with director Joanne Akalaitis of Mabou Mines, and Spalding Gray and the Wooster Group. Without this particular project, I might have stayed in New York, where my passion for the avant-garde was fed. The Canadian theatre scene would have missed the formation of Nightwood Theatre, but more importantly dozens and dozens of women theatre artists would not have had the chance or seen the possibility of producing theatre that was their own vision.

The Defining Moment for Me and for Nightwood Theatre

There are moments in life that you charge into, without realizing that a lifetime later you will be defined by this choice that you have made. I recall my first interview with the Toronto press, in 1979, as the enthusiastic director and producer of the first production of a company entitled Nightwood Theatre. *The Globe and Mail* reporter Ray Conologue had responded to our press release about the play. I was keen to speak of the imagist theatrical approach that we had taken, despite the fact that the work was based on a text. I'd just returned from New York City, full of talk of imagist theatre à la Mabou Mines, courtesy of my first individual grant. My imagined career involved the creation of post-structuralist/modern style and, like others that I had met or was about to meet in forming the Theatre Centre—Richard Shoichet, Thom Sokoloski, Richard Rose, and Sky Gilbert—I wanted to "turn on" the Toronto theatre community to new work with radical artistic visions.

Ray Conologue was more interested in what he saw as the "story" of Nightwood Theatre. He asked me why I had formed a women's theatre company. I was surprised that this was his focus. "'Where does it say that we've formed a women's company in the press release?" I asked. Well, it didn't, but the company, by virtue of who was directing and producing the piece—me, a female—about the story of a woman—a fictional Ida Johnson—presented as a women's theatre company. Hmm. This was the beginning of a "negotiating of identity" that continues for women artists. Yes, I've always been both a woman and a feminist, but I didn't realize that this would be in the forefront of how the world saw me as an artist. The interview with Ray Conologue was a harbinger of the life ahead ... whether I chose it or not.

The increased funding in the period of the early eighties allowed several of us to build companies. Together we formed the B.A.A.N.N. Theatre Centre with Sky Gilbert (founder of Buddies in Bad Times), Thom Sokoloski (founder of Autumn Leaf Theatre), Richard Shoichet (founder of A.K.A. Performance Interface), Richard Rose (founder of Necessary Angel), and Cynthia Grant (founder of Nightwood Theatre), the lone female on the founding Board of Directors.

Nightwood Theatre grew with each year, in scope, in funding, in numbers of women involved, in numbers of projects produced. For the first seven years, I directed and produced almost every project. Productions included *Mass/Age*, *Memories of Tomorrow/Memorias del Manana*, *The Medical Show*, *Peace Banquet*, *Pope*

Joan, Smoke Damage. Over time, we embraced our feminist positioning, as the feminist movement evolved. We also had an obligation to include a more diverse grouping of artists, despite our small size, which led us to process issues of sexual orientation, race, and class.

Much of my identity was wrapped up in Nightwood from 1979 until 1985. Nightwood Theatre was my life … my child, for whom I would sacrifice much else, in whom I would invest years of my most energetic creative and producing skills, and for whom I would publicly rail against the injustice of women's exclusion from the mainstream theatres.

When the child, Nightwood, was a teen, I let her go…

Moving On … The Company of Sirens

Company of Sirens was really a breakaway group from Nightwood, a grouping of more politically engaged women. At Sirens, my colleagues included artist-activists of varying descriptions: A number of the Sirens had more radical roots than I. Let me now remember Lina Chartrand, one of the founding Sirens, who had been a very active member of the Communist Party of Canada. Aida Jordao, whose article on the Sirens appeared in *Canadian Theatre Review* 115, was a member of the Portuguese Canadian Democratic Association, which seemed to be a euphemism for the Portuguese communists here in Toronto. Another influential member of the Sirens's activist work, Catherine Glen, joined us early on, bringing solid labour credentials and a beautiful voice and talent. Lib Spry had returned from working with Augusto Boal. Shawna Dempsey had worked with me for years and, at the Sirens's performance at the Sexuality conference at OISE, she premiered her *We're Talking Vulva* piece, which is documented in the *Five Feminist Minutes* film of the National Film Board. This was prior to forming her partnership with Lorri Milan and moving to Winnipeg, to create her awesome lesbian performance art work. Actually, Lina and Amanda Hale had created lesbian performance art work that had been uncomfortably rejected at Nightwood. Partly as an act of solidarity against the homophobic undertones, I left with them to form Sirens.

Company of Sirens produced plays for labour groups, forming an early alliance with the Organized Working Women, an umbrella group of women from various labour groups of the Ontario Federation of Labour. Soon, we were the hit of the labour circuit.

Context is important here, since it created the conditions of possibility for the social justice work for which the Sirens became best known. The late eighties and early nineties were a period of social change, particularly with the NDP coming to power in Ontario. Several of our projects became absolute hits in the touring-for-social-change network. As activists, our work was in demand from various sectors. Our play, the *Working People's Picture Show*, which was the breakaway project from Nightwood, went on to be performed literally hundreds of times, for audiences in the tens of thousands, over the years 1985 to 1995. We developed innovative partnerships. The Ministry of Housing commissioned our play, *Shelter from Assault*, originally designed to bring together shelter workers and Housing Authority staff, who were implementing a new policy on assaulted women. Our work in the feminist movement came to the table when the provincial government formed The Inter-Ministerial Committee on Wife Assault. *Shelter from Assault* toured the province each fall and spring. Soon, we were asked to produce a play for high school students on family violence. This play, co-authored by Susan Seagrove and myself, with a dynamite original cast, toured dozens of high schools from 1990 on.

Alison Sealy-Smith, Catherine Glen, and ahdri zhina mandiela spearheaded the creation of the anti-racist play *No Problems Here*, on the invitation of the Ministry of Citizenship, under the liberal government of the late eighties. That play really took off when, suddenly, the province elected an NDP government, and we knew several NDP cabinet ministers by first name. The play was shown both in the grassroots setting, with funding provided by a progressive government, and at Queens' Park, to the highest levels of governance, the Management Board of Cabinet. With the Coordinator of the Justices of the Peace and the Attorney General's office, we developed an incredibly daring anti-racist initiative, which dealt with the race and gender biases in the justice system, *Speak Legal*. Heck, even the corporate world was on-board. Xerox wanted to expose its people to ideas of workplace change; at this time, everybody seemed onside to see employment equity embraced voluntarily.

It was a promising time for the popular theatre movement right across the country. As with the popular education movement situated outside the spaces of formal schooling, the theatre of social transformation was taking place outside of traditional theatre spaces.

Oddly, my intense period of activist performance from 1986 until 1996 happened because government was committed to ideals of a just society (note the Trudeau-influenced language) that would seek to educate against racism, violence against women, and discrimination. The schools, the workplaces, the communities had money to commit to bringing the Company of Sirens's projects into their settings.

However, these were not the most high-stakes theatrical projects in which I was involved.

Street Activism and Performance

It is on the streets that you will find the hard-core activity, so to speak. For instance, I have been involved in organizing the theatrics of demonstrations, though friends at Greenpeace have been greater activists of a theatrical stripe than I. I have carried the cross of dead or disappeared people in Latin America in front of consulates in Toronto. In one street event that was carefully conceived, I worked as director with the Toronto Action for Chile, a solidarity support group. We planned the scenario to take place in front of the Cumberland theatre, where a film about Chile was premiering as part of the Toronto International Film Festival. Several of our people on the street would be the targets of an arrest and raid by people impersonating a Chilean army squad.

Scenario for a street performance at the Toronto International Film Festival: At the line-up for a film at the Cumberland Cinema during the Toronto International Film Festival, a van pulled up. There was pandemonium, as people were chased by men in helmets and uniforms, wielding clubs. Some were "arrested" and dragged off into the van. Spectators were startled. Others spectators may have just been confused. I suspect that almost everyone there understood this to be a simulation of the kind of street actions by the military that too often happened in Chile. The visceral experience of armed squads, their rapid intervention and their rough treatment of civilians, was the thrust of the piece. There is an article about this performance, written by Joan Simalchuk, the former director of the Centre for Victims of Torture and a key figure in the Toronto Action for Chile.

Should We Equate Activist Theatre with Street Theatre?

Here in Canada, I think that we need to understand activist theatre in broader terms. When we toured into non-traditional settings, this was activist theatre. When we presented women's sexuality at conferences where women were taking charge of the politics and representation of the body, this was activist theatre. I remember one of the Sirens's early performance-art-type pieces. This was a gem of a piece entitled *Sex Realité* and then *Mother Tongue* (with Vivine Scarlett, Patricia Wynter, Lina Chartrand, Amanda Hale, Rita Kohli, Cynthia Grant, and Shawna Dempsey).

The theatre of the streets is often created by people whom we would not normally speak of as theatre artists.

So, yes, the context is key and Canada has not always been the easiest place to enact activist theatre. I feel fortunate that there was a period of my life when I could work full-time, creating meaningful theatre for social change. The idea of context, political context, comes up a great deal in the interviews that I've just conducted with some awesome activist theatre artists. And it is context that I have on occasion tried to re-create for younger or international audiences when I've spoken about the impetus to form Nightwood Theatre or Company of Sirens.

(2004)

Note

[1] In a long Letter to the Editor Kim Renders disputes Cynthia Grant's account of the founding and early years of Nightwood Theatre, together with her account of Grant's departure from Nightwood to form The Company of Sirens —ed.

Work Cited

Renders, Kim. "Letter to the Editor." *Canadian Theatre Review* 119 (2004): 4.

Still Acting Out After 25 Years

by Jennifer O'Connor

Shortly after she became artistic director of Nightwood Theatre, Canada's oldest and largest professional women's theatre company, Kelly Thornton was asked by a reporter whether a feminist theatre company was still needed in the 21st century.

"Nightwood very much needs to exist," Thornton replied. "Feminism is not a dead movement."

This year marks the company's 25th season, which began in late August with Groundswell—a festival of new work by women playwrights. The celebration continues in October, when Sonja Mills's *The Danish Play* will be at the National Arts Centre. *Hysteria: A Festival of Women*, a Nightwood/Buddies in Bad Times Theatre co-presentation, runs from November 4 to 13, and a new play by Lisa Codrington, *Cast Iron*, runs from February 13 to March 15. FemCab, the annual five-minute feminist cabaret, will take the stage in May 2005.

Nightwood began with the September 1979 production of *The True Story of Ida Johnson*, based on the Sharon Riis novel. Formed by Cynthia Grant, Kim Renders, Mary Vingoe and Maureen White, the company has produced acclaimed work such as Djanet Sears's *Harlem Duet* and Ann-Marie MacDonald's *Goodnight Desdemona (Good Morning Juliet)*. Since 1983, FemCab has featured work by the likes of Brigitte Gall, Dionne Brand and Jackie Richardson. Besides Groundswell, Nightwood produces Write from the Hip, a playwright's workshop for women 18-29, and Busting Out, a new program for girls aged 12 to 16.

Thornton is well aware of how tough it can be for women. *The Status of Women in Canadian Theatre Report*, produced by Rina Fraticelli in 1982 for the Applebaum-Hébert Commission, looked at 1,156 productions by 104 theatres over three years. It found that women wrote 10 per cent of these plays and that women made up only 13 percent of directors and 11 percent of artistic directors.

Things have only improved marginally. A straw poll by Toronto producer Naomi Campbell looked at 26 Canadian theatre companies' 2004-2005 seasons. She found that 21 of the artistic directors are men, while only five are women. Of the 223 productions these companies will perform, 169 (75.8 percent) were written by men; 45 (20.2 percent) by women and nine (four percent) by collectives. With few exceptions, most companies' plays will also be directed by men this season.

Thornton says that an "old boys club" mentality and a generally blasé attitude in society contribute to the problem. She is part of a group of 15 women, theatre professionals and scholars from across the country that has pledged to update the 1982 study over the next three years. The new study on that status of women in Canadian theatre is called Equity in Canadian Theatre: The Women's Initiative (the partnering organizations are Playwrights Guild of Canada Women's Caucus, Professional Association of Canadian Theatres [PACT], and Nightwood). In the Fall of 2005, over 300 companies were surveyed nationally. The results will be presented in Spring 2006.

"Theatre is a huge tool in society," says Thornton. "I think because Nightwood is about feminism and women's empowerment, and focusing on our place in society, it keeps you aware that it has to be intellectually challenging, stimulating theatre. It has to shake your mind up and change your world."

(2004)

Suggested Further Reading

General Texts for Feminist Theatre/Theory

Canning, Charlotte. *Feminist Theaters in the USA.* London: Routledge, 1995.

Case, Sue-Ellen. *Feminism and Theatre.* London: Macmillan, 1988.

———, ed. *Performing Feminisms: Feminist Critical Theory and Theatre.* London and Baltimore: Johns Hopkins UP, 1990.

Dolan, Jill. *The Feminist Spectator as Critic.* Ann Arbor and London: UMI Research P, 1988.

Féral, Josette. "Ecriture et déplacement: la femme au théâtre." *The French Review* 56.2 (1982): 281-92.

Goodman, Lizbeth. *Contemporary Feminist Theatres: To Each Her Own.* London: Routledge, 1993.

———, ed. With Jane de Gay. *The Routledge Reader in Gender and Performance.* London: Routledge, 1998.

Hart, Lynda, ed. *Making A Spectacle: Feminist Essays on Contemporary Women's Theatre.* Ann Arbor: The U of Michigan P, 1989.

Hart, Lynda and Peggy Phelan, ed. *Acting Out: Feminist Performances.* Ann Arbor: The U of Michigan P, 1993.

Holledge, Julie and Joanne Tompkins. *Women's Intercultural Performance.* London and New York: Routledge, 2000.

Scolnicov, Hanna. *Woman's Theatrical Space.* Cambridge: Cambridge UP, 1994.

Tait, Peta. *Converging Realities: Feminism in Australian Theatre.* Sydney: Currency P, 1994.

Wandor, Michelene. *Carry On, Understudies.* London: Routledge, 1986.

Feminist Theatre in Canada

Bennett, Susan. "Feminist (Theatre) Historiography/Canadian (Feminist) Theatre: A Reading of some Practices and Theories." *Theatre Research in Canada* 13 (1992): 144-51.

Boyer, Ghislaine. "Théâtre des femmes au Québec, 1975-1985." *Canadian Literature* 118 (1988), 61-80.

Burnett, Linda. "Margaret Clark's *Gertrude & Ophelia*: Writing Revisionist Culture, Writing a Feminist 'New Poetics.'" *Essays in Theatre* 16 (1997): 15-32.

Butterwick, Shauna and Jan Selman. "Deep Listening in a Feminist Popular Theatre Project: Upsetting the Position of Audience in Participatory Education." *Adult Education Quarterly* 54.1 (2003): 7-23.

DiCenzo, Maria and Susan Bennett. "Women, Popular Theatre, and Social Action: Interviews with Cynthia Grant and the Sistren Theatre Collective." *ARIEL* 23.1 (1992): 73-96.

"Feminist Theatre." *Canadian Theatre Encyclopedia* (online): <http://www.canadiantheatre.com/dict.pl?term=Feminist%20Theatre>.

Forsyth, Louise. "Feminist Theatre." *Oxford Companion to Canadian Theatre.* Ed. Eugene Benson and L.W. Conolly. Toronto: Oxford UP, 1989: 206.

Fortier, Mark. "Shakespeare with Difference: Genderbending and Genrebending in *Goodnight Desdemona.*" *Canadian Theatre Review* 59 (1989): 47-51.

Fraticelli, Rina. "'Any black crippled woman can!': A feminist's notes from outside the sheltered workshop." *A Room of One's Own* 8.2 (1983): 7-18.

Godard, Barbara. "Between Repetition and Rehearsal: Conditions of (Women's) Theatre in Canada in a Space of Reproduction." *Theatre Research in Canada* 13 (1992): 18-33.

Jones, Heather. "Feminism and Nationalism in Domestic Melodrama: Gender, Genre and Canadian Identity." *Essays in Theatre* 8.1 (1989): 5-14.

Moss, Jane. "Women, History, and Theater in Québec." *Women Writing in Québec.* Ed. Paula Ruth Gilbert, et al. Plattsburgh: Plattsburgh State UP, 2000: 97-109.

Much, Rita. *Women on the Canadian Stage: The Legacy of Hrotsvit.* Winnipeg: Blizzard, 1992.

Rewa, Natalie. "Le Madonne Feministe: Italian Canadian Women Playwrights." *Canadian Theatre Review* 104 (2000): 24-28.

Rudakoff, Judith and Rita Much, ed. *Fair Play: 12 Women Speak. Conversations with Canadian Playwrights.* Toronto: Simon & Pierre, 1990.

Smith, Jane Orion. "Feminist Lesbian Aesthetics." *Canadian Theatre Review* 70 (1992): 23-26.

Stone-Blackburn, Susan. "Maenadic Rites on Stage in Calgary." *Canadian Theatre Review* 69 (1991): 28-33.

Zimmerman, Cynthia. *Playwriting Women: Female Voices in English Canada.* Toronto: Simon & Pierre, 1994.

Special Issues of Canadian Theatre Journals

Jeu 16 (1980): "Théâtre-femmes"

Canadian Theatre Review 43 (1985): "Feminism & Canadian Theatre"

Canadian Theatre Review 59 (1989): "Sexuality, Gender and Theatre"

Canadian Theatre Review 69 (1991): "Canadian Women Playwrights: (Inter)national Contexts"

Theatre Research in Canada 8.1 (1987): "Women in the Theatre of Québec and Canada"

Notes on Contributors

In 1992, **Patricia Badir** was completing her doctorate at the University of Leeds, England, in the area of Renaissance popular entertainments. She is now Associate Professor in the Department of English at the University of British Columbia. While most of her publications have been in the area of Reformation Theatre, she has continued to work on Canadian theatre. An article on Marjorie Pickthall's *The Wood-Carver's Wife* appeared in *Modern Drama* in 2001 and she is currently working on a project on Shakespeare at Hart House in the teens and twenties. A collection of essays, co-edited with Paul Yachnin, *Shakespeare and the Cultures of Performance* is forthcoming from Ashgate in 2006.

Susan Bennett is University Professor in the Department of English at the University of Calgary. She is widely published on a variety of theatre and performance topics, with especial interest in women's dramatic writing. She is a member of the Equity in Canadian Theatre initiative.

Kym Bird is Associate Professor of Drama at York University, Atkinson Faculty, School of Arts and Letters. Her book *Redressing the Past: the Politics of Early, English-Canadian Women's Theatre 1880-1920* (McGill-Queens UP, 2004) won the Association of Canadian Theatre Research Ann Saddlemyer book prize. She is also the recipient of two teaching awards, including the York, University-Wide Teaching Award. Presently she is working on an anthology of early Canadian Women's plays.

In 1984, **Cindy Cowan** was playwright and member of the Mulgrave Road Co-op Theatre Company of Guysborough, Nova Scotia, and the playwright-in-residence at the Neptune Theatre, Halifax.

Long-time collaborators **Shawna Dempsey and Lorri Millan** create feminist performances, films, videos, publications and public art projects. They are infamous for pieces such as *We're Talking Vulva, A Day in The Life of A Bull-Dyke, and Lesbian National Parks and Services*: multi-disciplinary projects that use humour to articulate political concerns. This duo tours nationally and abroad, but Winnipeg is their chosen home.

Celeste Derksen teaches at the University of Victoria, British Columbia.

In 1997, **Louise Forsyth** taught French, Women's Studies, and Drama at the University of Saskatchewan. She continues to research and publish widely in these fields. She is a member of the Equity in Canadian Theatre initiative.

In 2004, **Cynthia Grant** was completing a PhD at the Ontario Institute for Studies in Education, University of Toronto, and teaching in the Theatre & Film Programme of the School of the Arts at McMaster University. She is a member of the Equity in Canadian Theatre Initiative.

In 1985, **Kate Lushington** was a member of the Toronto Women's Cultural Building and a committed feminist who has directed at the National Theatre School and Theatre Passe Muraille.

Jane Moss is Associate Professor of Modern Foreign Languages and coordinator of Women's Studies at Colby College in Waterville, Maine. Her recent research has concentrated on women's theatre in Québec and in France. She has written numerous articles and reviews in the areas of French and Québec drama and fiction.

Jennifer O'Connor is a Toronto-based freelance writer.

Wendy Philpott conducted interviews for the 1991 article with each member of the Women's Circle Collective, a feminist theatre project sponsored by Edmonton's Catalyst Theatre.

Shelley Scott is an Associate Professor in the Department of Theatre and Dramatic Arts at the University of Lethbridge. In 2005-2006, while on her first study leave, she re-wrote and updated her thesis on Nightwood with the intention of publishing it. Shelley's other research interest has been in plays by Canadian women that deal with real-life incidents of violence by women. She has published a number of articles on this topic in journals such as *Modern Drama*, *Canadian Theatre Review*, and *Theatre Research in Canada*, and she has recently gathered them into a manuscript.

In 1989, **Donna E. Smyth** was a political activist and academic teaching at Acadia University.

Djanet Sears is an actor, director and playwright. Her one-woman show *Afrika Solo* premiered at the Factory Theatre Studio Café in Toronto in the fall of 1987. In 1992, she was an active member of the Black Film and Video Network in Toronto and was one of four black women filmmakers who constituted the Britain/Canada-based film and television production company Leda Serene, which won a gold medal for the debut film *I Is a Long Memoried Woman* at the New York Film and Televison Festival. She will direct her own play *Harlem Duet* at the Studio Theatre of the Stratford Festival of Canada in 2006.

Ann Wilson, as an undergraduate, majored in history at York University. The interests cultivated in those years have returned, and her scholarly interests now circulate around the consideration of late Victorian and Edwardian theatrical texts as artifacts which speak to the negotiation of issues around identity, in terms of gender, sexuality, class and race, in relation to English nationalism.